Supervision over Courts and Judges

Dia-Logos

Schriften zu Philosophie und Sozialwissenschaften
Studies in Philosophy and Social Sciences

Edited by
Piotr W. Juchacz

Vol. 30

Wojciech Piątek (ed.)

Supervision over Courts and Judges

Insights into Selected Legal Systems

Bibliographic Information published by the Deutsche Nationalbibliothek
The Deutsche Nationalbibliothek lists this publication in the Deutsche Nationalbibliografie; detailed bibliographic data is available in the internet at http://dnb.d-nb.de.

Library of Congress Cataloging-in-Publication Data
A CIP catalog record for this book has been applied for at the Library of Congress.

The monograph is a part of a research project no DEC-2017/25/B/HS5/00343, financed by the National Science Centre (Poland) devoted to the supervision over courts and judges.

This work has been reviewed by Professor Krisztina Rozsnyai (University ELTE Budapest).

ISSN 1619-005X
ISBN 978-3-631-83617-0 (Print)
ISBN 978-3-631-86011-3 (E-PDF)
ISBN 978-3-631-86041-0 (EPUB)
DOI 10.3726/b18615

Peter Lang – Berlin · Berlin · Bruxelles · New York · Oxford · Warszawa · Wien

This publication has been peer reviewed.

www.peterlang.com

Table of contents

Introduction 7

Stefan Haack
The supervision of judges throughout the history of the German judiciary 11

Katharina Pabel
Judicial independence and the court's organisation from the perspective of the European Convention on Human Rights 27

Jan Olszanowski
The shape of supervision over courts – reflections on the supervisory measures applied to courts and judges 51

Matej Horvat, Matúš Radosa
Considerations on the supervision exercised over courts and judges 77

Martin Sunnqvist
Public entities responsible for court administration and supervision over judges 101

Andrzej Skoczylas
The organisation of the work of a judge and the activities of judicial administration bodies (comments from the viewpoint of the administrative judiciary) 127

Andrzej Paduch
Supervision over a court as a tool to protect the right to have a court case heard within a reasonable time 149

Igor Gontarz
Electronic case distribution as a measure enhancing neutrality in the assignment of cases 171

Wojciech Piątek
Administrative supervision as a tool for building trust in the courts and judges 195

Final remarks 225

About the Authors 231

Introduction

An independent judiciary is a precondition for every analysis concerning the judicial adjudication of effectiveness, let alone professionalism. If courts are not impartial and judges are not independent, then the court's judgments will not create legal certainty and the fundament elements of the rule of law will not be stable. Though the role of judicial independence is stressed in many acts of international law, including Article 6 of the European Convention on Human Rights[1] and Article 47 of the Charter of Fundamental Rights of the EU,[2] for many legislators compliance with basic standards seems to be difficult.[3] In the era of populism, courts may be forced to serve as partners in cooperation with politicians, as the latter attempt to create an alternative world. In such circumstances, judicial independence depends not on structural guarantees, but solely on the internal attitude of each judge.

A significant instrument which has a lot in common with judicial independence and trust in the courts is supervision over the judiciary. Understood broadly, this term denotes the scope of legal measures which can make the courts' adjudication more effective, in the sense of ensuring better protection of individual rights. It is an indispensable element in any analysis concerning the internal organisation, management and administration of the courts. Though supervision may be used for negative purposes, as a tool for the courts' subordination, it has great positive potential for a more professional organisation of the judiciary.[4] The aim of this book is to present the conditions under which

---

1 Convention for the Protection of Human rights and Fundamental Freedoms adopted in Rome on 4 November 1950, available at https://www.echr.coe.int/documents/convention_eng.pdf (access date: 10.03.2021).

2 Official Journal of the EU 2012 C 326/391.

3 The phenomenon of the weakened importance of the rule of law is topic that has been subject to broad analysis in the literature. See A. von Bogdany, M. Ioannidis, Systemic deficiency in the rule of law: what it is, what has been done, what can be done, Common Market Law Review 2014, 59–96, S. Panov, The effect of populism on the rule of law, separation of powers and judicial independence in Hungary and Poland, in: J. Vidmar, European populism and human rights, Brill 2020, International Studies in Human Rights, Vol. 130, 256–288.

4 Judicial independence should not be perceived as a basis for the total freedom for courts and judges, who would be not subordinated to any verification. See A. Thiele, Die Unabhängigkeit des Richters – grenzenlose Freiheit? – Das Spannungsverhältnis zwischen richterlicher Unabhängigkeit und Dienstaufsicht, Der Staat 2013, pp. 417–418.

the positive role of supervision can be performed, and to shed light on what conditions have to be fulfilled in order to achieve the goal of creating an impartial and professional judiciary system. When analysing the positive significance of supervision, it will be beneficial to know how supervision can help judges in adjudication, and in which way this process can be organised more quickly and effectively.

There are several detailed grounds for conducting an analysis of the correlation between court adjudication and the supervision over courts. The topic of the supervision exercised over the courts and judges merits development and deepening, due to the legal and social reasons that are associated with this issue. The effective functioning of the courts has an impact on the quality of judicial decisions, and thus on the compliance and transparency of the legal system in a given country. For the proper conduct of their duties, courts should benefit from the normative guarantees that ensure the freedom of procedural activity. Supervision should lead to the achievement of this goal.

The effectiveness of judicial review is essential for the protection of the rights of the individual and the functioning of the state authorities in both the social and the economic realms.[5] From an extrajudicial viewpoint, its significance is reflected in the influence on the judiciary, which will not only be effective in its procedural activity but also in the level of trust and social prestige.

Another justification for this study is the increasingly important role of the judiciary in modern democratic societies. The direct expression of this is the gradual rise in the number of cases filed with the courts.[6] This increase is consistent with the growing expectations of citizens with regard to courts and judges, both in terms of the need to improve the efficiency and speed of the court proceedings, and to strengthen the assurance of objectivity in resolving disputes.

The basic research areas tackled in this publication concern such issues as: a detailed definition of supervision over courts and judges; the differences between various components of this supervision, mainly administrative and judicial; the scope of the supervision and the entities which are responsible for exercising it; the measures of supervision which are present in selected legal orders; the

5 The connection between judicial and economic realms is multifaceted and is not only evaluated positively in the literature. See F. Wittreck, Die Verwaltung deer dritten Gewalt, Tübingen 2006, pp. 24–27.

6 In Poland, this increase is significant. In 2002, 8,696,913 cases were lodged to ordinary courts. In 2017, this number was almost double: 15,782,479 cases. See A. Siemaszko, P. Ostaszewski, J. Włodarczyk-Madejska, Tendencje wpływu spraw do polskich sądów powszechnych. Analizy wymiaru sprawiedliwości 2019, pp. 9–10.

adoption of new technologies into the internal court organisation; and the trust placed in the courts. The analysis seeks to specify the boundary beyond which supervisory powers should not be exercised.[7] It is also necessary to analyse what areas of court action should be free from supervision. Hence, there are also other questions addressed in this study, such as: How does the regulation of supervision affect the judge's status and personal position? What is the relationship between the legal regulation of supervision and the financial independence of the courts? How does the legal regulation of supervision affect the level of trust which the courts have in a society?

It is understandable that the courts, which are organs of personal and material resources, must have their own administration. Nevertheless, administrative supervision should not enter the judicial area. Thus, it is justified to raise the question of the possibility of separating the judicial sphere from the administrative activities of the courts. Where is the boundary between them, if it is possible to designate it at all? In what areas of the courts' activity is administrative supervision indispensable, and when does this supervision begin to have an inappropriate influence on the decision-making role of the courts? What might the consequences be, in the event of non-compliance, or if supervision does not cover all areas of the courts' actions?

The analysis will be of an interdisciplinary, normative, and sociological nature, and will be presented from various points of view, including numerous insights into international and national legal systems with varied legal histories and cultures, such as Austria, Denmark, Germany, Poland, Slovakia, and Sweden. In the presented legal orders, there are various entities responsible for supervision over courts and judges. The measures of supervision are different. The level of trust placed in the courts varies between 40 % in Poland and Slovakia, to more than 80 % in the Scandinavian countries.[8] A closer look at the legal systems in other countries facilitates a better understanding of the domestic structures and enables the identification of common solutions for different legal orders. Presenting the different forms of administrative supervision that operate in different legislative systems will allow the advantages and disadvantages of native legal solutions to be highlighted. In this respect, special consideration will be

7 Though it is clear that the adoption of supervision measures cannot violate judicial independence, there is no clear border designating the point after which supervision should not be used. See E. Wiederin, Gedanken über die richterliche Unabhängigkeit, in: ed. M. Neumayr, Unabhängigkeit der Rechtsprechung. Nach außen und innen, Wien 2019, pp. 110–11.

8 The 2020 EU Justice Scoreboard, Publication Office of the EU 2020, p. 41.

given to the law in action. The study compares analogous situations that have arisen before the courts of the countries in question.

Poznań, 30 June 2021
Wojciech Piątek

Stefan Haack[1]

The supervision of judges throughout the history of the German judiciary

Abstract: In the paper the supervision over courts and judges is analysed from a historical perspective. Based on the presented facts, the basic components of supervision will be examined, such as the rule of law, the judge's independence, the judge's overload, and the judge's freedom of expression. In this study, the necessity and range of judicial supervision will be proved. The relation between supervision and judge's independence leads to the conclusion that these two components are essential for the court's effective functioning. A constitutional state without judicial independence is just as inconceivable, as is a constitutional state without the minimal supervision of judges. A minimum of control is indispensable, especially where a maximum of judicial independence is to be established.

Keywords: supervision of judges, judge's independence, overloaded judges, judge's neutrality, effective judicial protection

1. Introduction: The supervision of judges as a problem for the rule of law

How can judges be supervised, and by whom? Behind the issue of the supervision of judges loom key problems for the rule of law: What does it mean for the independence of the judiciary if the individual judge is subject to supervisory measures by higher authorities? How can judicial decisions be protected from manipulation by court presidents, ministers of justice or other supervisory authorities by way of supervision? It should be noted that a complete lack of effective supervisory instruments can lead to conditions unacceptable under the rule of law. Who will protect those seeking legal remedy from arbitrary jurisdiction and possible abuses of judicial authority in such instances? These questions are as old as the concept of a judiciary based on the rule of law and in some cases even older.[2] By drawing on a few examples from older and more recent history of

---

1 Stefan Haack, PhD, Professor of Law at Europa University Viadrina, (Germany). ORCID – 0000-0001-6178-6551.

2 For the history of supervision of the judiciary, see F. Baur, *Justizaufsicht und richterliche Unabhängigkeit*, Tübingen: J. C. B. Mohr (Paul Siebeck), 1954, pp. 5 ff., and R. Schmidt-Räntsch, *Dienstaufsicht über Richter*, Bielefeld: Gieseking, 1985, pp. 3 ff.

the German judiciary, this article will show that they are still relevant today and have only partially been resolved.

2. Supervision in former times: The dictum of the Prussian King concerning miller Arnold

The first case we will look at takes us back to a time before the constitutional state had been established, more precisely to the Kingdom of Prussia under Frederick the Great. The Prussian king himself is one of the protagonists in this story – along with various judges and one of his subjects, a miller named Christian Arnold from a village on the Oder river near Grünberg in Silesia (today's Zielona Góra), which at the time belonged to Prussia. What began as an ordinary legal dispute over the hereditary lease for a water mill developed into a historical power struggle between the king and the judiciary, which entered German and European legal history as the "case of the miller Arnold."[3] Miller Arnold, whose economic existence was at stake in the trial, succeeded in having Frederick the Great personally intervene in the proceedings before the civil courts by submitting several petitions to the Prussian king. When the Court of Appeal in Küstrin (today Kostrzyn) as well as the *Kammergericht*, the highest Prussian court – unimpressed by the interventions of the king – nevertheless ruled against the miller, the Prussian king ordered the arrest of the judges involved. In addition, he called on the *Kammergericht* to impose prison sentences no less than a year. Since the competent judges of the *Kammergericht* refused to impose such a sentence on their former colleagues, the Prussian king declared the arrested judges convicted by virtue of a so-called "*Machtspruch*" – a royal dictum of power.

In the present context, the wide-ranging consequences of the "case of the miller Arnold" for the Prussian judicial system[4] are less interesting than the theoretical implications for the problem of the supervision of judges. The "case of the miller Arnold" illustrates the tension between administrative supervision and judicial independence, by putting the issue under a magnifying glass.[5] What in the eyes

3 P. Prümm, "Friedrich II. von Preußen und das Recht – Das Interpretationsverbot im ALR, der Prozess des Müllers Arnold und der Überfall auf Sachsen," *Zeitschrift für das juristische Studium*, 2012, pp. 24, 29 ff., and H. Sendler, "Friedrich der Große und der Müller Arnold," *Juristische Schulung*, 1986, p. 759 are recommended as introductory reading for the "case of the miller Arnold."

4 See E. Schmidt, *Rechtsentwicklung in Preußen*, 2nd ed., Berlin: Springer, 1929, pp. 26 ff.

5 For the significance of the Müller Arnold trial for the problem of supervision see F. Baur, *Justizaufsicht und richterliche Unabhängigkeit*, p. 8.

of the Prussian king appeared as an unavoidable supervisory measure to correct a blatant injustice,[6] in the eyes of the judiciary presented itself as an outrageous and untimely interference with its independence, even at the time.[7] Frederick the Great based his claim on the authority to control abuses of judicial power. By holding the involved judges accountable for what – in his eyes – was obviously the wrong decision, he presented himself as protector of his subjects and as the supreme guardian of justice and law. It should be noted that not only did he want to enforce procedural standards, but that he also wanted a result that was found to be substantially correct: What seemed unacceptable to Frederick the Great was the defeat of the miller Arnold as such. This kind of influence on the content of a judgement constitutes the most serious interference with judicial independence conceivable. Where it happens, the supervising authority de facto assumes the function of the court (which is why we rightly speak of cabinet justice).[8]

Nowadays, supervisory measures aimed at the content of the judicial decision making are generally precluded[9] – a "miller Arnold scenario" is no longer imaginable under the German Basic Law (even if one disregards the royal dictum and the arbitrary condemnation). Nevertheless, a backdoor for the supervision of the substance of judicial decisions is left open: The German Federal Court of Justice (Bundesgerichtshof) allows supervisory measures with regards to the content of judicial decisions if their incorrectness is "jedem Zweifel entrückt" (beyond any doubt).[10] What would Frederick the Great have answered if he had

---

6 On the otherwise ambivalent practice of Frederick the Great in controlling the judiciary see F. Baur, *Justizaufsicht und richterliche Unabhängigkeit*, pp. 7 ff.

7 H. Sendler, "Friedrich der Große und der Müller Arnold …," pp. 760 ff. (who points out that Frederick the Great also made use of his authority to correct judicial decisions in numerous other cases).

8 For the further historical development with regards to a substantive control of judicial decisions in Prussia, see R. Schmidt-Räntsch, *Dienstaufsicht über Richter*, pp. 9 ff.

9 See instead of many N. Achterberg, "Die richterliche Unabhängigkeit im Spiegel der Dienstgerichtsbarkeit," *Neue Juristische Wochenschrift*, 1985, pp. 3041, 3043; H.-J. Papier, "Richterliche Unabhängigkeit und Dienstaufsicht," *Neue Juristische Wochenschrift*, 1990, pp. 8, 11; M. Redeker, "Die Dienstaufsicht über Richter," *Sächsische Verwaltungsblätter*, 2007, pp. 73, 74. In the relevant literature, there have been occasional attempts to relativise this principle; see for example H. Arndt, "Grenzen der Dienstaufsicht über Richter," *Deutsche Richterzeitung*, 1974, pp. 248, 252. Critical of this K. Rudolph, "Zur Dienstaufsicht über Richter," *Deutsche Richterzeitung*, 1978, p. 146.

10 Judgment of Bundesgerichtshof, *Neue Juristische Wochenschrift* 1977, p. 437; Judgment of Bundesgerichtshof, *Deutsche Richterzeitung*, 1995, p. 394; Judgment of Bundesgerichtshof, *Neue Juristische Wochenschrift – Rechtsprechungsreport*, 2001, pp. 498, 499; Judgment of Bundesgerichtshof, *Neue Juristische*

been asked whether this condition had been met in the decisions of the Prussian *Kammergericht* and the Regional Court in Küstrin in the "case of the miller *Arnold*"?

The example of the miller Arnold illustrates yet another problem of judicial supervision. The more the judicial system provides mechanisms for correcting its own errors, the less the need for supervisory measures can be justified. First of all, such a mechanism is to be seen in the stages of appeal. Where the unsuccessful party can appeal against an incorrect decision, it is not without legal protection and therefore does not require a corrective intervention by other state bodies.[11] In a jurisdiction based on the rule of law, which provides several stages of appeal, the chances of winning in court with a legitimate claim should generally be high enough, so that further control by bodies outside the judiciary do not seem necessary.[12] There is no reason to believe that a supervisory authority – be it a minister, a court president or Frederick the Great – has a better command of the law and more effective instruments for determining the truth than the judicial body whose judgments are in question. Likewise, it is not to be assumed that character traits such as honesty, decency and a sense of justice are more pronounced among officials outside the jurisdiction than among those within it – literary figures such as the village judge Adam do not represent the entire judiciary and are not limited to it; one meets them where mistakes have been made in the selection of officials and the exercise of sovereign power has been placed in the wrong hands. Although the possibility cannot be entirely ruled out that higher authorities, out of a misunderstood sense of collegiality or of misplaced trust, might uphold erroneous decisions of the lower courts in individual cases, it goes without saying that a constitutional state may not question the

---

Wochenschrift – Rechtsprechungsreport, 2008, pp. 1660, 1661. In the literature this exception is strongly criticised; cf. N. Achterberg, "Die richterliche Unabhängigkeit …," p. 3045 and A. Thiele, "Die Unabhängigkeit des Richters – grenzenlose Freiheit?," *Der Staat*, vol. 52, 2013, pp. 415, 426 ff. Detailed on the whole complex R. Schmidt-Räntsch, *Dienstaufsicht über Richter*, pp. 44 ff., 64 ff. (who also rejects such an exception in the conclusion).

11 Cf. C. Hillgruber, in: Maunz/Dürig, Grundgesetz-Kommentar, loose-leaf (updated October 2020), mn. 80 for Art. 97; H.-J. Papier, "Richterliche Unabhängigkeit …," p. 11; A. Thiele, "Die Unabhängigkeit des Richters …," p. 425.

12 It is therefore rightly emphasised that supervision is not a legitimate secondary or substitute instance; see W. Funk, "Grenzen der Dienstaufsicht über Richter im Hinblick auf deren verfassungsrechtlich geschützte Unabhängigkeit," *Deutsche Richterzeitung*, 1978, pp. 357, 363; K. Rudolph, "Zur Dienstaufsicht …," p. 146; id., "Richterliche Unabhängigkeit und Dienstaufsicht," *Deutsche Richterzeitung*, 1979, pp. 97, 101.

independence of the judiciary by means of comprehensive supervision. Who – if not the judiciary – is entitled to say how things stand in miller Arnold cases: do the judges involved really resemble the village judge Adam, who proved himself unworthy of office and deserved severe punishment – or has the former miller Arnold already become the horse trader Michael Kohlhaas? How does the miller Arnold's trial differ from the cases of those troublemakers who, having exhausted the legal procedure, bombard parliamentary boards, constitutional courts, and other state agencies with petitions and statements because they believe that the judges and other employees of the competent specialised courts have conspired with each other across all stages of appeal? Perhaps, only insofar as Frederick the Great wanted to listen to such an assertion – even at the expense (or with the aim[13]) of disavowing the high courts of Prussia.

3. Supervision today: What to do with overloaded judges?

Monarchs having rebellious judges imprisoned for the supposed sake of their subjects by dictum belong to the distant past – at least in Europe. Nevertheless, the question of how effective supervision and judicial independence relate to one another is still far from being resolved. This is illustrated by the following example: a trial concerning the work of a judge has been taking place in Baden-Württemberg for a period of over ten years already, with no end in sight.[14] The main person in question is Thomas Schulte-Kellinghaus, a judge at the Higher Regional Court of Karlsruhe, who, due to his extraordinarily meticulous approach, has found himself unable to hear and complete the number of proceedings required of him within a reasonable timeframe. The dispute arose when the president of the Higher Regional Court issued an order against him in which she

13 H. Sendler ("Friedrich der Große und der Müller Arnold …," p. 762) assumes that the Prussian king set an example "weil ihm die Gerichte insgesamt zu langsam zu arbeiten und zu sehr die Interessen der höheren Klassen zu bevorzugen schienen."

14 On this case, which has already been dealt with by numerous courts, see (in chronological order): Judgment of Dienstgericht Karlsruhe, BeckRS 2013, No. 942; Judgment of Dienstgerichtshof Stuttgart, BeckRS 2015, No. 11585; Judgment of Bundesgerichtshof, *Neue Juristische Wochenschrift*, 2018, p. 158; Judgement of Bundesverfassungsgericht, *Neue Juristische Wochenschrift*, 2018, p. 1532; Judgment of Bundesgerichtshof, BeckRS 2020, No. 10611; Judgment of Bundesgerichtshof, BeckRS 2020, No. 16578. Another decision of Bundesverfassungsgericht is still pending. The trial has also been commented on in legal literature; see, for example, A. Thiele, "Die Unabhängigkeit des Richters …," pp. 426 ff.; F. Wittreck, "Durchschnitt als Dienstpflicht?," *Neue Juristische Wochenschrift*, 2012, pp. 3287 ff.

reproached him for not having dealt sufficiently with many proceedings over the years, even if it was clear that those proceedings were very urgent. This allegation was substantiated by the assertion that his case handlings were equal to only 68 % of the cases handled by other judges at the Higher Regional Court. In a subsequent decision, the president of the Higher Court pointed out that his output did not even come up to the average output of a half-time employment. The judge in question believed that these decisions, which were measures of supervision in accordance with § 26 of the German Judiciary Act, violated his judicial independence as guaranteed by Article 97 of the Basic Law. In accordance with § 26 (3) of the German Judiciary Act (in conjunction with relevant state law), he filed a lawsuit against the decisions issued before the disciplinary courts, whose final instance is the Federal Supreme Court. In the end, the federal judges could not see any violation of judicial independence in the court president's decisions. The judge in question has lodged a constitutional complaint against this, which has not yet been decided.

Unlike in the "case of the miller Arnold," the circumstances do not concern correctness; that is, the substance of the judicial decision. Instead, the federal judges disapproved of how the judge had handled his workload and the way he had worked. In the history of the German judiciary, lawsuits against such or comparable supervisory measures based on a violation of judicial independence have occurred several times.[15] It is obvious why it seems necessary to differentiate between such circumstances and the substantial corrections discussed earlier: While the accusation that a judge makes wrong decisions with regard to content directly interferes with his original sphere of responsibility as a judge and allows the supervisory authority to at least partially replace the judiciary, supervisory measures relating to the workload do not affect the genuine judicial function (that is supposed to be shielded against undue influence) in the same way.[16] Whether or not they can endanger the independence of a judge is less obvious. Accordingly, the Federal Court of Justice differentiates between interventions in the core area of judicial activity, which includes the hearing of the case and the decision as such, and measures in the area of the "äußere Ordnung" (peripheral order), which essentially concern the modalities of

15 From previous case law, see Judgment of Bundesgerichtshof, *Neue Juristische Wochenschrift*, 1978, p. 760; Judgment of Bundesgerichtshof, *Neue Juristische Wochenschrift*, 1984, p. 2535; Judgment of Bundesgerichtshof, *Neue Juristische Wochenschrift – Rechtsprechungsreport*, 1999, pp. 426, 428.

16 Judgment of Bundesgerichtshof, *Neue Juristische Wochenschrift*, 2018, pp. 158, 160.

work.[17] In addition to the workload, the latter includes, for instance, the organisation of working hours,[18] the usage of technical aids, and the wearing of the official attire. The Federal Court of Justice attaches different legal consequences to this classification: While measures of supervision which affect the core area of judicial activity – up to the point of manifest error discussed above[19] – are not permissible in principle, the Federal Court of Justice generally does not qualify any measures outside this area as interference with judicial independence.[20] The jurisdiction of the Federal Court of Justice has been heavily criticised in legal literature. Numerous authors have criticised its inconsistency,[21] lack of practicability,[22] its methodological deficiencies[23] and circularity[24] (just to mention a few of the criticisms). The intricacies of this (rather convoluted) discussion left aside; in the present context, the only thing that matters is what fundamental

17 Judgment of Bundesgerichtshof, *Neue Juristische Wochenschrift*, 2018, pp. 158, 160 – settled case-law; cf. from the literature N. Achterberg, "Die richterliche Unabhängigkeit …," 1985, pp. 3043 ff.; H.-J. Papier, "Richterliche Unabhängigkeit und Dienstaufsicht …," pp. 10 ff.; J. N. Scheuer, "Dienstaufsicht und richterliche Unabhängigkeit," in: *Auf festem Fundament. Festschrift für Christean Wagner*, ed. M. Demel et al., Berlin: Duncker & Humblot, 2013, pp. 191, 194 ff.; R. Schmidt-Räntsch, *Dienstaufsicht über Richter*, pp. 33 ff.; A. Thiele, "Die Unabhängigkeit des Richters …," pp. 419 ff.

18 The Federal Court of Justice (Bundesgerichtshof) classifies the question of fixed working hours as falling under the scope of the protection of judicial independence; cf. Judgment of Bundesgerichtshof, *Neue Juristische Wochenschrift*, 1991, p. 1103. This extension of judicial independence is criticised in the literature; see C. Hillgruber, in: Maunz/Dürig, Grundgesetz-Kommentar, loose-leaf (updated October 2020), mn. 84 on Art. 97; M. Redeker, "Die Dienstaufsicht über Richter …," p. 73, 77.

19 See above: II.

20 Judgment of Bundesgerichtshof, *Neue Juristische Wochenschrift*, 2018, pp. 158, 160 – settled case-law; cf. fn. 17 on the issue of working hours.

21 H. Arndt, "Grenzen der Dienstaufsicht …," p. 250; R. Schmidt-Räntsch, *Dienstaufsicht über Richter*, pp. 73 ff.

22 H. Arndt, "Grenzen der Dienstaufsicht …," p. 250; W. Funk, "Grenzen der Dienstaufsicht über Richter im Hinblick auf deren verfassungsrechtlich geschützte Unabhängigkeit," *Deutsche Richterzeitung*, 1978, pp. 357, 362; R. Schmidt-Räntsch, *Dienstaufsicht über Richter*, pp. 61 ff.

23 W. Funk, "Grenzen der Dienstaufsicht …," pp. 361 ff.; R. Schmidt-Räntsch, *Dienstaufsicht über Richter*, p. 77.

24 N. Achterberg, "Die richterliche Unabhängigkeit …," p. 3045; A. Mayer, "Richterliche Unabhängigkeit und Dienstaufsicht," *Deutsche Richterzeitung*, 1978, p. 313; A. Thiele, "Die Unabhängigkeit des Richters …," p. 420 (in footnote 29).

questions arise when supervisory measures criticise the quantity of work and the way judges work.

When it is to be determined whether supervisory measures which concern the "äußere Ordnung" of judicial activity violate the constitutionally guaranteed independence of the judge, the effects of such measures must be considered and measured against the normative purpose of Article 97 of the Basic Law. Workload requirements (to stick with this example) can indirectly limit the judge's ability to handle the proceedings he has to decide.[25] He may be forced to schedule a trial even though he did not want to conduct it until later on. Similarly, the pressure to complete could be a reason for shortening the research on a particular legal problem, reducing the time and intensity of one's own deliberations, or targeting certain forms of completion (such as a settlement). In all these cases, a corresponding measure by the supervisory authority affects the core area of judicial activity. In such circumstances it is hardly possible to distinguish between the core area and the peripheral order[26] – in this regard, the criticism in the scholarly literature is to be endorsed. However, the protection of judicial independence is not an end in itself;[27] the independence of judges is not written into the constitution for its own sake nor for the judges' self-interest, but is guaranteed as a central component of a judiciary based on the rule of law.[28] Although the rule of law demands a sufficient consideration of the autonomy of legal work in developing the legal system and the judicial body, this must not lead to losing sight of the serving character of the rule of law in general, and of judicial independence in particular: The constitutional state and its judicial system are rooted in the protection and freedom of the citizen. Based on this insight, it must be understood that judicial independence as well as supervision are justified by one and the same purpose: Both are concerned with the functioning of a judiciary that appears to be bound solely by law and by justice, and that decides legal conflicts independently. The state owes its citizens this kind of judiciary as soon as it claims a monopoly on the use of force.[29] In other words: The independence of the

25 Cf. H.-J. Papier, "Richterliche Unabhängigkeit …," p. 13.

26 H. Arndt, "Grenzen der Dienstaufsicht …," p. 250; id., "Zur Dienstaufsicht über Richter," *Deutsche Richterzeitung*, 1978, p. 78; R. Schmidt-Räntsch, *Dienstaufsicht über Richter*, p. 63.

27 F. Baur, *Justizaufsicht und richterliche Unabhängigkeit*, p. 17; K. Rudolph, "Zur Dienstaufsicht …," *Deutsche Richterzeitung*, 1978, pp. 146 ff.

28 Cf. W. Funk, "Grenzen der Dienstaufsicht …," p. 360; H.-J. Papier, "Richterliche Unabhängigkeit …," p. 9; R. Schmidt-Räntsch, *Dienstaufsicht über Richter*, pp. 23 ff.

29 Cf. W. Funk, "Grenzen der Dienstaufsicht …," p. 363; M. Redeker, "Die Dienstaufsicht über Richter …," p. 74.

judiciary and its supervision are both based on the right[30] of access to justice.[31] The interest of the state and citizens in a functioning judiciary[32] also justifies the requirement that the judge completes a certain workload and the monitoring of a timely processing of cases by means of supervision:[33] Delayed hearings often amount to a denial of access to justice.[34] Furthermore, according to Article 6 (1) ECHR everyone is entitled to a fair and public hearing within a reasonable time by an independent and impartial tribunal established by law. There are several practical issues associated with the supervision of judicial work, on which the Federal Court of Justice has repeatedly taken a stand. How great a workload may be demanded of a judge?[35] According to the prevailing view, a violation of judicial independence by an excessive workload can only be assumed if the judge is required to perform services that cannot realistically be performed in a proper way within his due working hours. In such a case he would be forced to neglect parts of his judicial tasks and duties.[36] This seems to be the right approach, but it leads to the question of how this limit should be determined. As the German Federal Court of Justice has emphasised, the average number of cases handled by judges in comparable positions can be little more than an indication.[37] The outcomes of the Federal Court of Justice jurisdiction appear acceptable from a

30 For general information on the right of access to justice see C. Degenhart, *Staatsrecht I. Staatsorganisationsrecht*, Heidelberg: C.F. Müller, 36th ed., 2020, mn. 445.

31 N. Achterberg, "Die richterliche Unabhängigkeit …," p. 3042; C. Hillgruber, in: Maunz/Dürig, Grundgesetz-Kommentar, loose-leaf (updated October 2020), mn. 80 for Art. 97; H.-J. Papier, "Richterliche Unabhängigkeit …," p. 9; A. Thiele, "Die Unabhängigkeit des Richters …," p. 417; dissenting opinion on the anchoring of the supervision M. Redeker, "Die Dienstaufsicht über Richter …," p. 74.

32 For more information on this, see R. Schmidt-Räntsch, *Dienstaufsicht über Richter*, pp. 125 ff.

33 Cf. Judgment of Bundesgerichtshof, *Neue Juristische Wochenschrift*, 2018, pp. 158, 160; in detail J.N. Scheuer, "Dienstaufsicht und richterliche Unabhängigkeit …," pp. 200 ff.; R. Schmidt-Räntsch, *Dienstaufsicht über Richter*, pp. 121 ff.; A. Thiele, "Die Unabhängigkeit des Richters …," pp. 430 ff.; F. Wittreck, "Durchschnitt als Dienstpflicht …," p. 3287.

34 F. Baur, *Justizaufsicht und richterliche Unabhängigkeit*, p. 29; R. Schmidt-Räntsch, *Dienstaufsicht über Richter*, pp. 121 ff.

35 Cf. Judgment of Bundesgerichtshof, *Neue Juristische Wochenschrift*, 2018, pp. 158, 161; from the legal literature cf. A. Thiele, "Die Unabhängigkeit des Richters …," pp. 430 ff.; F. Wittreck, "Durchschnitt als Dienstpflicht …," p. 3287.

36 Judgment of Bundesgerichtshof, *Neue Juristische Wochenschrift*, 2018, pp. 158, 160 and H.-J. Papier, "Richterliche Unabhängigkeit …," p. 13.

37 Judgment of Bundesgerichtshof, *Neue Juristische Wochenschrift*, 2018, p. 161.

rule-of-law perspective: Judicial independence and the right of access to justice are to be reconciled in this way, with sufficient consideration being given to the particularities of the individual case.

4. Supervision in times of conflict: A means to enforce political neutrality?

Another case that deserves attention regarding the supervision of judges occurred last year, in the federal state of Hesse. The key actor in this case was a judge at the Administrative Court of Giessen named Andreas Höfer, who had used a relatively simple case of administrative law as an opportunity to vent his personal resentment about the federal government's migration policy and its (supposed) effects in an all-out attack that disregarded objectivity and a sense of proportion.[38] The underlying legal dispute concerned the election posters of a far-right party with the slogan "Migration tötet!" and the order of a local authority to remove these posters from the streets – according to the municipality the posters constituted an illegal act of incitement of the people ("*Volksverhetzung*") under § 130 of the Penal Code. The unlawfulness of this order was already apparent, since the party had not been heard, even though § 28 of the Hessian Law of Administrative Proceedings requires such a hearing.[39] Moreover, it would have been legally justifiable to qualify the incriminated slogan as a permissible expression of opinion.[40] Instead of admitting the party's claim for one of these obvious reasons, the administrative judge in Giessen used the opportunity to present his own answer to the (not very sensible) question of whether migration can kill. The result was a hodgepodge of assertions, data and facts to prove that the statement "Migration kills!" is true. Starting with the Romans, Huns and Goths, the judgement draws a distorted picture of historical "migration processes" and arrives at the Aztecs, the Incas and the bison populations of the USA, among others, followed by passages on Salafism, blood revenge, honour killings and

38 The decision of Verwaltungsgericht Gießen is available in the database Beck-Online. The reference is: BeckRS 2019, No. 23522. The judgement was strongly criticised in the public discussion as well as in legal literature; see in particular N. Austermann/A. Fischer-Lescano/J. Gelhaar/T. Vetter, "Rechte Ab-Gründe," *Kritische Justiz*, vol. 53, 2020, pp. 114 ff. and M. Wagner, "Rassismus tötet. Kommentar und Kontext zum Urteil des VG Gießen v. 9. August 2019," *myops*, Nr. 38, 2020, pp. 4 ff.

39 See M. Wagner, "Rassismus tötet...," pp. 8 ff.

40 On the controversial assessment of these and similar slogans on election posters by the courts, see M. Wagner, "Rassismus tötet...," pp. 6 ff. (with further references).

"no-go areas" in German cities. The grand finale of the whole piece is a doubtful constitutional reference to the right of resistance under Article 20 (4) of the Basic Law and the outrageous assertion that the request to remove the posters by the authorities is "dictatorial" and amounts to a "suppressive measure." All of this is written, it must be emphasised once again, in the reasoning of an administrative court decision. It goes without saying that this constituted a shameless abuse of the independence and authority of the judiciary. So far, it has remained without legal consequences. In the present context, it is necessary to consider whether such conduct could justify supervisory measures.

The abuse of judicial independence and authority to express political views is a phenomenon that has already been demonstrated in the history of the German judiciary and has often sparked discussions about the permissibility of appropriate supervisory measures (although the abuse has rarely reached such a level of brazenness as in the case of the Giessen judge).[41] The Prussian Grand Disciplinary Senate had already had to decide on such cases – for example in a case from the 1920s, in which a judge had described the expropriation of aristocratic families as "theft" in several judgments. In such circumstances, the Prussian Grand Disciplinary Senate considered supervisory measures against the judge regarding the abuse of his position to be lawful – also and especially when it came to formulations in the judgement itself.[42]

What are the supervisory powers of the authorities today when a judge uses the reasoning of a judgement to express political statements?[43] Or to put it another way: To what extent does the guarantee of judicial independence cover political statements made by a judge in the grounds for a judgment or during oral hearings? According to § 39 of the German Judiciary Act, within and outside of

41 References to relevant cases can be found – among others – in R. Schmidt-Räntsch, *Dienstaufsicht über Richter*, p. 689, 691. One particularly drastic case is mentioned by H. Arndt, "Grenzen der Dienstaufsicht ...," p. 301; the issue was a tirade against the political parties in a local court decision. Regrettably, the reference to jurisdiction (in footnote 34 of the article) proved to be incorrect, which is why the decision could not be found by the author. The weekly magazine DER SPIEGEL (22/1977, p. 18) also reported on the case at the time.

42 See the detailed description in R. Schmidt-Räntsch, *Dienstaufsicht über Richter*, pp. 7 ff. (with extensive references).

43 When reviewing the literature on the supervision of judges, it is rather perplexing that this problem area has seldom been addressed, although there have been repeated occurrences. More detailed explanations can be found in R. Schmidt-Räntsch, *Dienstaufsicht über Richter*, pp. 150 ff. and H. Sendler, "Was dürfen Richter in der Öffentlichkeit sagen?," *Neue Juristische Wochenschrift*, 1984, pp. 689, 691 ff.

his office a judge must behave in such a way that confidence in his independence does not appear to be jeopardised. The wording of § 39 German Judiciary Act explicitly states that this also applies to political activity. Based on the law of the civil service, this regulation is interpreted as the "rule of moderation."[44] First of all, it is worth noting that the legislator believes that such a requirement for moderation serves the independence of the judiciary (instead of impairing it). It is evident that judicial independence is not affected if political moderation (whatever that means) is demanded of him in his off-duty conduct. In the present case the situation is more complicated: § 39 of the German Judiciary Act requires that judges exercise political moderation in the execution of their office – this includes the writing of a judgement. It would seem only logical to regard the core area of judicial activity as always being affected – in this case, the principle of judicial independence would have to be applied in full (the same standards would however apply for the judge's verbal expressions of opinion throughout the oral hearing). Conversely, it has been suggested in the literature that a distinction should be made between the "what" and the "how" when formulating the reasons for a judgement:[45] Obiter dicta in the form of political opinions would not concern the substantive correctness of a judgment, but only its linguistic version and thus its form. This form would be subject to supervision. Whether this distinction is convincing and viable may be up for debate. There is cause for doubt, at least in so far as the linguistic version of the judgement would thus also be subject to supervision in other respects, too (for example in the case of stylistic deficiencies). In a case like the present one, the same result can also be justified based on the standards established by case law (as described above[46]). Since the core area of judicial activity appears to be affected, intervention by the supervisory authority can only be considered in the event of an obvious and unquestionable violation of the principle of rule of moderation. In the case of the Giessen administrative judge, this condition is fulfilled. However, it can be assumed that such a limit may be exceeded even in less serious cases:[47] As a rule, political statements do not belong in the reasoning of a judgement, so that such statements are usually obvious mistakes beyond any doubt (especially if they do

44 Cf. J.-F. Staats, *Deutsches Richtergesetz*, Baden-Baden: Nomos, 2012, mn. 1 on § 39.

45 In this vein, R. Schmidt-Räntsch, *Dienstaufsicht über Richter*, p. 152.

46 See above: II and III.

47 Ultimately, R. Schmidt-Räntsch (*Dienstaufsicht über Richter*, pp. 153 ff.) also considers supervisory measures to be permissible to a large extent if, under the guise of judicial independence, the reasoning behind decisions is abused as a forum for the expression of political opinions.

not directly relate to the subject matter of the judgement). Things might only be different if it is a political commentary on a legal provision relevant to the decision – in such a case it would depend on the scope and the respect for objectivity. These principles are also based on the consideration that judicial independence is guaranteed in the interest of the citizens and the state in a judiciary that is governed by the rule of law and not grounded in the private interest of the judge. A judge who uses the reasoning of his judgement to express his political views mixes up and confuses civil liberties and judicial independence; he speaks as a private person, but in his capacity as a judge he is asked as part of the state.

5. Conclusion: Juridification and the reduction of supervision in the judicial system of a constitutional state

What conclusions can be drawn from the historical and current conflicts over the relationship between judicial independence and administrative supervision? As the "case of the miller *Arnold*" has shown,[48] this is a traditional problem that dates back to a time before the rule of law was established. To the same extent that the rule of law has asserted itself as a constitutional principle, two things can be observed with regard to the aforementioned tension. One of these is the juridification of the supervision itself: While in times before the rule of law the ruler was able to intervene in the administration of justice in a corrective manner through "*Machtsprüche*" or similar instruments, the supervision of the judge is a legal institution with clear legal contours, which, in turn, is subject to judicial control by the disciplinary courts. At the head of this disciplinary jurisdiction is the highest ordinary court, the Federal Court of Justice. The final word on a supervisory measure against the judge is thus again had by a judge. This complies with the rule-of-law principle of the separation of powers.

At the same time, however, the intensity and scope of supervision measures are remarkable. It was common practice well into the twentieth century for the supervision of judges to extend to all aspects of judicial work and thus also to the substantial correctness of the content of judgments and decisions. In legal literature, it was said that the supervisory authority – meaning the practice in Prussia – had examined a judge's decisions "wie ein Ausbilder die Arbeiten des Referendars."[49] Where the judicial core competences are concerned, that is, in the settling of legal disputes, there is no place for such a comprehensive supervision

48 See above: II.

49 R. Schmidt-Räntsch, *Dienstaufsicht über Richter*, p. 9.

nowadays. Nevertheless, judicial independence cannot be limitless in this area either – as has been shown both by the trials on judicial workload[50] and the case of the Giessen Administrative Court.[51] The barriers are to be developed from the assumption that judicial independence must not be an end in itself and is not granted in the private interest of the judge. It draws its plausibility and justification from the right to be granted judicial protection; it must therefore end where this protection itself is endangered by serious misconduct on the part of the judge. A constitutional state without judicial independence is just as inconceivable as a constitutional state without such a minimum of supervision of judges. This minimum of control is indispensable, especially where a maximum of judicial independence is to be established.

References

Achterberg N., "Die richterliche Unabhängigkeit im Spiegel der Dienstgerichtsbarkeit," *Neue Juristische Wochenschrift*, 1985, pp. 3041ff.

Arndt H., "Grenzen der Dienstaufsicht über Richter," *Deutsche Richterzeitung*, 1974, pp. 248ff.

Arndt H., "Zur Dienstaufsicht über die Richter," *Deutsche Richterzeitung*, 1978, pp. 278ff.

Austermann N./Fischer-Lescano A./Gelhaar J./Vetter T., "Rechte Ab-Gründe," *Kritische Justiz*, vol. 53, 2020, pp. 114ff.

Baur F., *Justizaufsicht und richterliche Unabhängigkeit*, Tübingen: J. C. B. Mohr (Paul Siebeck), 1954.

Degenhart C., *Staatsrecht I. Staatsorganisationsrecht*, Heidelberg: C.F. Müller, 36th ed., 2020.

Funk W., "Grenzen der Dienstaufsicht über Richter im Hinblick auf deren verfassungsrechtlich geschützte Unabhängigkeit," *Deutsche Richterzeitung*, 1978, pp. 357ff.

Hillgruber C., in: Maunz/Dürig, *Grundgesetz-Kommentar*, loose-leaf (updated October 2020), commentary on Art. 97.

Mayer A., "Richterliche Unabhängigkeit und Dienstaufsicht," *Deutsche Richterzeitung*, 1978, p. 313.

Papier H.-J., "Richterliche Unabhängigkeit und Dienstaufsicht," *Neue Juristische Wochenschrift*, 1990, pp. 8ff.

50 See above: III.

51 See above: IV.

Prümm P., "Friedrich II. von Preußen und das Recht – Das Interpretationsverbot im ALR, der Prozess des Müllers Arnold und der Überfall auf Sachsen," *Zeitschrift für das juristische Studium*, 2012, pp. 24ff.

Redeker M., "Die Dienstaufsicht über Richter," *Sächsische Verwaltungsblätter*, 2007, pp. 73ff.

Rudolph K., "Zur Dienstaufsicht über Richter," *Deutsche Richterzeitung*, 1978, p. 146.

Scheuer J. N., "Dienstaufsicht und richterliche Unabhängigkeit," in: *Auf festem Fundament. Festschrift für Christean Wagner*, ed. M. Demel et al., Berlin: Duncker & Humblot, 2013, pp. 191ff.

Schmidt E., *Rechtsentwicklung in Preußen*, 2nd ed., Berlin: Springer, 1929.

Schmidt-Räntsch R., *Dienstaufsicht über Richter*, Bielefeld: Gieseking, 1985.

Sendler H., "Was dürfen Richter in der Öffentlichkeit sagen?," *Neue Juristische Wochenschrift*, 1984, pp. 689ff.

Sendler H., "Friedrich der Große und der Müller Arnold," *Juristische Schulung*, 1986, pp. 759ff.

Staats J.-F., *Deutsches Richtergesetz*, Baden-Baden: Nomos 2012.

Thiele A., "Die Unabhängigkeit des Richters – grenzenlose Freiheit? – Das Spannungsverhältnis zwischen richterlicher Unabhängigkeit und Dienstaufsicht," *Der Staat*, vol. 52, 2013, pp. 415ff.

Wagner M., "Rassismus tötet. Kommentar und Kontext zum Urteil des VG Gießen v. 9. August 2019," *myops*, No. 38, 2020, pp. 4ff.

Wittreck F., "Durchschnitt als Dienstpflicht?," *Neue Juristische Wochenschrift*, 2012, pp. 3287ff.

Judgments:

Bundesgerichtshof, *Neue Juristische Wochenschrift*, 1977, p. 437.

Bundesgerichtshof, *Neue Juristische Wochenschrift*, 1978, p. 760.

Bundesgerichtshof, *Neue Juristische Wochenschrift*, 1984, p. 2535.

Bundesgerichtshof, *Neue Juristische Wochenschrift*, 1991, p. 1103.

Bundesgerichtshof, *Deutsche Richterzeitung*, 1995, p. 394.

Bundesgerichtshof, *Neue Juristische Wochenschrift – Rechtsprechungsreport*, 1999, p. 426.

Bundesgerichtshof, *Neue Juristische Wochenschrift – Rechtsprechungsreport*, 2001, p. 498.

Bundesgerichtshof, *Neue Juristische Wochenschrift – Rechtsprechungsreport*, 2008, p. 1660.

Bundesgerichtshof, *Neue Juristische Wochenschrift*, 2018, p. 158.
Bundesgerichtshof, BeckRS 2020, No. 10611.
Bundesgerichtshof, BeckRS 2020, No. 16578.
Bundesverfassungsgericht, *Neue Juristische Wochenschrift*, 2018, p. 1532.
Dienstgericht Karlsruhe, BeckRS 2013, No. 942.
Dienstgerichtshof Stuttgart, BeckRS 2015, No. 11585.
Verwaltungsgericht Gießen, BeckRS 2019, No. 23522.

Katharina Pabel[1]

Judicial independence and the court's organisation from the perspective of the European Convention on Human Rights

Abstract: The aim of the paper is to analyse judicial independence and the court's organisation from the perspective of the European Convention on Human Rights and the jurisprudence of the ECtHR. In the paper, the following components of the art. 6 ECTHR are presented: the definition of "tribunal," the criterion of "established by law," the concept of an "independent" and "impartial" tribunal. The analysis demonstrates that judicial independence is not a goal that is successfully achieved at a given time. It must be observed, fostered and improved all the time. It is not enough to have the "perfect" legal framework for the organisation of the judiciary and the independent position of judges with all the requirements emanating from the case law fulfilled. The implementation of the law in every single proceeding with the mind-set of effective independence is at least as important as the legislation itself. Therefore, continuing the training of the judges, evaluating their independence with the existing tools and improving the overall understanding of the importance of an independent judiciary are prerequisites for the public's trust in the judiciary.

Keywords: European Convention on Human Rights, judicial independence, judicial impartiality, judicial functions, court organisation

1. The significance of Art. 6(1) ECHR

Art. 6 of the European Convention on Human Rights (ECHR) constitutes a significant manifestation of the principle of Rule of Law.[2] It is one of the provisions that were interpreted quite early on by the European Court of Human Rights (ECtHR). The respective case law goes back to the 1960s, like the case of *Neumeister*, which refers to a tribunal's independence of the executive and the parties to a case in the context of the principle of "equality of arms."[3] As early as 1971, the ECtHR further elaborated on the term of office of members of a

---

1 Katharina Pabel, PhD, Professor of Law at Vienna University of Economics and Business, (Austria), The Member of Venice Commission. ORCID – 0000-0002-5726-7633.

2 Grabenwarter, Ch., K. Pabel, "Europäische Menschenrechtskonvention," Munich: C.H. Beck, 2016, p. 470.

3 Ruling of ECtHR, 27.6.1968, *Neumeister v AT*, No. 1936/63, para. 22 f.

tribunal as well as "necessary guarantees" of national proceedings in the case of *Ringeisen*.[4] The court widened its approach in the 1980s, above all in the case of *Campbell and Fell*,[5] establishing the core criteria of an independent and impartial tribunal.

Judicial independence is guaranteed by Art. 6(1) ECHR, which reads as follows:

> In the determination of his civil rights and obligations or of any criminal charge against him, everyone is entitled to a fair and public hearing within a reasonable time **by an independent and impartial tribunal established by law**. Judgment shall be pronounced publicly but the press and public may be excluded from all or part of the trial in the interests of morals, public order or national security in a democratic society, where the interests of juveniles or the protection of the private life of the parties so require, or to the extent strictly necessary in the opinion of the court in special circumstances where publicity would prejudice the interests of justice." Therefore, all civil and criminal proceedings falling within its scope of application need to be decided by an independent and impartial tribunal established by law to inspire confidence in the public or in the accused, which is of "fundamental importance in a democratic society."[6]

Art. 6(1) ECHR additionally plays a role in the European Union, as the right to a fair trial constitutes a general principle of Union law, which is codified in Art. 6(3) of the Treaty on the European Union.[7] Moreover, Art. 6(1) ECHR is also relevant for the interpretation of Art. 47(2) of the Charter of Fundamental Rights of the European Union (CFR) concerning the right to a fair trial, equally calling for a decision-making body established by law and acting independently as well as impartially.[8] Art. 52(3) CFR states that if Charter rights correspond to the rights guaranteed by the ECHR, "the meaning and scope of those rights shall be

---

4 Ruling of ECtHR, 16.7.1971, *Ringeisen v AT*, No. 2614/65, para. 95.

5 Ruling of ECtHR, 28.6.1984, *Campbell and Fell v UK*, No. 7819/77 et al., para. 76 f.

6 Ruling of ECtHR (GC), 15.12.2005, *Kyprianou v CYP*, No. 73797/01, para. 118; Grabenwarter, Ch., *European Convention on Human Rights. Commentary*, Munich: C.H. Beck, 2014, Art. 6 para. 34; Harris, D., M. O'Boyle, Bades, E., and C. Buckley, *Law of the European Convention on Human Rights*, Oxford: Oxford University Press, 2018, p. 446.

7 Ruling of ECJ, 15.5.1986, *Johnston*, C-222/84, para. 18 f.

8 Ruling of ECJ, 17.7.2014, *Torresi*, C-58/13 a.o., para. 17; Ruling of ECJ, 6.10.2015, *Consorci Sanitari del Maresme*, C-203/14, para. 17; Ruling of ECJ, 16.2.2017, *Margarit Panicello*, C-503/15, para. 27; Ruling of ECJ, 27.2.2018, *Associação Sindical dos Juizes Portugueses*, C-64/16, para. 38; Pabel, K. in: *Europäischer Grundrechtsschutz. Enzyklopädie Europarecht*, ed. by Ch. Grabenwarter, Baden Baden: Nomos, 2014, No. 2(19), para. 53.

the same as those laid down by the said Convention." The explanations relating to the CFR illustrate that the reference to the ECHR covers the Convention itself, the Protocols, as well as the case law of the ECtHR.[9] Although it needs to be acknowledged that the overall scope of application of Art. 47(2) CFR is more broadly framed than Art. 6(1) ECHR, as the former is not limited to civil and criminal proceedings, the case law of the ECtHR, in terms of the definition of an independent and impartial tribunal, is broadly applicable.[10] The Court of Justice of the European Union (ECJ) has lately increasingly focused on Art. 47 CFR when deciding upon infringement proceedings pertaining to the Rule of Law, and in several cases in relation to an independent tribunal.[11]

2. The definition of a "tribunal" under Art. 6(1) ECHR

The notion of "tribunal" underlies the autonomous interpretation by the ECtHR and does not depend on the concept or classification in any domestic legal order.[12] Thus, any organ which satisfies the relatively strict criteria that stem from the Convention and the case law of the ECtHR, qualifies as a tribunal independent of their formal status as a court in the national legal framework.[13] This encompasses courts of ordinary jurisdiction as well as other decision-making bodies when meeting the following criteria:

First, the organ must have the competence to fully exercise judicial functions and, thus, "determining matters within its competence on the basis of rules of law and after proceedings conducted in a prescribed manner."[14] Second, it needs

9 Explanations Relating to the Charter of Fundamental Rights, *OJ C 303, 14.12.2007*, p. 17–35.

10 Pabel, K. in: *Europäischer Grundrechtsschutz. Enzyklopädie Europarecht*, ed. by Ch. Grabenwarter, Baden Baden: Nomos, 2014, No. 2(19), para. 24.

11 Ruling of ECJ, 24.6.2019, *EC v POL and HUN*, para. 57, 71 f. (lowering retirement age of judges, presidential prolongation of shortened term of office of Supreme Court judges); Ruling of ECJ, 5.11.2019, *EC v POL*, C-192/18, para. 100, 105 f. (lowering retirement age of judges, presidential prolongation of shortened term of office of ordinary court judges).

12 Grabenwarter, Ch., *European Convention on Human Rights. Commentary*, Munich: C.H. Beck, 2014, Art. 6 para. 34.

13 Grabenwarter, Ch., *European Convention on Human Rights. Commentary*, Munich: C.H. Beck, 2014, Art. 6 para. 34.

14 Ruling of ECtHR, 30.11.1987, *H v BE*, No. 8950/80, para. 50; Ruling of ECtHR, 29.4.1988, *Belilos v SUI*, No. 10328/83, para. 64; Ruling of ECtHR, 22.10.1984, *Sramek v AT*, No. 8790/79, para. 36; Ruling of ECtHR, 6.4.2004, *Rozsa v AT*, No. 67950/01; see also Ruling of ECtHR, 27.6.1968, *Neumeister v AT*, para. 24; Ruling of ECtHR,

to be competent to take binding decisions on questions of fact and law on the parties, meaning that the organ establishes the facts of a case itself, and applies the relevant legal provisions to the identified factual situation.[15] If the organ takes decisions solely on the admissibility of the re-opening of proceedings or if it is bound by non-contestable decisions of a political body, these standards are not met.[16] However, in case of doubt, the external appearance can be decisive.[17] Third, a tribunal's decision must not be altered by a non-judicial authority entailing a detriment to a party.[18]

Also, domestic legal systems must guarantee that judicial decisions are actually implemented.[19] It is not sufficient for a person seeking legal protection to obtain a binding judgment. Clear and admissible procedures for its prompt and effective implementation have to be set up, as well as bodies that are competent to execute the judgments. The Strasbourg case law shows that in some member states the implementation of judgments is a weak point in the judiciary.

3. The criterion of "Established by Law"

The requirement of "established by law" according to Art. 6(1) ECHR especially reflects the principle of Rule of Law and covers the composition of the bench of a tribunal, its organisation in general, and its competence.[20] This "law" has to be

---

16.7.1971, *Ringeisen v AT*, para. 95; Ruling of ECtHR, 23.6.1981, *Le Compte a.o. v BEL*, No. 6878/75, para. 51b, 55, 60; Ruling of ECtHR, 28.6.1984, *Campbell and Fell v UK*, para. 76.

15 Ruling of ECtHR, 28.6.1984, *Campbell and Fell v UK*, para. 76; Ruling of ECtHR, 23.10.1985, *Benthem v NED*, No. 8848/80, para. 40; *Grabenwarter*, Ruling of ECHR, Art. 6 para. 36; see also Ruling of ECtHR, 23.9.1982, *Sporrong and Lönnroth v SWE*, No. 7151/75 et al., para. 86; Ruling of ECtHR, 21.9.1993, *Zumtobel v AT*, No. 12235/86, para. 32.

16 Ruling of ECtHR, 23.9.1982, *Sporrong and Lönnroth v SWE*, para. 86; Ruling of ECtHR, 13.2.2003, *Chevrol v FRA*, No. 49636/99, para. 76–84.

17 Ruling of ECtHR, 29.4.1988, *Belilos v SUI*, para. 67.

18 Ruling of ECtHR, 28.10.1988 (GK), *Brumarescu v ROM*, No. 28342/95, para. 63; Ruling of ECtHR, 22.5.1998, *Vasilescu v ROM*, No. 27053/95, para. 39 f.; Ruling of ECtHR, 26.2.2002, *Morris v UK*, No. 38784/97, para. 73; as part of "*independence*" e.g. Ruling of ECtHR, 25.2.1997, *Findlay v UK*, No. 22107/93, para. 77.

19 Van Dijk P., F. van Hoof, A. van Rijn, L. Zwaak, *Theory and Practice of the European Convention on Human Rights*, Cambridge: Intersentia, 2018, p. 599.

20 Ruling of ECtHR, 4.3.2003, *Poshokhov v RUS*, No. 63486/00, para. 39 (lay judges); Ruling of ECtHR, 11.7.2006, *Gurov v MOL*, No. 36455/02, para. 35; Ruling of ECtHR,

a generally binding provision having a "higher degree of legal validity" in order to be capable of preventing arbitrary conduct.[21]

It is of a special importance whether a state's Constitution guarantees the right to a competent judge, as pointed out by the Venice Commission in its Rule of Law-Checklist.[22] The basic rules of the court system concerning its organisation and jurisdiction should be set out by legislation emanating from Parliament, while particular matters can be left to the executive and be subject to judicial review so that illegal or arbitrary actions can be prevented.[23] This also entails that the organisation of the judicial system cannot be left to the discretion of judicial authorities in countries where the law is generally codified, but a certain latitude to interpret the relevant domestic law can be left to the courts. The ECtHR recently repeated this approach in the case of *Miracle Europe Kft.*, which concerned the national procedure for designating cases to other courts as the territorially competent ones.[24]

A very prominent example in this context is provided by the *Coëme a.o.* case. The Belgian Constitution gave the Court of Cassation the competence to try government ministers for certain criminal offences, while non-ministers were tried before ordinary courts. However, the Court of Cassation decided to try all accusations of ministers and non-ministers together in a special case, due to the connection between the offences without a legislative basis for this course of action. This "connection rule" was merely the rule of the court itself. That is why the Court of Cassation was not "established by law."[25]

Moreover, "established by law" includes "established in accordance with the law." This means that a court has additionally to function according to the

---

20.7.2006, *Sokurenko and Strygun v UKR*, No. 29458/04, para. 27; Ruling of ECtHR, 12.1.2016, *Miracle Europe Kfz v HUN*, No. 57774/13, para. 47 f.

21 Grabenwarter, Ch., *European Convention on Human Rights. Commentary*, Munich: C.H. Beck, 2014, Art. 6 para. 40.

22 Ruling of ECtHR, 21.6.2011, *Fruni v SLK*, No. 8014/07, para. 134 f; European Commission for Democracy through Law (Venice Commission), Rule of Law Checklist, adopted at its 106th Plenary Session in Venice, 11–12 March 2016, Point E(1)(b) Independence of individual judges.

23 Ruling of ECtHR, 18.12.1980, *Crociani a.o. v IT*, No. 8603/79 et al.; Ruling of ECtHR, 28.6.1984, *Campbell and Fell v UK*, para. 76; ECtHR, 5.10.2010, *DMD Group, A.S. v SLK*, No. 19334/03, para. 58; Ruling of ECtHR, 12.1.2016, *Miracle Europe Kfz v HUN*, para. 51.

24 Ruling of ECtHR, 12.1.2016, *Miracle Europe Kfz v HUN*, para. 51.

25 Ruling of ECtHR, 22.6.2000, *Coëme a.o. v BEL*, No. 32492/96 et al., para. 107 f.

delegated statutory rules governing it. Hence, even internal rules, e.g. on the appointment of judges, have to be complied with.[26]

In principle, setting up arbitration courts is allowed under Art. 6(1) ECHR. If it is obligatory to address an arbitration court, the criteria of Art. 6(1) ECHR need to be respected, while in the case of voluntariness a party may waive its rights under Art. 6(1) ECHR. Apart from being voluntary, a waiver has, furthermore, to be explicit and lawful as well as to a certain extent procedurally safeguarded.[27] The ECtHR regularly accepts a voluntary agreement on arbitration clauses in the economic realm.[28] In sports-related cases, the ECtHR generally accepts an international arbitrational tribunal and a restricted judicial review by a national court as a last instance. However, the condition of accepting an arbitration clause in order to attend competitions or to work as a professional sportsman shows an obligatory arbitrational jurisdiction.[29]

4. The concept of an "independent" tribunal

The concept of an "independent" tribunal relates to the separation of powers, which is fundamental to the Rule of Law principle and concerns the tribunal as a whole.[30] It additionally refers to each single member and in general encompasses the independence of the executive and of the parties to the case.[31] Therefore, independence and impartiality are closely related and sometimes difficult to

26 Ruling of ECtHR, 4.3.2003, *Poshohkov v RU*, para. 39 f (lay judges); Ruling of ECtHR, 13.4.2006, *Fedotova v RU*, No. 73225/01, para. 38 f (lay judges); see further Harris, D., M. O'Boyle, Bades, E., and C. Buckley, *Law of the European Convention on Human Rights*, Oxford: Oxford University Press, 2018, p. 459.

27 Ruling of ECtHR, 28.10.2010, *Suda v CZE*, No. 1643/06, para. 49; Ruling of ECtHR, 2.10.2018, *Mutu and Pechstein v SUI*, No. 40575/10, para. 96.

28 Ruling of ECtHR, 16.12.2003, *Transportes Fluviais do Sado SA v PT*, No. 35943/02; Ruling of ECtHR, 1.3.2016, *Tabbane v SUI*, No. 41069/12, para. 23 f.

29 Ruling of ECtHR, 2.10.2018, *Mutu and Pechstein v SUI*, para. 109 f.

30 Grabenwarter, Ch., *European Convention on Human Rights. Commentary*, Munich: C.H. Beck, Art. 6 para. 42; Schabas W.A., "The European Convention on Human Rights. A commentary," Oxford: Oxford University Press, 2017, p. 294.

31 Ruling of ECtHR, 18.10.2018, *Thiam v FRA*, No. 80018/12, para. 71 f; Grabenwarter, Ch., *European Convention on Human Rights. Commentary*, Munich: C.H. Beck, Art. 6, para. 42; Grabenwarter, Ch., K. Pabel, "Europäische Menschenrechtskonvention", Munich: C.H. Beck, 2016, p. 487; Schabas W.A., "The European Convention on Human Rights. A commentary," Oxford: Oxford University Press, 2017, p. 294.

dissociate. Thus, both requirements are often collectively used and analysed by the ECtHR.[32] Nevertheless, independence constitutes a prerequisite for impartiality.[33]

All in all, the ECtHR assesses the criterion of independence, as first established in the case of *Findlay*, on the basis of the manner of appointment of the members of the organ, their term of office, as well as the existence of guarantees against outside pressure and the question of whether the body appears to be independent.[34] Also, adequate remuneration can be an indication.[35]

4.1 Appointment of the members of a tribunal

The appointment of the members of a tribunal has to entail that the judges sit in an individual capacity and perform their duties free from any instructions of the executive.[36]

On the one hand, there are various examples of permissible appointment procedures in the case law of the ECtHR. Appointment by the executive or parliament is not per se obstructive.[37] It may be legitimate that the executive appoints the members of the tribunal. Then, the judges should be able to perform their duties individually and independently.[38] This can be ensured e.g. by a previous consultation of judicial organs, obligatory compliance with the appointment

---

32 Ruling of ECtHR, 25.2.1997, *Findlay v UK*, para. 73; Ruling of ECtHR, 9.10.2008, *Moiseyev v RUS*, No. 62936/00, para. 175; Ruling of ECtHR, 6.10.2011, *Agrokompleks v UKR*, No. 23465/05, para. 128.

33 *Grabenwarter*, ECHR, Art. 6 para. 52.

34 Ruling of ECtHR, 23.6.1981, *Le Compte a.o. v BEL*, para.55; Ruling of ECtHR, 28.6.1984, *Campbell and Fell v UK*, para. 78; Ruling of ECtHR, 22.6.1989, *Langborger v SWE*, para. 32; Ruling of ECtHR, 22.11.1995, *Bryan v UK*, No. 19178/91, para. 37; Ruling of ECtHR, 25.2.1997, *Findlay v UK*, para. 73.

35 Schabas W.A., "The European Convention on Human Rights. A commentary," Oxford: Oxford University Press, 2017, p. 294.

36 Ruling of ECtHR, 28.6.1984, *Campbell and Fell v UK*, para. 79; Ruling of ECtHR, 22.10.1984, *Sramek v AT*, para. 38.

37 Ruling of ECtHR, 16.7.1971, *Ringeisen v AT*, para. 95 f; Ruling of ECtHR, 1.10.1982, *Piersack v BEL*, No. 8692/79, para. 27; Ruling of ECtHR, 28.6.1984, *Campbell and Fell v UK*, para. 78 f.

38 Ruling of ECtHR, 28.6.1984, *Campbell and Fell v UK*, para. 79; Ruling of ECtHR, 22.10.1984, *Sramek v AT*, para. 38.

proposals put forward by the judiciary, or the establishment of general selection criteria.[39]

On the other hand, the ECtHR has also dealt with cases showing impermissible appointments. If the judges are appointed or nominated by an interest group and the tribunal has to decide on their interests or of its members respectively, legitimate doubts as to independence (or impartiality) can arise.[40]

The Venice Commission considers it appropriate to establish an independent judicial council that has decisive influence over decisions on the appointment and career of judges. While the Venice Commission is aware of the variety of legal systems, it recommends that states, which have not yet done so, consider the establishment of an independent judicial council or similar body.[41] In all cases the council should have a pluralistic composition with a substantial part, if not the majority, of members being judges. Though this approach is widely accepted among European states, experience shows that the mere existence of a judicial council cannot guarantee the independence of the judiciary. The ECJ established that the participation of such a body, in the context of a process for the appointment of judges, could contribute to making that process more objective only if that body is itself sufficiently independent of the legislature and executive, and of the authority to which it is required to deliver such an appointment proposal.[42]

4.2 The term of office of members of a tribunal

Regarding the term of office, the duration does not need to be for a lifetime, but generally for a period of time sufficient to guarantee a certain level of stability. Ordinary courts usually need judges for life or a fixed term.[43]

Besides, the ECtHR considers a minimum term of office of 5 or 6 years as adequate.[44] Shorter terms of office can be justified in the case of understandable

---

39 Grabenwarter, Ch., *European Convention on Human Rights. Commentary*, Munich: C.H. Beck, 2014, Art. 6 para. 43; Grabenwarter, Ch., K. Pabel, "Europäische Menschenrechtskonvention", Munich: C.H. Beck, 2016, p. 488.

40 Ruling of ECtHR, 29.4.1988, *Belilos v SUI*, para. 67; Ruling of ECtHR, 22.6.1989, *Langborger v SWE*, para. 35.

41 Venice, Commission Report on the Independence of the Judicial System Part I: The Independence of Judges, 16.3.2010, para. 32.

42 Ruling of ECJ, 19.11.2009, *A.K.*, para. 137 f.

43 Harris, D., M. O'Boyle, Bades, E., and C. Buckley, *Law of the European Convention on Human Rights*, Oxford: Oxford University Press, 2018, p. 446.

44 Ruling of ECtHR, 23.6.1981, *Le Compte a.o. v BEL*, para. 57; Grabenwarter, Ch., *European Convention on Human Rights. Commentary*, Munich: C.H. Beck, Art. 6 para. 44.

reasons, like the performance of duties free of charge or as a mere secondary function. This was primarily established in the case of *Campbell and Fell*, which constitutes one of the landmark cases on the element of judicial independence;[45] also, the Venice Commission refers to this judgment in its Rule of Law-Checklist on the issue of judicial independence.[46] In this ruling, a prison Board of Visitors acted as a disciplinary tribunal for a period of 3 years, which was justified because the members were unpaid and it was difficult to find candidates for a longer term.

However, a 4-year term of office of military judges with the possibility of renewal was problematic.[47]

4.3 The irremovability of members of a tribunal

Another significant aspect constitutes the **irremovability** of judges, which is a "corollary" of their independence.[48] In general, it may be possible to remove a member of a tribunal, but this has to be limited to exceptional cases and specific reasons that should be incorporated into law.[49] However, a practical irremovability suffices as long as it is recognised in fact and the other necessary guarantees are preserved, which is also derived from *Campbell and Fell*.[50]

The ECtHR recognises several procedures as permissible. There is no problem if the decision-making organ does not re-elect a judge. Moreover, there are no doubts concerning independence if the judge performs other tasks within the

45 Ruling of ECtHR, 28.6.1984, *Campbell and Fell v UK*, para. 80.

46 European Commission for Democracy through Law (Venice Commission), Rule of Law Checklist, adopted at its 106th Plenary Session in Venice, 11–12 March 2016, Point E(1)(a) Access to justice.

47 Ruling of ECtHR (GK), 9.6.1998, *Incal v Turkey*, No. 22678/93, para. 68.

48 Ruling of ECtHR, 28.6.1984, *Campbell and Fell v UK*, para. 80; Schabas W.A., "The European Convention on Human Rights. A commentary," Oxford: Oxford University Press, 2017, p. 294; Reid, K., *A practitioner's Guide to the ECHR*, London: Sweet & Maxwell, 2012, p. 215.

49 Ruling of ECtHR, 28.6.1984, *Campbell and Fell v UK*, para. 80; Ruling of ECtHR, 22.10.1984, *Sramek v AT*, para. 38; ECtHR, 21.7.2009, *Luka v ROM*, No. 34197/02, para. 44; Ruling of ECtHR, 30.11.2010, *Henryk Urban a Ryszard Urban v POL*, No. 23614/08, para. 53.

50 Ruling of ECtHR, 28.6.1984, *Campbell and Fell v UK*, para. 80; see also Ruling of ECtHR, 16.7.1971, *Ringeisen v AT*, para. 95, Ruling of ECtHR, 8.6.1976, *Engel a.o. v NED*, No. 5100/71 et al., para. 68; Ruling of ECtHR, 22.10.1984, *Sramek v AT*, para. 38; ECtHR, 22.6.1989, *Langborger v SWE*, para. 22.

judicial branch.[51] If a judge is simultaneously employed in other state functions, it depends on the nature of the task whether there is an infringement of the requirement of independence.[52] Moreover, a problem does not necessarily arise in theory if a member of the executive has an influence on a resignation, but in practical terms this is limited to exceptional circumstances or the decision is subject to judicial review.[53]

However, examples of impermissible procedures can be found in the ECtHR's case law as well. In *Henryk Urban and Ryszard Urban*, an assessor (trainee judge) in a criminal court was not satisfactorily independent, as she – although there was no exercise in practice – could have been removed by the Minister of Justice at any time during her term of office. In addition, there were not any adequate guarantees of protection from the arbitrary exercise of the Minister's power or a full judicial review of the decision of the assessor.[54] The same applied to members of a maritime dispute division, namely the president and the vice-president who were subject to removal from office by the Minister of Justice and were additionally in a position of hierarchical subordination.[55]

4.4 Carrying out functions free from instructions

It is especially important that judges are able to carry out their judicial functions free from instructions and without being subject to accountability.[56] The essence of this aspect is that a judge must come to a decision in compliance with the law and their conscience.[57] This does not affect a hierarchical structure in the context

51 Ruling of ECtHR, 1.10.1982, *Piersack v BEL*, para. 30.

52 Grabenwarter, Ch., *European Convention on Human Rights. Commentary*, Munich: C.H. Beck, Art. 6, para. 45; Grabenwarter, Ch., K. Pabel, "Europäische Menschenrechtskonvention", Munich: C.H. Beck, 2016, p. 488.

53 Ruling of ECtHR, 28.6.1984, *Campbell and Fell v UK*, para. 80; Ruling of ECtHR, 25.8.2005, *Clarke v UK*, No. 23695/02.

54 Ruling of ECtHR, 30.11.2010, *Henryk Urban and Ryszard Urban v POL*, para.53 f; see further Schabas W.A., "The European Convention on Human Rights. A commentary," Oxford: Oxford University Press, 2017, p. 295; Reid, K., *A practitioner's Guide to the ECHR*, London: Sweet & Maxwell, 2012, p. 215.

55 Ruling of ECtHR, 3.3.2005, *Brudnicka v POL*, No. 54723/00, para. 41.

56 Ruling of ECtHR, 28.6.1984, *Campbell and Fell v UK*, para. 78; Ruling of ECtHR, 22.10.1984, *Sramek v AT*, para. 38; Ruling of ECtHR, 8.7.1986, *Lithgow a.o. v UK*, No. 9006/80 et al., para. 202; Ruling of ECtHR, 24.11.1994, *Beaumartin v FRA*, No. 15287/ 89, para. 38 f.

57 Grabenwarter, Ch., *European Convention on Human Rights. Commentary*, Munich: C.H. Beck, Art. 6, para. 46.

of service law.[58] However, if a person functions as an official or office-holder and also as a judge, it is necessary to examine whether the independence is called into question by obligations under service law.[59] Additionally, judges need to be free from illegal influence within the judiciary itself, e.g. directives or pressure from other judges or the president of a court.[60] Again, installing lay judges does not hinder independence but actually contributes to adequate decision-making, frequently due their special expertise.[61]

There are various examples of allowed restrictions. According to the ECtHR, a disciplinary court for medical practitioners which was composed of exactly the same number of medical practitioners as of the judiciary – the latter had the casting vote in case of deadlock – is acceptable.[62] A court can be bound by a decision of an administrative authority on a preliminary question if a judicial review – in the event of a direct effect on civil rights and obligations – of the preliminary question is provided, which complies with Art. 6 ECHR.[63]

In any event, there are many examples for impermissible restrictions in the Court's case law. In general, problems arise if the judiciary and the executive closely intertwine, as the proceedings are then classified as administrative in nature (though falling within the scope of Art. 6 ECHR), or a certain relation between a court and a prosecution authority occurs.[64] The court considers tribunals dealing with social security cases as not independent if the executive controls the appointment of the decision-making organ, the organs have the

---

58 Grabenwarter, Ch., *European Convention on Human Rights. Commentary*, Munich: C.H. Beck, Art. 6, para. 46.

59 Ruling of ECtHR, 22.10.1984, *Sramek v AT*, para. 40 ff.

60 Ruling of ECtHR, 22.12.2009, *Parlov and Tkalic v CRO*, No. 24810/06, para. 86 f.; *van Dijk/van Hoof/van Rijn/Zwaak*, ECHR, p. 601.

61 Ruling of ECtHR, 23.6.1981, *Le Compte a.o. v BEL*, para. 55 f; Ruling of ECtHR, 22.10.1984, *Sramek v AT*, para. 39; Ruling of ECtHR, 22.6.1989, *Langborder v SWE*, No. 11179/84, para. 30; Ruling of ECtHR, 23.4.1996, *Remli v FRA*, No. 16839/90, para. 46–48; Ruling of ECtHR, 28.1.2010, *Puchstein v AT*, No. 20089/06, para. 53 f; Ruling of ECtHR, 28.1.2010, *Stechauner v AT*, No. 20087/06, para. 52 f.

62 Ruling of ECtHR, 23.6.1981, *Le Compte a.o. v BEL*, para. 57 (also an issue of impartiality).

63 Grabenwarter, Ch., *European Convention on Human Rights. Commentary*, Munich: C.H. Beck, Art. 6 para. 50; corresponding Ruling of ECtHR, 28.6.1990, *Obermeier v AT*, No. 11761/85, para. 70; Ruling of ECtHR, 20.11.1995, *British-American Tobacco Company Ltd. v NED*, No. 19589/92, para. 82 f.

64 Ruling of ECtHR, 23.10.1985, *Benthem v NED*, para. 41; Grabenwarter, Ch., *European Convention on Human Rights. Commentary*, Munich: C.H. Beck, Art. 6 para. 50.

legal status of employees, and there is no guarantee against outside pressure.[65] Also, cases under military law are deemed to be problematic. For example, a military tribunal conducting proceedings in which a convening officer played a key prosecuting role and, moreover, appointed the members of the court, who were at the same time subordinate and within his chain of command, was not accepted as independent.[66] What is more, the facts that members of a tribunal working as military and state judges at the same time violates the criterion of independence.[67] The same goes for a military officer as a judge without legal qualifications if he is still hierarchically linked to superior officers and thus subject to military discipline.[68] A court that is exclusively composed of military officers but puts civilians on trial cannot be considered as independent either.[69]

5. The concept of an "impartial" tribunal

Impartiality means the "absence of prejudice or bias" and is particularly important, because a person needs to be able to trust in the impartiality of a tribunal determining of the question of right and wrong.[70] Thus, a court must not be biased when deciding; it must act without being influenced by information gathered outside the courtroom, and it is not allowed to go by popular feeling, or any other pressure. A judge's opinion has to exclusively rest on objective arguments put forward at a trial without being led by personal emotions or attitudes.[71] Again, the ECtHR and also the Venice Commission look at whether

---

65 Ruling of ECtHR, 2.9.1998, *Lauko v SVK*, No. 26138/95, para. 64; Ruling of ECtHR, 2.9.1998, *Kadubec v SVK*, No. 27061/95, para. 57.

66 Ruling of ECtHR, 25.2.1997, *Findlay v UK*, para. 73 f.

67 Ruling of ECtHR (GK), 9.6.1998, *Incal v TUR*, para. 72; Ruling of ECtHR, 6.3.2001, *Mehdi Zana v TUR*, No. 29851/96, para. 22.

68 Ruling of ECtHR, 17.11.2015, *Tanisma v TUR*, No. 32219/05, para. 83; Reid, K., *A practitioner's Guide to the ECHR*, London: Sweet & Maxwell, 2012, p. 217.

69 Ruling of ECtHR, 22.11.2011, *Ercep v TUR*, No. 43965/04, para. 68 f.

70 Ruling of ECtHR, 24.2.1993, *Fey v AT*, No. 14396/88, para. 27 ff; Ruling of ECtHR, 21.12.2000, *Wettstein v SUI*, No. 33958/96, para. 42; Ruling of ECtHR (GC), 15.10.2009, *Micallef v MLT*, No. 17056/06, para. 95; Grabenwarter, Ch., *European Convention on Human Rights. Commentary*, Munich: C.H. Beck, Art. 6, para. 52; Harris, D., M. O'Boyle, Bades, E., and C. Buckley, *Law of the European Convention on Human Rights*, Oxford: Oxford University Press, 2018, p. 451.

71 Van Dijk, P., G. van Hoof, A. van Rijn, L. Zwaak, ECHR, p. 602.

there are specific constitutional and legal rules providing for the impartiality of the judiciary.[72]

To assess the concept of impartiality, the actual and procedural circumstances as well as the specific questions at the various stages of the proceedings in every individual case need to be analysed.[73] As stated above, the notion of impartiality is often functionally linked to and, therefore, difficult to distinguish from the concept of independence. The objectivity of proceedings and of the decision is determined by the independence and the impartiality of the members of the tribunal.[74] As an example, if a tribunal is dependent of the executive, it is also likely to be violating impartiality if the executive is a party. The same applies to a judge who shares a connection with a private party to a case.[75] Although closely linked to each other, impartiality constitutes an autonomous requirement for the objectivity of judicial conduct and the assessment of that conduct. It therefore forms the core of the right under Art. 6(1) ECHR and needs to be prescribed by law.[76]

It is possible that an individual – even implicitly – can waive his/her right to an impartial judge, but only if there was legal counsel prior to the waiver, as a layperson cannot fully assess the legal consequences.[77] Further minimum requirements are that the individual concerned was sufficiently notified and that the waiver is not contrary to any important public interest; a mere presumption is not enough.[78] There had been no violation of the concept of impartiality if an applicant was adequately notified and subject to the right to challenge the composition of the court but did not take the opportunity to do so.[79]

---

72 Ruling of ECtHR (GC), 15.10.2009, *Micallef v MLT*, para. 99–100; European Commission for Democracy through Law (Venice Commission), Rule of Law Checklist, adopted at its 106th Plenary Session in Venice, 11–12 March 2016, Point E(1)(c), Impartiality of the judiciary.

73 Grabenwarter, Ch., K. Pabel, "Europäische Menschenrechtskonvention," Munich: C.H. Beck, 2016, p. 499; see further ruling of ECtHR, 24.2.1993, *Fey v AT*, para. 27 ff.

74 Grabenwarter, Ch., K. Pabel, "Europäische Menschenrechtskonvention," Munich: C.H. Beck, 2016, p. 491.

75 Harris, D., M. O'Boyle, Bades, E., and C. Buckley, *Law of the European Convention on Human Rights*, Oxford: Oxford University Press, 2018, p. 446.

76 Ruling of EComHR, 2.1.1983, *Bramelid and Malmström v SWE*, No. 8588 a.o.; Grabenwarter, Ch., *European Convention on Human Rights. Commentary*, Munich: C.H. Beck, Art. 6, para. 53.

77 Ruling of ECtHR, 25.2.1992, *Pfeifer and Plankl v AT*, No. 10802/84, para. 37; see also Ruling of ECtHR, 24.5.1991, *Oberschlick v AT*, No. 11662/85, para. 51.

78 Ruling of ECtHR, 12.2.1985, *Colozza v IT*, No. 9024/80, para. 28; Ruling of ECtHR, 24.2.2008, *Dorozhko a.o. v EST*, No. 14659/04 et al., para. 45 f.

79 Ruling of ECtHR, 22.2.1996, *Bulut v AT*, No. 17358/90, para. 34.

To assess impartiality, all the actual and procedural circumstances, as well as concrete questions pertaining to the individual stages of the proceeding, have to be examined in the individual case.[80] Therefore, the ECtHR looks at both the personal and objective impartiality of a judge.[81] Although those tests are sometimes difficult to distinguish,[82] there are certain criteria for differentiation. The subjective approach looks at whether the judge is prejudiced or partial in a concrete case. The objective approach considers ascertainable facts that may put the impartiality of the court in question and investigates whether the judge offered sufficient guarantees to exclude any legitimate doubts.[83] A request of one party to exclude a judge does not automatically trigger the need to exclude the judge, as long as the parties' arguments are answered and a decision is reached as to whether or not the challenge to a judge was justified.[84]

5.1 Personal (subjective) impartiality

Whether or not a judge acts personally in an impartial manner has to be determined in the particular case and the judge's conduct has to be seen in the overall context.[85] There is a general presumption that a judge acts impartially until proof is provided to the contrary; this is reflected in the principle that the tribunal's decision is final and binding unless set aside by a superior court.[86] However, impartiality as an inner attitude is hard to prove. It is not enough to refer to the subjective feelings of ill-will or hostility, but the allegation of a judge's partiality has to be objectively justified.[87]

---

80 Ruling of ECtHR, 24.2.1993, *Fey v AT*, para. 27; Grabenwarter, Ch., K. Pabel, "Europäische Menschenrechtskonvention", Munich: C.H. Beck, 2016, p. 492.

81 Most recently ruling of ECtHR, 3.10.2019, *Pastörs v GER*, No. 55225/14, para. 55 f.

82 E.g. Ruling of ECtHR (GC), 15.10.2009, *Micallef v MLT*, para. 95.

83 Ruling of ECtHR (GC), 15.10.2009, *Micallef v MLT*, para. 96; ECtHR, 15.12.2005 (GK) *Kyprianou v CYP*, para. 118 f.

84 Ruling of ECtHR, 20.11.2012, *Harabin v SVK*, No. 58688/11, para. 136 f.

85 Grabenwarter, Ch., *European Convention on Human Rights. Commentary*, Munich: C.H. Beck, Art. 6 para. 56.

86 Ruling of ECtHR, 1.10.1982, *Piersack v BEL*, para. 30; Ruling of ECtHR, 24.5.1989, *Hausschildt v DEN*, No. 10486/83, para. 47; Ruling of ECtHR, 10.6.1996, *Pullar v UK*, No. 22399/93, para. 32; Ruling of ECtHR (GC), 15.12.2005, *Kyprianou v CYP*, para. 119.

87 Ruling of ECtHR, 26.10.1984, *De Cubber v BEL*, No. 9186/80, para. 25; Grabenwarter, Ch., *European Convention on Human Rights. Commentary*, Munich: C.H. Beck, Art. 6 para. 57.

On rare occasions, the ECtHR has acknowledged personal bias when it was evident from the attitude of the judge during the proceeding or from the content of the judgment, as in *Kyprianou*, in which several factors played a role. The applicant, a lawyer, personally insulted and offended the judges with empathetic language conveying indignation and shock during a criminal trial. Subsequently, the same judges sentenced the applicant to five days' imprisonment.[88]

The majority of the existing case law on personal impartiality concerns the members of jury tribunals. In case of allegations, national tribunals have to examine if they are substantiated. The lack of an examination constitutes a violation of Art. 6(1) ECHR, unless the allegations are manifestly and directly ill-founded.[89] Nevertheless, the nature of the degree of familiarity in question needs to be analysed in each individual case.[90] For example, there is a violation if a juror expresses racist comments.[91] As a consequence, it may ultimately be necessary to dismiss the old jury and appoint a new one, or, in less severe situations, to redirect the jury in a forceful manner.[92]

5.2 Objective impartiality

As it is often difficult to rebut the presumption of a judge's subjective impartiality, it is the requirement of objective impartiality that provides another important guarantee and especially focuses on hierarchical or other links between the judge and participants of the proceeding or on rules for the withdrawal of judges.[93] It has to be decided in each individual case whether "the relationship in question is of such a nature and degree as to indicate a lack of impartiality."[94]

---

88 Ruling of ECtHR (GC), 15.12.2005, *Kyprianou v CYP*, para. 130; Schabas W.A., "The European Convention on Human Rights. A commentary," Oxford: Oxford University Press, 2017, p. 296; Van Dijk, P., G. van Hoof, A. van Rijn, L. Zwaak, ECHR, p. 603.

89 Ruling of ECtHR, 23.4.1996, *Remli v FRA*, para. 48; Grabenwarter, Ch., *European Convention on Human Rights. Commentary*, Munich: C.H. Beck, Art. 6, para. 58.

90 Ruling of ECtHR, 10.6.1996, *Pullar v UK*, para. 36; ECtHR, 20.12.2011, ruling of *Hanif and Khan v UK*, No. 52999/08 et al., para. 142 ff (relation to a witness).

91 Ruling of ECtHR, 23.4.1996, *Remli v FRA*, para. 47 f; Ruling of ECtHR, 9.5.2000, *Sander v UK*, No. 34129/96, para. 33 f.

92 Ruling of ECtHR, 25.2.1997, *Gregory v UK*, No. 22299/93, para. 47, 49; Ruling of ECtHR, 9.5.2000, *Sander v UK*, para. 34.

93 Ruling of ECtHR (GC), 15.10.2009, *Micallef v MLT*, para. 95 f; Ruling of ECtHR, 21.12.2000, *Wettstein v SUI*, para. 44 f.

94 Ruling of ECtHR (GC), 15.10.2009, *Micallef v MLT*, para. 97; see also Ruling of ECtHR, 10.6.1996, *Pullar v UK*, para. 38.

It is the legislator's task to adopt procedural laws that safeguard impartiality; also, when there is a bench of judges.[95] In general, a tribunal lacks (independence and) impartiality if there is no legal basis for the replacement of judges or any procedural safeguard.[96] The composition of ordinary courts usually does not seem to be a problem. In the case of other tribunals, there is a strong indicator for impartiality, when at least half of the members of a tribunal are judges, including the chairperson with a casting vote.[97]

In order to assess whether there was an infringement of the framework of the objective impartiality, the internal organisation and the functions of a judge in a certain trial exercised are at stake.[98] It is sufficient that ascertainable facts may raise doubts as to impartiality.[99] For this purpose, it is decisive whether there is a legitimate reason to fear that judges lack impartiality and whether this fear can be held to be objectively justified.[100] The standpoint of the accused in a criminal procedure is important but not the decisive factor.[101] To secure the public's trust in the courts of a democratic society, a court needs to review partiality, unless the grounds appear to be manifestly devoid of merit and the judge, legitimately fearing a lack of impartiality, must withdraw.[102] In this respect, "appearances" also play a certain role, meaning that impartiality has to be ensured in law and in practice, as explained by the ECtHR and adapted by the Venice Commission,

---

95 Grabenwarter, Ch., *European Convention on Human Rights. Commentary*, Munich: C.H. Beck, Art. 6 para. 59; Ruling of ECtHR (GC), 23.4.2015, *Morice v FRA*, No. 29369/10, para. 89.

96 Ruling of ECtHR, 9.10.2008, *Moiseyev v RUS*, para. 177 f.

97 Ruling of ECtHR, 23.6.1981, *Le Compte a.o. v BEL*, para. 43 (close link to the concept of independence).

98 Ruling of ECtHR, 26.10.1984, *De Cubber v BEL*, para. 26; Ruling of ECtHR, 25.7.2000, *Tierce a.o v SMR*, No. 24954/94 et al., para. 78; Ruling of ECtHR, 2.6.2016, *Mitrov v MKD*, No. 45959/09, para. 48 f; Ruling of ECtHR, 4.6.2019, *Sigurdur a.o. v ICE*, No. 39757/15, para. 55 f; Ruling of ECtHR, 3.10.2019, *Pastörs v GER*, para. 55 f.

99 Ruling of ECtHR, 26.10.1984, *De Cubber v BEL*, para. 26; Ruling of ECtHR, 19.3.1991, *Morel v FRA*, No. 11069/84, para. 42; Ruling of ECtHR (GC), 15.10.2009, *Micallef v MLT*, para. 98; Ruling of ECtHR, 3.10.2019, *Pastörs v GER*, para. 55 f.

100 Ruling of ECtHR (GC), 15.10.2009, *Micallef v MLT*, para. 96; Ruling of ECtHR, 21.12.2000, *Wettstein v AT*, para. 44.

101 Ruling of ECtHR, 1.10.1982, *Piersack v BEL*, para. 31; Ruling of ECtHR, 24.5.1989, *Hauschildt v DEN*, para. 48; Ruling of ECtHR (GC), 15.12.2005, *Kyprianou v CYP*, para. 118; ECtHR (GC), 15.10.2009, *Micallef v MLT*, para. 96.

102 Ruling of ECtHR, 24.5.1989, *Hauschildt v DEN*, para. 48; Ruling of ECtHR, 23.4.1996, *Remli v FRA*, para. 48; ECtHR, 21.6.2018, *Aviso Zeta AG v AT*, No. 5734/14, para. 47 f.

such that "justice must not only be done, it must also be seen to be done."[103] There is quite a broad range of situations in which problems of objective impartiality may arise.

First of all, adverse publicity as well as a virulent media campaign accompanying a trial are deemed to be problematic, as they might influence public opinion, including the jury's point of view.[104] Generally, there is a strong presumption that professional judges are not influenced by the media or hostile public opinions. In *Buscemi*, however, the president of the court reacted to a letter published by the applicant in the press concerning a court order, which placed the applicant's daughter in a children's home. The president of the court publicly reacted to that letter and used expressions from which it was implicitly clear that he had already formed an unfavourable opinion of the applicant's case before the court had formed a decision. This course of action was a clear violation of the concept of objective impartiality.[105] The ECtHR, however, generally acknowledges that the nature of the trial process and the directing role of the trial judge ensure a fair proceeding.[106]

Second, a judges' connection or affiliation may pose an obstacle. A close family relationship, such as one between siblings, can doubtlessly hinder impartiality.[107] Another example is provided by the *Sigurdsson* case, in which there was a strong financial link between a judge's husband and one of the parties of the proceeding, the National Bank of Iceland.[108] Moreover, family relations between the presiding judge and a person that is significantly involved in pre-trial investigation (of the case of the applicant or the opposing party's advocate) or a confusion between the functions of prosecutor and judge may raise serious doubts that the tribunal

103 Ruling of ECtHR, 26.10.1984, *DeCubber v BEL*, para. 26; Ruling of ECtHR (GC), 15.10.2009, *Micallef v MLT*, para. 98; Ruling of ECtHR, 9.1.2013, *Oleksandr Volkov v UKR*, No 21722/11, para. 106; Ruling of ECtHR, 21.6.2018, *Aviso Zeta AG v AT*, para. 45; European Commission for Democracy through Law (Venice Commission), Rule of Law Checklist, adopted at its 106th Plenary Session in Venice, 11–12 March 2016, Point E(1)(c), Impartiality of the judiciary.

104 Ruling of ECtHR, 5.12.2002, *Craxi v IT* (No. 1), No. 34896/97, para. 98; Reid, K., *A practitioner's Guide to the ECHR*, London: Sweet & Maxwell, 2012, p. 218.

105 Ruling of ECtHR, 16.9.1999, *Buscemi v IT*, No 29569/95, para. 67–69.

106 Ruling of ECtHR, 18.1.2011, *Akay (Abu Hamza) v UK*, No. 31411/07, para. 39.

107 Ruling of ECtHR (GC), 15.10.2009, *Micallef v MLT*, para.102.

108 Ruling of ECtHR, 10.4.2003, *Sigurdsson v ICE*, No 39731/98, para. 39 f.

is impartial.[109] A conflict with objective impartiality might also occur if jurors are or have been members of a political party.[110]

Mitrov can serve as a good example of a case in which the applicant was tried before judges that were former colleagues of the victim of a family tragedy caused by the applicant. The ECtHR repeated its established impartiality criteria and concluded that due to their status as full-time judges, their similar functions, as well as their professional collaboration, a personal link could have existed. Also, the domestic law did not offer the possibility of transferring a case to another competent court. Thus, doubts as to the impartiality of the court were objectively justified.[111] In another even more recent example, the case of *Aviso Zeta AG*, one of the judges sitting on the case had intended to file an action against the applicant company for financial losses caused by a share purchase and had for the same reason withdrawn of his own motion in comparable cases. Moreover, the judge offered shares to a litigation funder to bring possible claims against the applicant company. In comparable cases, the judge had reported his possible incompatibility and was subsequently excluded. Here, the ECtHR focused on the importance of appearances; also, in the light of the fact that the Supreme Court decided in a closed meeting, there was a violation of Art. 6(1) ECHR.[112]

Third, another situation that may pose a problem occurs whenever a judge takes differing roles or is involved in the case before the trial. Impartiality is definitely not established if the plaintiff is – as the head of the Association of Judges – involved in disciplinary proceedings against judges or takes career-related decisions.[113] The same applies to organs that are responsible for disciplinary proceedings against judges if they are mostly composed of members of the legislative or the executive.[114]

Concerning criminal cases, the roles of a judge commonly conflict when a judge additionally takes an investigating role, or when an overlap between the prosecution and the trial court occurs.[115] Judges must not be involved in a trial

---

109 Ruling of ECtHR, 24.4.2008, *Dorozhko a.o. v EST*, No. 14659/04 et al., para. 56 f; Ruling of ECtHR (GC), 15.10.2009, *Micallef v MLT*, para. 56 f; Ruling of ECtHR, 18.5.2010, *Ozerov v RUS*, No. 64962/01, para. 50.

110 Ruling of ECtHR, 25.11.1993, *Holm v SWE*, No. 14191/88, para. 30 f.

111 Ruling of ECtHR, 2.6.2016, *Mitrov v FYROM*, No. 45959/09, para. 52 f.

112 Ruling of ECtHR, 21.6.2018, *Aviso Zeta AG v AT*, para. 47 f.

113 Ruling of ECtHR, 15.7.2010, *Gazeta Ukraina-Tsentr v UKR*, No. 16695/04, para. 34.

114 Ruling of ECtHR (GC), 25.9.2018, *Denisov v UKR*, No. 76639/11, para. 60 f; Ruling of ECtHR, 27.5.2013, *Oleksandr Volkov v UKR*, para. 110 f.

115 Reid, K., *A practitioner's Guide to the ECHR*, London: Sweet & Maxwell, 2012, p. 219.

if they have already formed an opinion before the main proceedings, e.g. when they have dealt with a question that is in connection with the issue of the main proceedings.[116] Again, at this stage, a judge is personally biased if he/she presides over a case in which he/she has already been involved as a prosecutor; even if a former head of the section of a public prosecutor's department later acts as a judge without any knowledge of the concrete investigation of the applicant.[117]

Ruling on similar charges or on a co-accused is not problematic, while findings that actually prejudge the question of guilt in a subsequent proceeding or the imposition of a fine for contempt of court can objectively impair the bias of the judge.[118] The same may apply if it is a judge that fulfils the function of both an examining judge and the trial judge, depending on the scope of the judges' competences that are independent of the prosecution. For example, this was the case in *De Cubber*, in which a judge had previously been involved in the investigation and then acted as the president of a chamber.[119] A judge is not per se partial if he/she takes decisions on pretrial detention or other trial related questions and has a detailed knowledge of the case before the trial takes place. The scope and nature of the measures taken before the trial are decisive.[120] Partiality especially concerns the question of indictment and guilt of the applicant, not the collection of simple information and transmittance of the case-file.[121]

The impartiality of a judge is further violated if the judge of first instance also participates in the appeal trial. A lay judge must not additionally function as a legal representative of the opposing party in a parallel proceeding detached from

---

116 Ruling of ECtHR, 26.10.1984, *De Cubber v BEL*, para. 29; Ruling of ECtHR, 19.3.1991, *Morel v FRA*, para. 48; Ruling of ECtHR, 27.8.1991, *Demicoli v MLT*, No. 13057/87, para. 41.

117 Ruling of ECtHR, 1.10.1982, *Piersack v BEL*, para. 30 f.

118 Ruling of ECtHR (GC), 15.12.2005, *Kyprianou v CYP*, para. 123 f; Ruling of ECtHR, 24.3.2009, *Poppe v NED*, No. 32271/04, para. 26.

119 Ruling of ECtHR, 26.10.1984, *De Cubber v BEL*, para. 29; also Ruling of ECtHR, 10.8.2006, *Schwarzenberger v GER*, No. 75737/01, para. 43 f.

120 Ruling of ECtHR, 19.3.1991, *Morel v FRA*, para. 145; Ruling of ECtHR, 24.2.1993, *Fey v AT*, para. 30; Ruling of ECtHR, 24.8.1993, *Nortier v NED*, No. 13924/88, para. 33; Ruling of ECtHR, 22.4.1994, *Sraiva de Carbalho v PT*, No. 15651/89, para. 35; Grabenwarter, Ch., *European Convention on Human Rights. Commentary*, Munich: C.H. Beck, Art. 6 para. 61.

121 Ruling of ECtHR, 24.5.1989, *Hausschildt v DEN*, para. 50; Ruling of ECtHR, 24.2.1993, *Fey v AT*, para. 32.

any material link and the proceedings partly overlap in time.[122] However, it is in accordance with Art. 6(1) ECHR if, in the event of annulment of a decision, the same judge has to decide on the case again.[123]

6. Final remarks

The scope of a state's obligation to ensure a trial by an independent and impartial tribunal also entails that the executive, the legislature, and any other State authority has to respect and abide by the judgments as well as decisions of the court in any circumstances. This is a necessary precondition for the confidence of the public in the courts and generally in the Rule of Law.[124]

This confidence can be jeopardised if the independence of the judiciary or specific parts of it are constantly and publicly challenged by other state organs or institutions. To be sure, criticism of the judiciary and judgments is permissible in a democratic society and forms a part of the public debate. However, in order to safeguard the indispensable public trust in the judiciary, any other authority should express criticism against it with due restraint.

Judicial independence is not a goal that is successfully achieved at a given time but stays on the scoreboard. It must be observed, fostered and improved all the time. The case law of the ECtHR developed over decades with a view to different European judiciary systems and forms a strong basis for the assessment of structural and other newly emerging challenges with regard to the independence of judges.

One of the challenges faced by the judiciary is actual influence from members of the executive branch, be it members of the government or persons belonging to the authorities. Their influence is often strongly interlinked with public opinion and the role of the media. This is especially true for criminal proceedings related to offences committed by well-known persons (such as athletes, actors or politicians) or to crimes that are sensational due to the grievance associated with them or their exceptional modality. Such settings may entail that the public expects a specific outcome of the proceedings that may lead to some pressure on

---

122 Ruling of ECtHR, 21.12.2000, *Wettstein v SUI*, para. 46 f; Van Dijk, P., G. van Hoof, A. van Rijn, L. Zwaak, ECHR, p. 609.

123 Ruling of ECtHR, 16.7.1971, *Ringeisen v AT*, para. 97; Ruling of ECtHR, 26.9.1995, *Diennet v FRA*, No. 18160/91 et al., para. 37, 38.

124 Ruling of ECtHR, 6.10.2011, *Agrokompleks v UKR*, para. 136; Grabenwarter, Ch., *European Convention on Human Rights. Commentary*, Munich: C.H. Beck, Art. 6 para. 51.

the judges. The same is true for court proceedings dealing with administrative permission for large infrastructure projects, where the interests of economy, on the one hand, have to be weighed against the interests of environmental protection, on the other hand. Often, such cases lead to controversies, which again can lead to pressure from members of the executive branch, the media, or the public.

Nevertheless, expectations expressed by politicians as to the outcome of a court proceeding are not *a priori* a threat to judicial independence. Moreover, of course, the media should report on proceedings, and the public should be interested in the judiciary, in specific proceedings, and its outcomes. However, it can be observed that the general expectations vis-à-vis the court have amounted to actual pressure on the judges in duty. Naming such examples of possible pressure does not mean shaming the judges for not acting independently. It is about promoting measures to improve independence by supporting the mind-set and the attitude of judges. Judges should perceive their own role as independent.

Experience shows that it is not enough to have the "perfect" legal framework for the organisation of the judiciary and the independent position of judges with all the requirements emanating from the case law fulfilled. The implementation of the law in every single proceeding with the mind-set of effective independence is at least as important as the legislation itself. Therefore, continuing the training of the judges, evaluating their independence with the existing tools and raising overall understanding for the importance of an independent judiciary are prerequisites for the public's trust in the judiciary.

References

Publications

Grabenwarter, Christoph, *Europäischer Grundrechtsschutz. Enzyklopädie Europarecht*, Baden Baden: Nomos, 2014.

Grabenwarter, Christoph, *European Convention on Human Rights. Commentary*, Munich: C.H. Beck, 2014.

Grabenwarter, Christoph, Katharina Pabel, "Europäische Menschenrechtskonvention," Munich: C.H. Beck, 2016.

Harris, David, Michael O'Boyle, Bades, Ed, and Carla Buckley, *Law of the European Convention on Human Rights*, Oxford: Oxford University Press, 2018.

Reid, K., *A practitioner's Guide to the ECHR*, London: Sweet & Maxwell, 2012.

Schabas William A., "The European Convention on Human Rights. A commentary," Oxford: Oxford University Press, 2017.

Van Dijk, Pieter, Godefridus van Hoof, Arjen van Rijn, Leo Zwaak, ECHR.

Van Dijk Pieter, Fried van Hoof, Arjen van Rijn, Leo Zwaak, *Theory and Practice of the European Convention on Human Rights*, Cambridge: Intersentia, 2018.

Jurisprudence

European Court of Justice

Ruling of ECJ, 15.5.1986, *Johnston*, C-222/84.

Ruling of ECJ, 19.11.2009, *A.K.*, para. 137.

Ruling of ECJ, 17.7.2014, *Torresi*, C-58/13 a.o.

Ruling of ECJ, 6.10.2015, *Consorci Sanitari del Maresme*, C-203/14.

Ruling of ECJ, 16.2.2017, *Margarit Panicello*, C-503/15.

Ruling of ECJ, 27.2.2018, *Associação Sindical dos Juizes Portugueses*, C-64/16.

Ruling of ECJ, 24.6.2019, *EC v POL and HUN*.

Ruling of ECJ, 5.11.2019, *EC v POL*, C-192/18.

European Court of Human Rights

Ruling of ECtHR, 27.6.1968, *Neumeister v AT*, No. 1936/63.

Ruling of ECtHR, 16.7.1971, *Ringeisen v AT*, No. 2614/65.

Ruling of ECtHR, 8.6.1976, *Engel a.o. v NED*, No. 5100/71 et al.

Ruling of ECtHR, 18.12.1980, *Crociani a.o. v IT*, No. 8603/79.

Ruling of ECtHR, 23.6.1981, *Le Compte a.o. v BEL*, No. 6878/75,

Ruling of ECtHR, 23.9.1982, *Sporrong and Lönnroth v SWE*, No. 7151/75 et al.

Ruling of ECtHR, 28.6.1984, *Campbell and Fell v UK*, No. 7819/77 et al.

Ruling of ECtHR, 22.10.1984, *Sramek v AT*, No. 8790/79.

Ruling of ECtHR, 26.10.1984, *De Cubber v BEL*, No. 9186/80.

Ruling of ECtHR, 12.2.1985, *Colozza v IT*, No. 9024/80.

Ruling of ECtHR, 23.10.1985, *Benthem v NED*, No. 8848/80.

Ruling of ECtHR, 30.11.1987, *H v BE*, No. 8950/80.

Ruling of ECtHR, 29.4.1988, *Belilos v SUI*, No. 10328/83.

Ruling of ECtHR, 28.10.1988 (GK), *Brumarescu v ROM*, No. 28342/95.

Ruling of ECtHR, 28.6.1990, *Obermeier v AT*, No. 11761/85.

Ruling of ECtHR, 24.5.1991, *Oberschlick v AT*, No. 11662/85.

Ruling of ECtHR, 25.2.1992, *Pfeifer and Plankl v AT*, No. 10802/84.

Ruling of ECtHR, 21.9.1993, *Zumtobel v AT*, No. 12235/86.

Ruling of ECtHR, 24.11.1994, *Beaumartin v FRA*, No. 15287/89.

Ruling of ECtHR, 26.9.1995, *Diennet v FRA*, No. 18160/91 et al.

Ruling of ECtHR, 20.11.1995, *British-American Tobacco Company Ltd. v NED*, No. 19589/92.

Ruling of ECtHR, 22.2.1996, *Bulut v AT*, No. 17358/90.

Ruling of ECtHR, 25.2.1997, *Findlay v UK*, No. 22107/93.

Ruling of ECtHR, 25.2.1997, *Gregory v UK*, No. 22299/93.

Ruling of ECtHR, 22.5.1998, *Vasilescu v ROM*, No. 27053/95.

Ruling of ECtHR (GK), 9.6.1998, *Incal v Turkey*, No. 22678/93.

Ruling of ECtHR, 2.9.1998, *Lauko v SVK*, No. 26138/95.

Ruling of ECtHR, 2.9.1998, *Kadubec v SVK*, No. 27061/95.

Ruling of ECtHR, 22.6.2000, *Coëme a.o. v BEL*, No. 32492/96 et al.

Ruling of ECtHR, 21.12.2000, *Wettstein v SUI*, No. 33958/96.

Ruling of ECtHR, 6.3.2001, *Mehdi Zana v TUR*, No. 29851/96.

Ruling of ECtHR, 26.2.2002, *Morris v UK*, No. 38784/97.

Ruling of ECtHR, 13.2.2003, *Chevrol v FRA*, No. 49636/99.

Ruling of ECtHR, 4.3.2003, *Poshokhov v RUS*, No. 63486/00.

Ruling of ECtHR, 10.4.2003, *Sigurdsson v ICE*, No 39731/98.

Ruling of ECtHR, 16.12.2003, *Transportes Fluviais do Sado SA v PT*, No. 35943/02.

Ruling of ECtHR, 6.4.2004, *Rozsa v AT*, No. 67950/01.

Ruling of ECtHR, 3.3.2005, *Brudnicka v POL*, No. 54723/00.

Ruling of ECtHR, 25.8.2005, *Clarke v UK*, No. 23695/02.

Ruling of ECtHR (GC), 15.12.2005, *Kyprianou v CYP*, No. 73797/01.

Ruling of ECtHR, 13.4.2006, *Fedotova v RU*, No. 73225/01.

Ruling of ECtHR, 11.7.2006, *Gurov v MOL*, No. 36455/02.

Ruling of ECtHR, 20.7.2006, *Sokurenko and Strygun v UKR*, No. 29458/04.

Ruling of ECtHR, 10.8.2006, *Schwarzenberger v GER*, No. 75737/01.

Ruling of ECtHR, 24.2.2008, *Dorozhko a.o. v EST*, No. 14659/04 et al.

Ruling of ECtHR, 24.4.2008, *Dorozhko a.o. v EST*, No. 14659/04 et al.

Ruling of ECtHR, 9.10.2008, *Moiseyev v RUS*, No. 62936/00.

Ruling of ECtHR, 24.3.2009, *Poppe v NED*, No. 32271/04.

Ruling of ECtHR (GC), 15.10.2009, *Micallef v MLT*.

Ruling of ECtHR, 22.12.2009, *Parlov and Tkalic v CRO*, No. 24810/06.

Ruling of ECtHR, 18.5.2010, *Ozerov v RUS*, No. 64962/01.

Ruling of ECtHR, 15.7.2010, *Gazeta Ukraina-Tsentr v UKR*, No. 16695/04.

Ruling of ECtHR, 28.10.2010, *Suda v CZE*, No. 1643/06.

Ruling of ECtHR, 30.11.2010, *Henryk Urban a Ryszard Urban v POL*, No. 23614/08.

Ruling of ECtHR, 18.1.2011, *Akay (Abu Hamza) v UK*, No. 31411/07.

Ruling of ECtHR, 21.6.2011, *Fruni v SLK*, No. 8014/07.

Ruling of ECtHR, 6.10.2011, *Agrokompleks v UKR*, No. 23465/05.

Ruling of ECtHR, 22.11.2011, *Ercep v TUR*, No. 43965/04.

Ruling of ECtHR, 20.11.2012, *Harabin v SVK*, No. 58688/11.

Ruling of ECtHR, 9.1.2013, *Oleksandr Volkov v UKR*, No 21722/11.

Ruling of ECtHR, 17.11.2015, *Tanisma v TUR*, No. 32219/05.

Ruling of ECtHR, 12.1.2016, *Miracle Europe Kfz v HUN*, No. 57774/13.

Ruling of ECtHR, 1.3.2016, *Tabbane v SUI*, No. 41069/12.

Ruling of ECtHR, 2.6.2016, *Mitrov v MKD*, No. 45959/09.

Ruling of ECtHR (GC), 25.9.2018, *Denisov v UKR*, No. 76639/11.

Ruling of ECtHR, 2.10.2018, *Mutu and Pechstein v SUI*, No. 40575/10.

Ruling of ECtHR, 18.10.2018, *Thiam v FRA*, No. 80018/12.

Ruling of ECtHR, 4.6.2019, *Sigurdur a.o. v ICE*, No. 39757/15.

Ruling of ECtHR, 3.10.2019, *Pastörs v GER*, No. 55225/14.

Sources of law

Explanations Relating to the Charter of Fundamental Rights, OJ C 303, 14.12.2007.

European Commission for Democracy through Law (Venice Commission), Rule of Law Checklist, adopted at its 106th Plenary Session in Venice, 11–12 March 2016, Point E(1)(b) Independence of individual judges.

European Commission for Democracy through Law (Venice Commission), Rule of Law Checklist, adopted at its 106th Plenary Session in Venice, 11–12 March 2016, Point E(1)(a) Access to justice.

European Commission for Democracy through Law (Venice Commission), Rule of Law Checklist, adopted at its 106th Plenary Session in Venice, 11–12 March 2016, Point E(1)(c), Impartiality of the judiciary.

Jan Olszanowski[1]

The shape of supervision over courts – reflections on the supervisory measures applied to courts and judges

Abstract: The aim of this study is to examine the means of supervising courts and judges from a comparative perspective. The analysis will consider both subjective and objective elements. First of all, it is necessary to present how the common courts in Poland operate and how they are constructed. It is also necessary to describe how the Polish legal doctrine defines the term "supervision over courts." This is followed by a presentation of concrete measures which the authorities responsible for administrative supervision can apply. Moreover, there is a short description of the shape of disciplinary proceedings against judges. To create a broader idea of the problems associated with supervision, the supervisory models in four countries are presented, namely Sweden, Germany, Denmark, and Slovakia.

Keywords: supervision over courts and judges, measures of supervision over courts, independence of the courts, impartiality of judges, the doctrine of the separation of powers

1. Introduction

The independence of the judiciary shall be guaranteed by the State and enshrined in the Constitution or the law of the country. It is the duty of all governmental and other institutions to respect and observe the independence of the judiciary.[2] The system of organisation and creation of the courts fall under every country's internal discretion. From the perspective of the EU, the independence, quality and efficiency of justice systems are key for the implementation of EU law and for the strengthening of mutual trust.[3] Moreover, it is necessary to emphasise

---

1 Jan Olszanowski, PhD, Adam Mickiewicz University in Poznań, (Poland). ORCID – 0000-0003-3072-3413.

2 Basic Principles on the Independence of the Judiciary Adopted by the Seventh United Nations Congress on the Prevention of Crime and the Treatment of Offenders held at Milan from 26 August to 6 September 1985 and endorsed by General Assembly resolutions 40/32 of 29 November 1985 and 40/146 of 13 December 1985

3 Communication from the EU Commission: The 2018 EU Justice Scoreboard COM(2018) 364 final; https://eur-lex.europa.eu/legal-content/EN/TXT/HTML/?uri=CELEX:52018DC0364&from=pl (access date: 27.10. 2020).

that article 6 of the European Convention on Human Rights protects the right to a fair trial.[4] It protects the right to a public hearing before an independent and impartial tribunal within a reasonable time. The organisation of the judiciary, especially the organisation of the management or supervision bodies enacted into the system of the courts has great significance from the perspective of the quality of the rule of law.[5] Every country should create the system of judiciary in a way that leads to ensuring the realisation of the right to a fair trial. The role of the courts is to dispense justice, which results in the implementation of concrete legal norms aimed at protecting legal principles.[6]

The aim of this study is to examine the means of supervising courts and judges from a comparative perspective. The analysis will consider both subjective and objective elements. First of all, it is necessary to present how the common courts operate and how they are constructed. It is also necessary to describe how the Polish legal doctrine defines the term "supervision over courts." It is necessary to point out that there is a distinction between administrative supervision and other forms of supervision, especially judicial supervision (exercised by the courts of higher instance as part of the established procedure).[7] In the second part of the article, concrete supervisory measures will be presented. The third part of the analysis will describe the judiciary in four different legal systems and the supervisory measures which are related to the administration of the judiciary. It is also obvious that while engaged in court proceedings judges should be free from the activity of the other two branches of power.[8] The organisation of the courts (and their structural creation) should ensure that the judges and court personnel have proper working conditions, that the work of judges is reliably evaluated, and that they are assisted in their professional development – because all of these factors

4 Convention for the Protection of Human Rights and Fundamental Freedoms Rome, 4.XI.1950

5 G. Yein Ng, M. Velicogna, C. Dallara, *Monitoring and Evaluation of Court System: A Comparative Study (CEPEJ Report),* 2007 (https://rm.coe.int/european-commission-for-the-efficiency-of-justice-cepej-monitoring-and/16807882ba), p. 28.

6 S. Dąbrowski, "Władza sądownicza – definicja, funkcja, atrybuty," in: *Pozycja ustrojowa sędziego*, ed. by *R. Piotrowski*, Warszawa: Wolters Kluwer Polska, 2015, p. 21.

7 Judgement of Polish Constitutional Tribunal from 15.1.2009, K 45/07, OTK-A 1/3, 2009; A. Łazarska, "Niezawisłość sędziowska w sprawowaniu urzędu," in: R. Piotrowski, *Pozycja ustrojowa sędziego*, Warszawa: Wolters Kluwer Polska 2015, p. 27.

8 Z. Fleck, "A Comparative Analysis of Judicial Power, Organizational Issues in Judicature and the Administration of Courts," in: Fair Trial and Judicial Independence ed. by EA. Bado, Cham Heidelberg New York Dordrecht London: Springer, 2014, p. 4.

can help to ensure the right of the parties to a fair trial. Depending on the legal system, there are different models for the administration or management of the courts and various possibilities for exercising supervision over the activities of courts. Therefore, there are also different ways of organising and structuring the entities responsible for the administration, management and supervision of the courts. These entities have various kinds of measures at their disposal to ensure the efficiency of the courts' operation. However, these measures should not have an impact on the dispensation of justice. In this regard, the courts should be completely independent. It is also quite clear that the independence of the judiciary requires extensive safeguards to be put in place to shield the judiciary from undue influence from, in particular, the other branches of government. Further issues relate to the terms and conditions on which judges operate. The resources allocated to the courts need to be adequate, and the security of office provided by tenure and similar mechanisms, as well as the level of remuneration afforded the judiciary, need to be guaranteed in law.[9]

Moreover, the effectiveness of judicial review and the shape of supervision over courts' activities are essential for the protection of individual rights and the functioning of the state authorities in both the social and the economic realm. From an extrajudicial point of view, its significance is reflected in the influence on the judiciary, which will not only be effective in its procedural activity but also in the level of trust and social prestige. The position and powers of judges enable them to contribute to an efficient and fair legal system and encourage them to commit themselves actively to the functioning of the judicial system.[10] When the system of supervision of the courts is complete and consistent, it is possible to guarantee every person the fundamental right to have their case decided in a fair trial, on legal grounds only, and without any improper influence.

The administration of the courts, their management and the technical aspects of their functioning, as well as the supervision of these activities, are often exercised by specific organs which should not encroach upon the structure of the judicial power.[11] The concept of supervision or administration of

9 F. van Dijk, G. Vos, "A Method for Assessment of the Independence and Accountability of the Judiciary," *International Journal for Court Administration*, December 2018, p. 4. See also: UN Basic Principles on the Independence of the Judiciary of 1985 (UN General Assembly resolution 40/146, 1985).

10 F. van Dijk, "Improved Performance of The Netherlands Judiciary: Assessment of the Gains for Society," *International Journal for court administration*, No. 1 vol.6, 2014, p. 16.

11 P. Mikuli, "Current Debates on the Supervision over the Administrative Activity of the Common Courts," *European Public Law* Vol. 20, no 3., 2014, p. 521

the courts is understood differently in different legal systems. In some cases, it is understood more as management or support. The concept of supervision which is directly expressed in the Polish legal system is thus not the only option available.[12]

There are also different ways of understanding the administration, management and supervision of the courts. In the literature it is stated that administration encompasses the administration of the judiciary and the administration of court units. Court administration is the set of measures, legal regulations and legal powers in court performance which are based on constitutional principles that determine the main organisational provisions of the court system and the performance of court activity.[13] From another viewpoint, the typical meaning of supervision over the courts is understood more broadly. Supervision may be defined as all the actions pertaining to the organisational and financial functioning of the courts (administrative supervision), or to the appellate procedures of a higher court concerning the judgment of a lower court (judicial supervision). It is thus not necessarily limited to controlling the aspects of formal adherence to proper administrative procedures including budget management, but can also involve the examination of trends in adjudication and the appraisal of legislative success and effectiveness, or even gathering information about court judgments and rulings, the inspection of court files and the material study of court judgments to ensure that judgements are consistent.[14] It is obvious that a proper understanding of the shape of the administration or supervision of courts and judges is dependent on analysing the measures which the management (supervision) authorities have at their disposal.

The dependence between the model of administration and the supervision of the judiciary may have an influence on the efficiency of the courts, as well as on how the public perceive them. It is also essential to discuss whether this supervision is not abused by the public authorities who exercise it in order to achieve other (i.e. political) aims, rather than to make the activity of the courts more effective.

12 K. Gonera in: *Model nadzoru nad działalnością sądów i pracą orzeczniczą sędziów*, ed. by P. Zientarski, Warszawa: Kancelaria Senatu 2015, p. 36.

13 M. Simunis, "Effective Court Administration and Professionalism of Judges as Necessary Factors Safeguarding the Mother of Justice – The Right to a Fair Trial," *International Journal for Court Administration* / Winter 2019, p. 51.

14 A. Lienhard, "Oberaufsicht und Justizmanagement," *Justice – Justiz – Giustizia* 1, 2009, p. 2.

2. Supervision over courts in Poland

Before beginning the analysis of the situation in Poland, it is necessary to acknowledge that it is difficult to separate the administrative tasks of the courts from the administration of justice. The tension that arises in this context involves, within the framework of supervision, the simultaneous consideration of judicial independence and the efficiency of the court's activity, the separation of the judiciary from the other authorities, and the need for its co-operation with the legislative and executive powers. In the Polish legal system, there is a distinction between administrative and judicial supervision. Administrative supervision is usually understood as management of the courts and personnel of the courts, including judges. It is focused on the courts' financial and administrative activity. In the Polish legal doctrine, judicial supervision is usually understood as a part of court proceedings.[15] In the judgments of the Constitutional Tribunal, the judicial administration, in a narrow sense, consists of the direct disposal of the court's material resources and personnel to the extent necessary to ensure the proper and continuous functioning of the court (including activities and decisions related to the court's finances, accounting, offices, court equipment).[16] Administrative activities also include a certain range of employee relationships, such as those between judges and court officials, and the activities performed during a trial or directly related to adjudication (e.g. issuing copies, certificates). On the other hand, by the judicial administration, the Constitutional Tribunal understands, in a broad sense, the activity of administration and administrative (official) supervision resulting from official subordination, consisting in controlling the proper course of office, checking the application of orders and instructions by judicial administration bodies, ensuring that judges and other court employees comply with their duties, and on analysing judicial decisions.[17]

From the perspective of the legal correctness of applying the law (judicial supervision), supervisory authorities are different in the two main branches of the judiciary (common and administrative courts). The Supreme Court exercises

---

15 S. Dąbrowski in: *Aurea praxis. Aurea theoria. Księga pamiątkowa ku czci Profesora Tadeusza Erecińskiego* ed. by J. Gudowski K. Weitz Karol, Vol. 2, Warszawa: LexisNexis, 2011, Lex/el.

16 Judgement of Polish Constitutional Tribunal, 7.11.2013, K 31/12, OTK-A 2013/8/121, Judgement of Polish Constitutional Tribunal, 15.1.2009, K 45/07, OTK-A 1/2009

17 Judgement of Constitutional Tribunal, 15.1.2009, K 45/07, OTK-A 1/3/2009.

supervision over common and military courts regarding judgments.[18] The Supreme Administrative Court has the same role in reviewing the judgments of administrative courts of the first instance.[19] The judgements of the courts of higher instances or the judgements or resolutions of Supreme Courts are the result of this kind of supervision.

It is necessary to clearly emphasise that the term "supervision over courts" is not expressly established in the Polish Constitution.[20] On the contrary, it follows from the Constitution that the legal system is based on the principle of the separation of powers.[21] However, the institution of supervision is included in the basic law. It is indicated that the Supreme Court exercises supervision over the common and military courts with regard to adjudication.[22] Supervision of the administrative activities in the ordinary courts is exercised by the Minister of Justice, by judges delegated to the Ministry, as well as by the presidents of the courts. It is described as an expression of the functional relationship between the judiciary and the executive.[23]

In administrative courts, this role is played by the President of Supreme Administrative Court. Judicial supervision over administrative courts is conducted by the Supreme Administrative Court itself.

The administrative activities of the ordinary courts are defined in article 8 of the Law on the System of Common Courts[24] as:

(1) the assurance of the proper technical, organisational and material conditions of the courts' work.

---

18 Art. 183 p. 1 of the Polish Constitution.

19 Art. 3 § 2 of the Law on the system of Administrative Courts from 25.7.2002 (Journal of Laws 2019, item 2167).

20 A. Machnikowska, *O niezawisłości sędziów i niezależności sądów w trudnych czasach*, Warszawa: Wolters Kluwer Polska, 2017, p. 316.

21 For more detailed discussion of the concept of the separation of powers from a Polish perspective, see: P. Mikuli, G. Kuca, "The Separation Versus the Cooperation of Powers in the Contemporary Democratic State," *Studia i Materiały Trybunału Konstytucyjnego* Vol. LV, Warszawa: Wydawnictwo Trybunału Konstytucyjnego 2015, pp. 125–136.

22 A. Górski in: *Model nadzoru nad działalności sądów i pracą orzeczniczą sędziów* ed. by P. Zientarski, Warszawa: Kancelaria Senatu 2015, p. 11.

23 J. Sobczak, "Niezawisłość sędziowska i niezależność sądów. Problem ważny i ciągle aktualny (Judicial independence – a vital and still up-to-date issue)," in: *Gdańskie Studia Prawnicze – Przegląd Orzecznictwa* 1, 2015, p. 85.

24 The Act from 27.7.2001 – Law on the system of common courts (Consolidated text Journal of Laws Journal of Laws 2020, item 2072).

(2) the assurance of the proper internal functioning of the courts directly connected with the dispensation of justice.[25]

This definition has great importance, for two reasons. First, it is necessary to emphasise that the administration of the courts or the supervision activity relating to the courts' activities are only the ways to ensure the dispensation of justice. The administration and supervision of the courts are only the tools that guarantee that the parties to the proceedings will have the fair trial they are entitled to and – in a broader sense – that citizens will have access to a fair and independent court. This is of great importance because the administration or supervision over courts is not an aim in itself. Second, the supervision should not be connected with the procedural aspects of the court case, but only with the technical, organisational and material aspects and the functioning of the courts' work. Therefore, in the event of any doubts as to the scope of supervisory activities, taking into account the rule of law, it should be assumed that no activities should be undertaken that could exceed the scope of supervisory activities.[26] In particular, this concerns activities falling within the scope of judicial independence.

In the most general way, the Minister of Justice exercises only general administrative supervision of common courts. This supervision covers issues connected with the financial and administrative activity of the courts. The external supervision concerns the technical, organisational and material conditions of the courts' work. It is executed by the Ministry of Justice through a competent supervising service composed of judges delegated to the Ministry of Justice. The role of the Minister consists mainly in reviewing whether this supervision is exercised correctly by these presidents, and in issuing appropriate orders to them. Thus, he is, in a way, a supervisor of the presidents of individual courts who supervise the courts and the judges working in them. The so-called internal administrative supervision over the common courts is exercised by the presidents of these courts. This supervisory activity should ensure the adequate internal operation of the courts. These activities may also be focused on problems concerning efficient reviewing of cases and the proper execution of judgements.

---

25 For more in this definitione, see: M. Radajewski, "Stwierdzenie uchybienia w zakresie sprawności postępowania sądowego," *Przegląd Sądowy*, No. 11–12, 2018, p. 57–70.

26 R. Piotrowski, Status ustrojowy sędziego a zakres i charakter zarządzeń nadzorczych in: *Pozycja ustrojowa sędziego* ed. by R. Piotrowski, Warszawa:Wolters Kluwer Polska 2015, p. 186.

Article 9b of the Law on the Common Courts Organization creates the most basic rule concerning the boundaries between the judicial independence and supervision over the courts, and emphasises that supervisory activities cannot encroach on the scope in which judges are independent. However, despite the reservation contained in this provision, it is not always easy to separate the sphere of adjudication from administrative matters.[27]

This means that the supervisory power of the Minister of Justice may not interfere with the independence of judges. Administrative supervision cannot be connected with judgements and decisions whose correctness may be examined only according to the procedure stipulated by law.

One of the most controversial problems discussed in Poland is the relationship between the Minister of Justice and the common courts in terms of the supervision over courts and the way judiciary is being reformed in Poland.[28] Generally, the supervision over the administrative activity of the courts executed by the Minister of Justice has a long tradition in Poland.[29] It was present before the Second World War, under the Constitutions of 1921 and 1935.[30] Each of those constitutions shaped the political system of the country in a completely different manner, but despite these differences the legal status of judges remained basically unchanged. The governmental administrative supervision over the courts

27 A. Górski, *The Law of the System of Common Courts. Commentary to art. 9b*, Warszawa: Lex 2013, Lex/el.

28 P. Mikuli, p. 528; M. Zubik, "Organizacja sadownictwa" in *Przyszłość polskiego wymiaru sprawiedliwości,* ed. by A. Zielinski Warszawa 2002, p. 33. S. Dąbrowski, "Władza sądownicza – definicja, funkcja, atrybuty" in: *Pozycja ustrojowa sędziego*, ed. by R., Warszawa: Wolters Kluwer Polska, 2014, p. 28; M. Matczak, *Poland: From Paradigm to Pariah? Facts and Interpretations of Polish Constitutional Crisis*, 12 March 2018, pp. 3–9, https://ssrn.com/abstract=3138541 (access date: 3.10.2002); P. Radziewicz, P. Tuleja, *Konstytucyjny spór o granice zmian organizacji i zasad działania Trybunału Konstytucyjnego: czerwiec 2015 – marzec 2016,* Warszawa: Wolters Kluwer Polska 2017; G. Skąpska, "The decline of liberal constitutionalism in East Central Europe," in: *The Routledge International Handbook of European Social Transformations* ed. by P. Vihalemm, A. Masso, S. Opermann, London–New York: Routledge 2018, pp. 130–145; J. Zajadło, "Constitution-hostile Interpretation," *Przegląd Konstytucyjny 2, 2018*, pp. 5–15; M. Ziółkowski, "Constitutional Moment and the Polish Constitutional Crisis 2015–2018 (a few Critical Remarks)," *Przegląd Konstytucyjny* 4, 2018, pp. 76–106.

29 P. Mikuli, "Poland: Current Debates on the Supervision over the Administrative Activity of the Common Courts," *European Public Law*, January 2014, p. 531.

30 For a more detailed discussion, see: Judgement of Constitutional Tribunal 15.1.2009, K 45/07, OTK-A 1/3, 2009.

continued in the People's Republic of Poland (1947–1989). The current legislation has increased the powers of the Minister of Justice. In particular, this concerns the internal organisation of the courts, especially the appointment and dismissal of the presidents and deputy presidents of the courts. In 2017–2018, the Ministry of Justice had the competence to dismiss every president of the common court in Poland. This competence was the result of the special act adopted in July 2017.[31] Moreover the reforms extend the competences of the Minister of Justice in the areas of promotion and disciplinary supervision of judges. The reforms of the last few years have also reduced the self-governmental judicial bodies. Generally, restrictions have been placed on the powers of the Colleges of Courts (elected by the judges) and the Assemblies of Judges of particular courts. Moreover, the Minister of Justice currently enjoys the power to discretionarily appoint, without a prior contest, a Court Director. This person manages the administrative personnel. However, this role is not directly connected with the supervision over judges, but more strictly involves managing the courts as an institution.

3. Measures of administrative supervision over the common courts

The common court system has a threefold structure, comprising district (*rejonowe*), regional (*okręgowe*), and appeal courts (*apelacyjne*). The most important role regarding to supervision activities is played by the presidents of these courts. The president of a Court of Appeal executes the internal supervision over the administrative activity of this court, the regional courts and the district courts operating in the territory of an appellate region. In turn, the president of a regional court executes the same supervision over the regional court and the district courts operating in the territory of the region, while the president of a district court is competent in terms of the administrative supervision over the respective district court.

As was mentioned above, the Minister of Justice is the authority when it comes to supervision over the common courts and the judges in these courts of general competence. The Minister of Justice is obliged to ensure the functioning of adequate, effective and efficient management control in the department of government administration under his management, in the field of matters not reserved by separate provisions for the competence of other state bodies and taking into

31 Act of 12 July 2017 amending the act – on the system of common courts and certain other acts (Journal of Laws 2017, item 1452).

account the principle of judicial independence.[32] External administrative supervision over the operation of courts is exercised by the Minister of Justice through a supervision service composed of judges delegated to the Ministry of Justice. The Minister of Justice also has the competence to establish and abolish courts, and determines their seats and local competence areas guided by the need to secure reasonable organisation of the courts, by adapting the number of courts, their size and local competence areas to the backlog of cases, and considering the economy of court proceedings and the need to guarantee the citizen's right to have their case heard within a reasonable time (art. 20 of LCCO). Moreover, the Minister of Justice assigns new posts of judges and deputy judges to individual courts, taking into consideration the rational use of common court personnel and the needs resulting from the workload of particular courts. The Minister of Justice, or the president of the court, may order the immediate interruption of a judge's duties if the judge is detained after having committed an intentional crime, or if it is necessary, due to the nature of the judge's behaviour, to preserve the reputation of the judiciary, or if the essential interests of the service require his or her immediate removal from the performance of his or her duties.[33]

The Minister of Justice also has the competence to manage the court personnel. He may appoint and dismiss the president and the vice president of the courts during the term of office. The presidents of the Court of Appeal prepare annual information about the activity of courts acting in the appellate area, within the scope of tasks entrusted thereto, which, after an opinion thereon is delivered by the general assembly of appellate judges, the president submits to the Minister of Justice not later than by the end of April each year. Negative assessment of the activity of a specific court may result in the dismissal of the president of the court.

The authorities which are on a lower level than the Ministry of Justice are the Presidents of the Appellate courts. They have the general competences of supervision over lower courts (regional and district) in the area of Appellate court activity. Apart from general competences, the president of the appellate court has the right to conduct supervision activities in relation to the court over which he presides. First of all, it is necessary to emphasise the general competences, which are:

32 T. Niemiec, "Nadzór zewnętrzny nad działalnością administracyjną sądów powszechnych," *Kwartalnik KRS*, No. 4, 2012, pp. 5–9.

33 M. Radajewski, "Zarządzenie natychmiastowej przerwy w czynnościach służbowych sędziego," *Przegląd Sądowy* 5, 2020, pp. 34–35.

- determining the directions, coordination and control the internal administrative supervision performed by the presidents of regional and district courts acting in the appeal court area (art. 37b § 3 LCCO),
- providing the president of the lower courts with a written comment in the event of a deficiency in the management of the court, internal administrative supervision, or performance of other administrative activities (art. 37e § 1 LCCO),
- recommending a change of activities in the event of irregularities or irrationality in allocating cases to judges (art. 37e § 2 LCCO),
- reducing the functional allowance corresponding with the seriousness of the default, in the range from 15 % to 50 % of the allowance, for a period from one month to six months (art. 37e § 9 LCCO).

Apart from these competences, the presidents of the appellate, regional and district courts have competences which are connected with the direct supervision over the lower courts in terms of their activities. These competences may be:

- general inspection of the activities of the courts (art. 37b § 2 LCCO),
- the possibility to request explanations or demand deficiencies in the administrative activities of the courts be remedied (Article 37 § 1 LCCO),
- the right to be present at a court hearing which is held in camera (Article 37 § 1 LCCO),
- annulling illegal or ineffective administrative actions during court proceedings (Article 37 § 3 LCCO),
- providing the judge with written notice about the failure in administrative activity and demand the removal of consequences of such a default (Article 37 § 4 LCCO),
- examining the efficiency of the proceedings in individual cases (Article 37b § 1.1 1 LCCO),
- controlling the activity of the office of the court's division (article 37b § 1.2 LCCO),
- examining the correctness of assigning cases to judges and ensuring their equal workload (Article 37b § 1.3 LCCO),
- visiting the courts (presidents of courts of appeal and presidents of regional courts):
  - visit, covering the full administrative activity of a court or court division (Article 37b § 2 point 1 LCCO),
  - inspection, covering selected issues from the administrative activity of a court or court division (Art. 37b § 2 point 2 LCCO).

To conclude, the competences also include an examination of trends in adjudication as well as the appraisal of legislative success and effectiveness, as well as inquiries in the case of gross infringements of the law or administrative violations of procedures (e.g. delays). Of course, these activities cannot encroach upon judicial independence. For example, it may be questionable whether supervisory authorities being present at a court case (which is a point of political discussion) would not improperly influence the judge presiding over the case. What is crucial and may have negative impact on the independence of judges is that there is a lack of a clear separation of the sphere in which the intervention of supervisory authorities is no longer possible because of the need to respect judicial independence.[34]

The supervisory measures at the disposal of the Minister of Justice are of a general nature. They are related to the structure of the judiciary (the creation and liquidation of courts or assigning new judicial positions) or they are related to the personnel aspect, in relation to persons managing the court (appointing and dismissing court presidents or directors). With regard to the scope of the supervisory powers of court presidents, it is definitely broader. In particular, it deals with issues related to the efficiency of the process itself. However, it is doubtful whether this will affect the independence of courts and judges. Some of these powers may affect the possibility of maintaining the principle of independence of a judge from factors such as the influence of the executive authority (their superiors appointed by a representative of the executive authority).

4. Disciplinary proceedings against judges

Apart from reforms of the judiciary, the Polish Government has introduced extensive changes to the disciplinary proceedings for judges.[35] The Polish legislator has created a special chamber in the Supreme Court which is devoted to such proceedings.[36] All the justices in this chamber are chosen by the new National Council of the Judiciary. It is designed to adjudicate as:

34 M. Radajewski, "Stwierdzenie uchybienia w zakresie sprawności postępowania sądowego," *Przegląd Sądowy* 11–12, 2018, p. 69.

35 For a more detailed discussion, see: W. Jasiński, "Charakterystyka zmian w ustroju i organizacji sądownictwa powszechnego w Polsce w latach 2016–2018," *Krajowa Rada Sądownictwa* 1, 2018, pp. 62–78.

36 The Act of Supreme Court 8.12.2017 (Journal of Laws 2018, item 5).

- the second instance court for disciplinary cases involving judges of the ordinary courts and members of other legal professions (prosecutors, attorneys and notaries),
- the first instance disciplinary court for disciplinary cases involving Supreme Court judges,
- the first and second instance court for cases involving Supreme Court judges,
- the second instance court recognising appeals from resolutions of the National Council of the Judiciary.[37]

This Chamber has a separate President (completely independent in terms of competences and not subordinated to the First President of the Supreme Court), a separate budget and a separate office. These new disciplinary proceedings were criticised by representatives of the legal doctrine and were contested by the ECJ and the Polish Supreme Court.[38] Apart from the creation of the Disciplinary Chamber, there are also some new regulations pertaining to disciplinary proceedings against judges. The main changes are as follows:

- members of first instance disciplinary courts (situated at the level of Appellate Courts) are elected by the Minister of Justice, and the judge appointed for the position in the disciplinary court is obliged to take up this position even if it is against his/her will and does not have any remedy against such an appointment (art. 110a § 1 LCCO),
- it is permissible to carry out a hearing in disciplinary proceedings in the absence of a judge or her/his counsel if this is justified (art. 115 § 3 LCCO),
- extensive powers are granted in matters of disciplinary proceedings to representatives of the Minister of Justice. He can appoint a disciplinary prosecutor for a particular judge. Such a disciplinary prosecutor can be appointed not only from among judges but also from among public prosecutors who are directly subordinate to the Minister of Justice, who is at the same time the General Public Prosecutor (art. 112b LCCO),
- the possibility to repeal a judge's immunity under the accelerated 24-hours mode of procedure (art. 80 § 2da LCCO).

---

37 Art. 27 § 1 of The Act of the Supreme Court (consolidated text Journal of Laws 2019, item 825).

38 Judgment of the CJEU, 19.11.2019 (Independence of the Disciplinary Chamber) in joined cases C-585/18, C-624/18, C-625/18.

The next step of the political authorities was to expand the basis of judges' disciplinary liability.[39] This was related to contesting the possibility of appointing to the post of judges those elected by the National Council of the Judiciary which was elected by the Parliament in 2018. The new regulations were criticised in the doctrine.[40] The shape and creation of the Disciplinary Chamber of the Supreme Court was also the subject of a case before the ECJ.

In the decision of April 8, 2020, the Court of Justice of the European Union obliged Poland to suspend the application of the provisions constituting the jurisdiction of the Disciplinary Chamber of the Supreme Court, both in the first and in the second instance, in disciplinary cases against judges.[41]

5. Measures of administrative supervision in selected European countries

As was mentioned above, the phenomenon of supervision over courts is not understood in the same way in different countries. The understanding prevailing in a specific country is strongly related to the legal culture, and to the structure of the courts and the authorities which are responsible for the administration, management or the supervision over judiciary. It is also obvious that the differences between the countries (even in the members of the EU) are the result of historical, legal and political aspects; however, the way that administration or supervision over courts is conducted should follow the same direction. It is also obvious that supervision measures cannot be a tool which can be used to put pressure on a judge or to question individual judgments. It is especially difficult to balance the need to safeguard the judicial process from distortion and pressure from political sources with the need for open discussion of matters of public interest concerning the administration of justice.[42] However, from the perspective of Polish experiences it is crucial to compare the domestic legal system with the regulations in other countries. Germany, Denmark, Sweden and Slovakia

39 The Act amending the act – the Law on the Common Courts system, the Supreme Court Act and certain other acts of 20. 12.2019 (Journal of Laws 2020, item 190).

40 A.Grzelak, A. Sakowicz, "Wymóg niezależności sądu krajowego jako element skutecznej ochrony sądowej (uwagi na tle wyroku TS z 19.11.2019 r. dla polskiego wymiaru sprawiedliwości)," *Państwo i Prawo* 5, 2020, pp. 74–75.

41 Order of the Court in Case C-791/19 R Commission v Poland, ECLI:EU:C:2020:277.

42 Opinion of Consultative Council of European Judges (CCJE) No. 18 (2015) "The position of the judiciary and its relation with the other powers of state in a modern democracy;" https://rm.coe.int/16807481a1.

were chosen for comparison. The choice of these four countries is not accidental. With regard to Sweden and Denmark, it should be remembered that these countries are perceived as guaranteeing the greatest degree of judicial independence.[43] In the case of Germany and Slovakia, the selection criterion was related to the geographic location and historical conditions. On the one hand, Slovakia has similar political experiences to Poland, while Germany, on the other hand, has a legal system which in many cases was a source of inspiration for the solutions adopted in Poland.

5.1 Germany[44]

5.1.1 General remarks

In Germany, judges are subject to a multilevel supervision. At the lowest level, administrative supervision is exercised by the president of the court. Highest authorities for supervision are the ministers of justice in the federal states (for judges of the lower courts) and the federal minister of justice (for judges of the federal courts, with the exception of the Federal Constitutional Court). If judicial independence is affected, supervisory measures can be challenged by legal recourse to special courts (*Dienstgerichte*). Furthermore, the rules of civil service law (*Beamtenrecht*) are applicable, which include disciplinary measures. These rules are implemented by the same supervision authorities and special courts (*Dienstgerichte*). Most of these rules have proved themselves in practice.

5.1.2 Measures of supervision

The measures of supervision over judges are allegations (*Vorhalte*) and reprimands (*Ermahnung*). If it comes to an official procedure according to civil service law, the authority can issue a letter of censure (*Verweis*). If it brings the case to the court (*Dienstgericht*), the court could impose rigorous sanctions, such as administrative fines, reduction in salary, demotion, and termination of employment. Furthermore, in severe cases the Public Prosecutor can bring

---

43 For more detailed discussion, see: The EU Justice Scoreboard, Communication from the Commission to the European Parliament, the Council, the European Central Bank, the European Economic and Social Committee and the Committee of the Regions COM(2020) 306, https://ec.europa.eu/info/sites/info/files/justice_scoreboard_2020_en.pdf, p. 41 (accesse date: 27.12.2020).

44 S. Haack, *Questionnaire "administrative supervision over courts and judges" in Germany*, Frankfurt(Oder) 2020, unpublished.

criminal charges against the judge on grounds of "judicial perversion of justice" in accordance with the German Criminal Code § 339. In the event of conviction, he or she can no longer work as a judge. If a judge is involved in anti-constitutional activities, impeachment is possible. For this, a special procedure before the Federal Constitutional Court exists (*Richteranklage*). In the history of the Federal Republic of Germany, this never had happened.

5.2 Denmark[45]

5.2.1 General remarks

In Denmark, there are a few intuitions which help in the administration and supervision of the courts. The Judicial Appointments Council handles applications for the vacant positions of judges. The Council makes a recommendation to the Minister of Justice and may nominate one candidate for each position. The only position exempt from this is the President of the Supreme Court, appointed by the judges of that Court.[46] This is a totally different solution to that in place in Poland, where the President of the Supreme Court is appointed by the President of the Republic. Judges must apply to the External Activity Review Board for permission to take a secondary job with a fixed income. The Board registers judges' salaries from such activities and may enforce sanctions against judges not complying with its rules. The Board publishes an annual account of its activities.[47] This authority may decide that a judge is subjected to a lower limit of secondary income from secondary jobs in the coming year and that he or she is included in a specific scheme of reporting and permissions.[48] The Danish Court Administration is an independent agency responsible for managing the courts' budgets, staff matters, IT, buildings, and the allocation of resources to the courts. The Court Administration is the supervisory authority in relation to courts' processing of data, which falls outside the competence of the Danish Data Protection Authority. Formally and in terms of funding, the Administration is an agency under the Ministry of Justice, but the Minister cannot change decisions made by the Administration.[49]

---

45 S. Kinge, *Questionnaire "administrative supervision over courts and judges" in Denmark*, Kopenhagen 2020, unpublished.

46 https://www.domstol.dk/dommerudnaevnelsesraadet/.

47 https://www.domstol.dk/bibeskaeftigelsesnaevnet/.

48 The Administration of Justice Act, art. 47 b (3).

49 https://www.domstol.dk/om-os/domstolsstyrelsen/.

5.2.2 Measures of supervision

Moreover, there are some measures which are designated to the presidents of the courts. A President of Court may issue a warning to a judge guilty of neglect or carelessness in the performance of his or her duties. This covers only less grave cases, as the Danish Penal Code lays down criminal sanctions (a fine or up to 4 months in prison) for judges and other public servants guilty of "gross or repeated neglect or carelessness" while performing in their public capacity.[50] The president may similarly issue warnings for judges' improper or indecent behaviour.[51] Warnings are issued on the presidents' own initiative or after receiving a complaint about a judge. In some cases, the president will refer complaints to the Special Court of Indictment and Revision.[52] A judge receiving a warning from a president of court may appeal against it to the Special Court of Indictment and Revision.[53]

Disciplinary cases against judges may also begin with a complaint directly to the Special Court of Indictment and Revision from "anyone offended by the improper or indecent behaviour of a judge" acting in his or her judicial capacity, or – in special cases where a judge is considered to be unworthy of the office due to e.g. being convicted for tax fraud – on request from the Minister of Justice.[54] If a complaint is found to be well-founded, the Special Court may state in its decision its disapproval of the judge's behaviour or issue a fine. If the case concerns a grave offence, or if the judge has been previously convicted for the same type of offence, he or she might be dismissed.[55] The decisions of the Special Court may be appealed to the Supreme Court.[56]

5.3 Sweden[57]

5.3.1 General remarks

In Sweden, the administration of the courts is designated to the National Courts Administration. This is an authority which supports the courts with administrative issues, such as payments of salaries, and arranging computer systems,

50 The Danish Penal Code, art. 157.
51 The Administration of Justice Act, art. 48 (1).
52 Ibid., art. 48 (3).
53 Ibid., art. 48 a (1).
54 Ibid., art. 49 (1) and (2).
55 Ibid., art. 49 (6).
56 Ibid., art. 49 (8).
57 M. Sunnqvist, Questionnaire "administrative supervision over courts and judges" in Sweden, Lund 2020, unpublished.

court buildings, technology, etc. The problem with this authority is that it is an authority under the government. The courts are independent authorities but have no decisive influence over the National Courts Administration. At the same time, however, Swedish administrative authorities are generally independent from the government, so the government is not able to interfere with the decision-making of the National Courts Administration. However, the Director General of the National Courts Administration is appointed by the government. The Director General is, by tradition, chosen from among senior judges or government officials who have previously been judges.

5.3.2 Measures of supervision

The supervisory measures in Sweden can be divided into three parts: critique, disciplinary proceedings, and prosecution. Critique from the ombudsman of justice or the chancellor of justice can deal with any question about due process and fair trial. The ombudsman and chancellor do not discuss the outcome of the case – that is a thing for the higher courts to assess – but rather the handling of the procedure as such. As mentioned above, such a critique is most often used as a guideline for the courts in later cases that are similar. Disciplinary proceedings concern cases where a judge has intentionally or negligently has set aside his/her duties as a judge, unless the mistake is less severe (i.e. there is an overlap with the cases of disciplinary proceedings, but these two types of proceedings exclude each other). Prosecution will most commonly consider a breach of duty/official misconduct (*tjänstefel*). The most common cases in the Supreme Court regarding official misconduct of judges relate to not adhering to the correct time frames for hearing issues of detention, mistakes relating to lengths of punishments, and other formal issues related to detentions and punishments.[58] There are also examples of judges that did not finalise their judgments in due time,[59] and a judge that applied a criminal delict in the wrong way.[60] Other examples are the slow handling of cases,[61] and the overly hasty handling of cases (the parties did not get the chance to finalise their arguments).[62]

58 NJA 1990, p. 542, 1994 p. 304, 1996 p. 237, 1996 p. 307, 1996 p. 806, 1997 p. 186, 1997 p. 368, 2002 p. 342, 2004, p. 164, 2016 p. 453, 2017 p. 842, RH 1997:23.

59 NJA 2001, p. 35, 2002 p. 336, cf. also 2011 not. 24.

60 NJA 1983, p. 644.

61 Appeal court cases according to God domarsed – om tjänsteansvar och tillsyn, 2011, p. 21.

62 NJA 2000 B 1.

5.4 Slovakia[63]

5.4.1 General remarks

In Slovakia, various bodies are entrusted with administrative supervision. Most of those bodies are elected by judges themselves and are judges. These include the Judicial Council of the Slovak Republic, court councils of each court, and a chairperson of a court. The state body with several important competences in the matter is the Ministry of Justice. Each court also has a Director of Court Administration who is responsible for the daily operation of a court, and for court security or public procurement. The Judicial Council's competencies include: ensuring the public control of the judiciary; declaring whether the candidate for a judge fulfils the preconditions for judicial competence, which guarantees that he/she will perform the function of a judge properly; submitting to the President of the Slovak Republic proposals of candidates in the formal act of appointing judges and submitting proposals for the dismissal of judges; deciding on the transfers of judges between courts; electing members of the disciplinary chambers and their chairpersons; commenting on the draft court budgets; supervising that the judge meets the conditions for judicial competence, which guarantees that he/she will perform the function of a judge properly for the entire duration their appointment; and issuing the principles of judicial ethics in cooperation with judicial self-government bodies. Court councils are judicial self-government bodies consisting of judges of respective courts. Court councils comment on draft court budgets; discuss the report of the chairperson of a court on budget use; discuss the draft of the court's work schedule. The Chairperson of a court ensures that the administration of the court follows the work schedule; exercises supervision over the dignity and fluency of court proceedings and the principles of judicial ethics; makes decisions based on the results of the internal review; and handles complaints. The Ministry of Justice is responsible for supervising competences in personnel, financial, organisational and economic matters. The lawful decision-making of the courts/judges is secured via a system of remedies. In matters of inconsistent decision making, special motions by court itself (Supreme Court), or by the General Prosecutor, or a special proceeding, may follow. This proceeding ends in a Unifying Opinion of the Supreme Court that binds the Supreme Court itself as well as all the other courts.

---

63 M. Horvat, Questionnaire "administrative supervision over courts and judges" in Slovakia, Bratislava 2020, unpublished.

5.4.2 Measures of supervision

Two of the most important measures of supervision in Slovakia are complaints and disciplinary proceedings.

A complaint may be lodged by a party to the proceedings. The complaint may be lodged in case of violation of the right to a public hearing without undue delay, or in the case of a violation of the principles of dignity of court proceedings conducted by judges, court clerks or court staff while performing their judicial tasks. The competent body to assess the merits of the complaint is the chairperson of the court.[64]

It is necessary to distinguish a motion for inappropriate behaviour from a complaint. Any natural or legal person may lodge a motion in which he/she points out the inappropriate behaviour of judges, court clerks or court staff outside the court proceedings, and or any other deficiencies which are not related to the proceedings and decisions in the present cases. The competent body to assess the merits of the motion is also the chairperson of the court.[65]

The complaints and their assessment, together with other factors, form the basis for the judge's evaluation, which takes place at regular intervals.[66]

Judges are held accountable for disciplinary offenses. Disciplinary offenses are stipulated by law.[67] The law distinguishes between disciplinary offenses,[68] serious disciplinary offenses[69] and disciplinary offenses incompatible with the judicial profession.[70]

In the area of measures of supervision, there have been, and will be, several changes in the Slovak legislation. On January 1, 2021, an amendment of the Constitution came into effect and established the Supreme Administrative Court. The Supreme Administrative Court will become responsible for disciplinary proceedings over judges, prosecutors and, if a law establishes it, other law professions too, on August 1, 2021.[71]

---

64 Art. 62 of Slovak Act on Courts.

65 Ibid., art. 69.

66 See art. 27c of Slovak Act on Judges.

67 Ibid., art. 115 and subsequent.

68 Examples of disciplinary sanctions are: reprimand, or a reduction of salary by up to 30 %, for a maximum period of three months.

69 Examples of disciplinary sanctions are: transferring a judge to a lower court, or a reduction of salary by 50 % to 70 %, for a period of three months to one year.

70 Only one sanction is applicable: termination of the judge's employment.

71 See art. 142(2)(c) of the Constitution of Slovak Republic.

A second new measure comes from criminal law. As of January 1, 2021, Criminal Code enacted a new crime called "bending the law"[72] punishable by the criminal courts. Pursuant to art. 326 of the Slovak Criminal Code whoever, as a judge, a lay judge or arbitrator of the arbitral tribunal, arbitrarily exercises the law in his/her decision and thereby harms or favours another, shall be punished by imprisonment for one to five years.

6. Final conclusions

The judiciary must remain independent from the other powers. It is also obvious that, in spite of their independence, judges do not operate in a vacuum.[73] It should be emphasised that purely from legal point of view, courts and judges must remain independent. The current legislation and reforms do not introduce any mechanisms which would let the legislative or executive branch directly affect judicial verdicts. It is true that the proceedings before the Polish courts (common and administrative) are lengthy and might seems complicated and ineffective. However, the reform of the judiciary is generally focused on personnel changes within the justice system. The pressure on judges is rather focused on their position as employees than directly on the court's proceedings. The reforms conducted from 2015 have had a negative impact on the perception of the courts in society, as well as on the certainty of professional stability of judges.

The system of administration and supervision over the courts in Poland shows similarities with the systems of the countries considered for comparison. Each of these systems has supervisory bodies, and it is also possible to implement disciplinary consequences. What distinguishes the Polish legal system from the above-mentioned countries is the different system of entities responsible for supervision (especially in contrast to Sweden and Denmark) and the relatively high influence of the executive power on the structure and functioning of the judiciary. However, the problem of judicial independence and impartiality, in the functional aspect and from the institutional perspective, particularly concerning interference with judicial bodies, is a topic of discussion in the legal doctrine of many countries.[74]

72 Art. 326a of the Slovak Criminal Code.

73 R. Kiener, "Judicial Independence in Switzerland" in: *Judicial Independence in Transition*, ed. by A. Seibert-Fohr, Heidelberg, New York: Springer, 2012, p. 433.

74 A. Ryser, *Swiss Justice in Comparison. An outline of the Swiss Judicial System According to the Approach by Devlin and Dodek*, Bern 2018, p. 11.

It is vitally important in a democracy that individual judges and the judiciary as a whole are impartial and independent of all external pressures. Participants of the proceedings should have confidence that their cases will be decided fairly and in accordance with the law. When carrying out their judicial function, they must be free of any improper influence. Such influence could come from any number of sources, such as:

- improper pressure by the executive or the legislature,
- individual litigants,
- particular pressure groups or the media,
- other judges or the management body of the courts.

The fundamental feature of a court that enables it to dispense justice is its independence. The supervisory measures which can be used by the presidents of the courts have a wide range. This might affect judicial independence, especially taking into account the influence of the Ministry of Justice on appointing the presidents of the common courts and the wide shape of supervisory measures of the administrative authorities acting in the courts.

References

Publications

Dąbrowski, Stanisław, "Władza sądownicza – definicja, funkcja, atrybuty" in: *Pozycja ustrojowa sędziego*, ed. by Piotrowski, Ryszard, Warszawa: Wolters Kluwer Polska, 2015.

Dąbrowski, Stanisław, in: *Aurea praxis. Aurea theoria. Księga pamiątkowa ku czci Profesora Tadeusza Erecińskiego*, Vol. 2, ed. by Gudowski, Jacek and Karol Weitz, Warszawa: LexisNecis 2011, Lex/el.

Fleck, Zoltan, "A Comparative Analysis of Judicial Power, Organisational Issues in Judicature and the Administration of Courts," in: *Fair Trial and Judicial Independence*, ed. by Bado Atilla, Cham Heidelberg New York Dordrecht London: Springer 2014, pp. 3–25.

Gonera, Katarzyna, in: *Model nadzoru nad działalnością sądów i pracą orzeczniczą sędziów*, ed. by. P. Zientarski, Warszawa 2015, pp. 35–40.

Górski, Antoni., Prawo o ustroju sądów powszechnych – Komentarz do art. 9b (The Law of the System of Common Courts. Commentary to art. 9b), Warszawa: Lex 2013, Lex/el.

Jasiński, Wojciech, Charakterystyka zmian w ustroju i organizacji sądownictwa powszechnego w Polsce w latach 2016–2018 in: *Krajowa Rada Sądownictwa* 1/2018, pp. 62–78.

Grzelak, Agnieszka and Andrzej, Sakowicz, "Wymóg niezależności sądu krajowego jako element skutecznej ochrony sądowej (uwagi na tle wyroku TS z 19.11.2019 r. dla polskiego wymiaru sprawiedliwości)," *Państwo i Prawo* 5, 2020, pp. 62–78.

Kiener, Regina, "Judicial Independence in Switzerland," in: *Judicial Independence in Transition, Springer*, ed. by Anja Seibert-Fohr, Heidelberg, New York: Springer, 2012.

Lienhard, Andreas, "Oberaufsicht und Justizmanagement," *Justice - Justiz - Giustizia* 1, 2009.

Łazarska, Aneta "Niezawisłość sędziowska w sprawowaniu urzędu," in: *Pozycja ustrojowa sędziego* ed. by Piotrowski Ryszard, Warszawa: Wolters Kluwer Polska 2015.

Machnikowska, Anna, *O niezawisłości sędziów i niezależności sądów w trudnych czasach*, Warszawa: Wolters Kluwer Polska 2018.

Mikuli, Piotr, "Current Debates on the Supervision over the Administrative Activity of the Common Courts", *European Public Law*, Vol. 20, No.3, 2014, No.3, pp. 521–537.

Mikuli, Piotr and Grzegorz, Kuca, "The Separation Versus the Cooperation of Powers in the Contemporary Democratic State", *Studia i Materiały Trybunału Konstytucyjnego Vol. LV, Warszawa: Wydawnictwo Trybunału Konstytucyjnego, 2015*, pp. 125–136.

Niemiec, Tomasz, "Nadzór zewnętrzny nad działalnością administracyjną sądów powszechnych", *Kwartalnik KRS*, No. 4, 2012, pp. 5–9.

Piotrowski, Ryszard, "Status ustrojowy sędziego a zakres i charakter zarządzeń nadzorczych" in: *Pozycja ustrojowa sędziego*, ed. by Piotrowski Ryszard, Warszawa: Wolters Kluwer Polska, 2014.

Radajewski, Mateusz, "Zarządzenie natychmiastowej przerwy w czynnościach służbowych sędziego", *Przegląd Sądowy* 5, 2020, pp. 32–45.

Radajewski, Mateusz, "Stwierdzenie uchybienia w zakresie sprawności postępowania sądowego," *Przegląd Sądowy* 11–12, 2018, pp. 57–70.

Radziewicz, Piotr and Piotr, Tuleja, *Konstytucyjny spór o granice zmian organizacji i zasad działania Trybunału Konstytucyjnego: czerwiec 2015 - marzec 2016*, Warszawa: Wolters Kluwer Polska, 2017.

Ryser, Anabelle, *Swiss Justice in Comparison. An outline of the Swiss Judicial System According to the Approach by Devlin and Dodek*, Bern 2018.

Sadurski, Wojciech, *Poland's Constitutional Breakdown*, Oxford 2019.

Simunis, Mindaugas, "Effective Court Administration and Professionalism of Judges as Necessary Factors Safeguarding the Mother of Justice – The Right to a Fair Trial," *International Journal for Court Administration* / Winter 2019, pp. 47–58.

Sobczak, Jacek, "Niezawisłość sędziowska i niezależność sądów. Problem ważny i ciągle aktualny," *Gdańskie Studia Prawnicze – Przegląd Orzecznictwa*, No. 4, 2015, pp. 79–115.

Skąpska, Grażyna, "The decline of liberal constitutionalism in East Central Europe," in: *The Routledge International Handbook of European Social Transformations* ed. by Vihalemm Peeter and Anu Masso and Signe Opermann, London–New York: Routledge, 2018, pp. 130–145.

Van Dijk, Frans and Geoffrey, Vos, "A Method for Assessment of the Independence and Accountability of the Judiciary," *International Journal for Court Administration*, December 2018, pp. 1–21.

Van Dijk, Frans, "Improved Performance of The Netherlands Judiciary: Assessment of the Gains for Society," *International Journal for court administration*, No. 1, Vol. 6, 2014, p. 16.

Zajadło, Jerzy, "Constitution-hostile Interpretation," *Przegląd Konstytucyjny* 2018/2, pp. 5–15.

Ziółkowski, Michał, "Constitutional Moment and the Polish Constitutional Crisis 2015–2018 (a few Critical Remarks)," *Przegląd Konstytucyjny* 4, 2018, pp. 76–106.

Zubik, Marek, "Organizacja sądownictwa," in: *Przyszłość polskiego wymiaru sprawiedliwości*, ed. by Zielinski Adam and Marek Zubik, Warszawa: CH Beck, 2002, p. 33.

Jurisprudence

CJEU

Order of the CJEU in Case C-791/19 R Commission v Poland, ECLI:EU:C:2020:277.

Judgment of the CJEU of 19..11.2019 (Independence of the Disciplinary Chamber) in joined cases C-585/18, C-624/18, C-625/18.

Polish Constitutional Tribunal

Judgement of Polish Constitutional Tribunal, 15.1.2009, K 45/07, OTK-A 2009/ 1/3.

Judgement of Polish Constitutional Tribunal, 7.11.2013, K 31/12, OTK-A 2013/8/121.

Judgement of Danish Supreme Court, 13.10.1983, 1983 p. 644.

Judgement of Danish Supreme Court, 18.9.1990, 1990 p. 542.

Judgement of Danish Supreme Court, 31.5.1994, 199r, 1994 p. 304.

Judgement of Danish Supreme Court 1.4.1996, 1996 p. 237.

Judgement of Danish Supreme Court from 14.6.2002 p. 342.

Judgement of Danish Supreme Court from 17.11.2017 p. 842.

Judgement of Court of Appeal for Lower Norrland 10.3.1997, RH 1997:23.

Sources of law

The Constitution of the Republic of Poland of 2.4.1997, Journal of Laws 1997, No. 78, item 483 with subsequent amendments.

The Act from 27th of July 2001 – Law on the system of common courts (Consolidated text Journal of Laws Journal of Laws 2020, item 2072).

The Act from 25th of July 2002 – Law on the system of Administrative Courts from 2 (Consolidated text Journal of Laws 2019, item 2167).

The Act from 8th of December 2017 of the Supreme Court (consolidated text Journal of Laws 2019, item 825).

The Act from 12 July 2017 amending the act – on the system of common courts and certain other acts (Journal of Laws 2017 item 1452).

The Act amending the act – the Law on the Common Courts system, the Supreme Court Act and certain other acts of 20.12.2019 (Journal of Laws 2020, item 190).

Convention for the Protection of Human Rights and Fundamental Freedoms Rome, 4.XI.1950.

UN Basic Principles on the Independence of the Judiciary of 1985 (UN General Assembly resolution 40/146, 1985).

Act No 757/2004 on courts in Slovakia.

The Administration of Justice Act in Denmark (Consolidated Act no. 1069 of 6.11.2008).

The Danish Penal Code (Order No. 909 of 27.9.2005, as amended by Act Nos. 1389 and 1400 of December 21, 2005).

Constitution of Slovak Republic from 1.9.1992 460/1992 Zb.

Act 300/2005 from 20 May 2005 – Slovak Criminal Code.

Basic Principles on the Independence of the Judiciary Adopted by the Seventh United Nations Congress on the Prevention of Crime and the Treatment of Offenders held at Milan from 26 August to 6 September 1985 and endorsed by General Assembly resolutions 40/32 of 29 November 1985 and 40/146 of 13 December 1985.

Internet sources

M. Matczak, Poland: From Paradigm to Pariah? Facts and Interpretations of Polish Constitutional Crisis, 12 March 2018, pp. 3–9, https://ssrn.com/abstract=3138541 (access date: 3.10.2020).

Communication from the EU Comission: The 2018 EU Justice Scoreboard COM(2018) 364 final; https://eur-lex.europa.eu/legal-content/EN/TXT/HTML/?uri=CELEX:52018DC0364&from=pl (access date: 27.12.2020).

The EU Justice Scoreboard, Communication from the Commission to the European Parliament, the Council, the European Central Bank, the European Economic and Social Committee and the Committee of the Regions COM(2020) 306, https://ec.europa.eu/info/sites/info/files/justice_scoreboard_2020_en.pdf, p. 41 (access date: 27.12.2020).

Opinion of Consultative Council of European Judges (CCJE) no. 18 (2015) "The position of the judiciary and its relation with the other powers of state in a modern democracy;" https://rm.coe.int/16807481a1

Website about Danish system of judiciary: https://www.domstol.dk/dommerudnaevnelsesraadet/ (access date: 27.12.2020).

Matej Horvat,[1] Matúš Radosa[2]

Considerations on the supervision exercised over courts and judges

Abstract: The subject of this chapter is the definition of the supervision exercised over courts and judges, i.e. what should be subject to supervision and who should perform this supervision. We will describe the issue from the point of view of the definition of supervision in administrative law, define the specific features of administrative supervision of the judiciary, its objectives and functions, followed by a section on administrative supervision and instance supervision, and conclude this chapter by describing the relationship between administrative supervision and the disciplinary liability of judges. The authors of this chapter do not aim to define the supervision exercised over courts and judges in exhaustive detail, but rather this chapter presents their personal reflection on this issue, which is influenced by the specifics of their country of their origin.

Keywords: judiciary control, judiciary supervision, supervision over courts, supervision over judges, instance supervision, principles of judicial ethics, disciplinary liability

1. Introduction

From the viewpoint of the traditional three divisions of state power,[3] it follows that the individual components of state power have a defined position within society. Each of these components has specific tasks which it must fulfil. Although their classification within the state is unambiguous (i.e. obvious), there exist inaccuracies and ambiguities in practical life. These are related to the political maturity, quality and stability of legislation, the material security of representatives of the state, but also to the subjective factors inherent for each individual. It must therefore be acknowledged at the same time that, on this basis, the clear boundaries between the various components of state power are partially blurred. The state

---

1 Matej Horvat, PhD, Professor of Law at Comenius University in Bratislava, (Slovakia). ORCID – 0000-0002-8249-4029.

2 Matúš Radosa, PhD, Comenius University in Bratislava, (Slovakia). ORCID – 0000-0003-3188-9829.

3 Partially mentioned, for example, in Aristotle's Politics; see Aristoteles. Politika. 1298a. Praha 1998. In modern form, in particular, Ch. Motesquieu. O duchu zákonů. Plzeň, 2003.

therefore necessarily creates a mechanism of mutual checks and balances. Its aim is to ensure a balance in the division of power. It ensures that none of the branches of state power acquires such a privileged position that it could jeopardise the democratic nature of the political system of the state. The separation of the individual components of power is complemented here by a mechanism of the limitation of power.

If we want to analyse the subject of supervision over courts and judges (judicial power, the judiciary), it is always necessary to start from the basic idea of the mutual separation of individual branches of power.

In the case of the judiciary, it is emphasised that it does not have the power to legislate; its role is seen in particular in the interpretation of legislation. It can issue individual legal acts (decisions), but only on the basis of law. For this reason, judges must be bound in this activity only by the constitution and laws.[4] Judges are not even bound by by-laws if these are in conflict with higher-level legislative regulations.[5] In the context of the judicial review of the decisions of executive bodies (especially public authorities), due to the system of checks and balances, the rule applies that a court decision may not change (or replace) a decision of an executive body,[6] but only reviews it from the point of view of its legality.

Unlike other branches of state power, the guarantee of independence and impartiality of judges and the judiciary is enshrined in the legislation of the highest legal force – the constitutions of individual states. Such guarantees can be found, for example, in Art. 173 of the Polish Constitution, Art. 97 of the German Constitution, Chapter 11, Art. 3 of the Swedish Instrument of Government, or Art. 141 of the Slovak Constitution. All these provisions have a common idea – the independent exercise of judicial power in a democratic and legal state.

We are convinced that the independence and impartiality of the judiciary is one of the fundamental principles of the rule of law. The independence and

---

4 See for example J. Prusák. Teória práva. Bratislava 1999, p. 91 ff.

5 For example, according to Section 2 para. 3 of Act no. 385/2000 Coll. on Judges, a judge is independent in the performance of his or her duties and is bound only by the Constitution of the Slovak Republic, a constitutional law, an international treaty pursuant to Art. 7 para. 2 and 5 of the Constitution of the Slovak Republic and by law.

6 Exceptions are permissible, but not the rule. In the case of the Slovak Republic, these are, for example, decisions in the field of administrative punishment (see Section 198 of the Administrative Procedure Code). In the case of the Czech Republic, for example, decisions in the area of the right to free access to information (see Section 16 (5) of Act no. 106/1999 Coll. on Free Access to Information).

impartiality of the exercise of judicial power is an important limit in formulating considerations on the definition of the object of supervision over courts and judges.

In this chapter, we will focus on a number of issues related to this topic, namely:

a) the concept of supervision in administrative law and its relation to the supervision over the exercise of judicial power and judges;
b) specific features of administrative supervision of the judiciary, its objectives and functions;
c) differences between administrative supervision and instance supervision in relation to the judiciary;
d) the exercise of disciplinary authority over judges.

2. Supervision in administrative law

At the beginning of the section on supervision, we consider it necessary to comment on the terminology that arises from the Slovak language. In Slovak, in addition to the term supervision (*dozor*), similar (often synonymous) terms are used, such as control (*kontrola*), audit or inspection (*inšpekcia*). In principle, legal theory uses these terms equally (interchangeably), under the influence of legislation, although it also points to their differences. Legislation does not make a fundamental distinction between those concepts. If we were to analyse the legislation governing these legal concepts, we would conclude that the term audit[7] is most often used in the sense of financial control. The terms inspection[8] and supervision[9] are most often used when it comes to the performance of these activities between non-subordinate entities.[10] In the case of inspections, they are carried out by specially established bodies whose competence is the performance of inspections. The term control means in particular internal control,[11] i.e. control between mutually subordinate entities, which for this reason most often also fulfils a repressive function (i.e. controlling authorities also specify liability

7 For example, Act no. 357/2015 Coll. on financial control and audit.
8 For example, Act no. 125/2006 Coll. on labour inspection.
9 For example, Act no. 541/2004 Coll. on the Peaceful Use of Nuclear Energy (Atomic Act), which regulates the conditions for the performance of state administration, the conditions for the performance of state supervision and the competence of the Nuclear Regulatory Authority of the Slovak Republic.
10 Cf. D. Hendrych et al. Správní právo. Obecná část. Praha 2009, p. 300.
11 For example, Act no. 10/1996 Coll. on control in state administration.

for their findings). However, the term control is often used as a concept that is the most general of the terms we present. In that case control also encompasses supervision, inspection, audit, or even instance supervision. In this way, the differences between these individual concepts become blurred.[12] For this reason, in the following text we will first analyse the term control and then we will point out the differences between it and the concept of supervision.

Control in general is part of the activities of any organised unit that shows signs of management. In the field of public law, it is also a guarantee of legality. It is also true in administrative law that it involves control of public administration and that public administration itself is subject to control.

Therefore, it is not only the public administration that is subject to control, but it is specific to the whole of society, not excluding the private sphere. Its general task is to point out mistakes and give an impetus to eliminate them and thus improve the individual and society as a whole.[13] In general, it is usually not enough to legally regulate some (specific) activity of natural persons or legal entities, and thus to direct it. To achieve the desired result, i.e. in order for persons to behave in accordance with the law and to fully respect it, it is also necessary to control the specific behaviour of persons in the given area.[14]

The importance of control in public administration is seen mainly in the fact that it is one of the basic preconditions for compliance with the law in the performance of public administration tasks.[15] In the context of control relations, it is ascertained whether or not the action of a certain entity was in accordance with the applicable procedure, which is established by law.[16] If it was not, there was a violation of the relevant law, and the control should reveal the reasons for this action and propose a solution so that it does not occur in the future.

Control activity is thus one of the basic preconditions and legal guarantees of compliance with the law.

The definition of control is often not the subject of legislation. From the point of view of legal theory, control means the exercise of the power to compare the

---

12 See for example B. Cepek et al. Správne právo hmotné. Všeobecná časť. Bratislava 2018, pp. 289 ff,

13 K. Tóthová et al. Základy správneho práva hmotného. Bratislava 1992, p. 126.

14 V. Sládeček. Obecné správní právo. Praha 2009, pp. 213 ff.

15 Cf. T. Seman, R. Jakab, J. Tekelli. Správne právo hmotné. Všeobecná časť. Košice 2020, p. 180.

16 Cf. M. Kopecký. Správní právo. Obecná část. Praha 2019, p. 203.

actual and required state of a particular activity and to set out measures to ensure their compliance.[17]

Unlike the definition of the term "control," there exists a consensus on the definition of control functions. Control functions include cognitive, comparative, analytical, reparative and repressive functions.[18]

The essence of the cognitive function is to know the factual state of affairs. This means that observation determines the state of affairs that really exists and that is there. The comparative function is a comparison of the actual state of affairs with the required state, i.e. the state defined in the legislation. The analytical function is connected, on the one hand, with the analysis of the results obtained by the control – i.e. whether or not this situation is in line with the expected state of affairs – and, on the other hand, it is also related to the analysis of the identified deficiencies, so that the control body can submit proposals for remediation to the controlled entity. This also fulfils the reparative function of the control. In a situation where the control findings show deficiencies in the activities of the controlled entity, it is the task of the control authority to propose measures to remedy this situation. Although it might seem that the repressive function contradicts the definition of control as such, it does not. Control must also necessarily have a repressive nature, especially in a situation where remedial action has not produced the desired effect.[19] Control without a possible repressive component would be "powerless" and could not fulfil its basic objective of protecting the rule of law.

Legal theory – in relation to the characteristics of control – states that control should be objective, professional, systematic and timely.[20]

The basic precondition for a properly performed control is that the control is objective. This means that the controller's approach to the findings, the controlled entity and its employees is unbiased, impartial and professional. In such a case, it evaluates all the facts, regardless of its subjective stance. In this way, the control becomes factual and corresponds to reality. The legal regulation of

---

17 P. Škultéty in P. Škultéty et al. Správne právo hmotné. Všeobecná časť. Bratislava 2005, p. 117.

18 E.g. B. Pekár. Kontrola vo verejnej správe v kontexte európskeho správneho práva. Bratislava 2011, p. 21.

19 Compare for example J. Machajová et al. Všeobecné správne právo. Žilina 2009, pp. 237–238; M. Vrabko et al. Správne právo hmotné. Všeobecná časť. Bratislava 2018, p. 151.

20 Cf. P. Škultéty in P. Škultéty et al. Správne právo hmotné. Všeobecná časť. Bratislava 2005, p. 118; P. Průcha. Správní právo. Obecná část. Brno 2007, p. 325.

reporting the bias of persons authorised to perform control serves to ensure the objectivity of the control.[21]

The professionalism of the control mainly concerns the position of the persons authorised to perform the control. It is essential that these persons have certain professional qualifications necessary to perform the control. The controlling person must therefore be a specialist in the given section of the control, and it should not happen that he or she is a person without any professional prerequisites for performing the control in the given area. For this reason, the legal regulations stipulate the professional prerequisites that the controlling person must meet, and which consist mainly in achieving a certain level of education and years of experience, or examinations that he or she must pass and their possible renewal.[22]

Systematic control means that the control is conceptual, has its rules in place and is performed according to plan. In order to achieve this, the scope of rights and obligations of the controlled entity, but also of the controlling person, must be established mainly by legal regulations. Likewise, the control should not interfere with the controlled entity's normal activities beyond the necessary extent.[23]

The timeliness of the control emphasises its preventative nature. The control should not highlight deficiencies after the deficiencies have already become obvious. The control should reveal such shortcomings in their early stages, point them out and suggest solutions so that they do not occur at all. Where deficiencies have already arisen, the control should be flexible enough to detect and rectify these deficiencies as soon as possible; it is unacceptable for these deficiencies to increase during the control.[24]

We believe that most of these ideas also apply to the supervision which is carried out in relation to the exercise of judicial power and judges. Also in this case, supervision must be objective, professional, systematic and timely. However, supervisory activities tend to also include procedures aimed at correcting the identified deficiencies.[25] We also see a difference in the case of functions. It is true that supervision must fulfil a cognitive, comparative, analytical and reparative

---

21 See, for example, Section 10 of Act no. 10/1996 Coll. on control in state administration; Section 26 of Act no. 357/2015 Coll. on financial control and audit; Section 43 para. 7 of Act no. 581/2004 Coll. on health insurance companies, health care supervision.

22 In the case of Slovakia, see for example Sections 12 to 14 of Act no. 357/2015 Coll. on financial control and audit.

23 B. Cepek et al. Správne právo hmotné. Všeobecná časť. Bratislava 2018, p. 280.

24 B. Cepek et al. Správne právo hmotné. Všeobecná časť. Bratislava 2018, p. 280.

25 M. Kopecký. Správní právo. Obecná část. Praha 2019, p. 203

function. The difference will lie in the case of the repressive function. We believe that, in order to preserve the independence of the judiciary and judges, the repressive component must be strictly separated. Liability relationships that arise as a result of findings must be regulated so as not to interfere with the independence of the judiciary, must be established by law and, depending on who implements them, their outcome must be subject to independent judicial review.[26]

As the control processes in the area of the exercise of judicial power are provided by bodies which cannot be subordinated to each other and which do not have a directly repressive function, the control of the judiciary always involves supervision, as defined in the introduction to this chapter.

3. Specific features of administrative supervision of the judiciary, its objectives and functions

The attempt to define the specific features of administrative supervision of the judiciary must be based on two factors. The first is the exercise of judicial power and the question of whether administrative supervision can also be exercised over it. The second concerns administrative supervision over activities other than the exercise of judicial power.

Administrative supervision over the exercise of judicial power.
If we are talking about administrative supervision of the exercise of judicial power, it must be seen at the level of providing effective guarantees in accordance with which the exercise of supervision will not interfere with the exercise of judicial power. The decision-making activity of a judge cannot be influenced by the performance of supervision. This type of supervision must be carried out by bodies that we classify as the judiciary itself (i.e. they "come" from the judiciary), but also by bodies that are outside the scope of the judiciary. The combination of these two components is important from the point of view of preventing the judiciary from closing itself off to the outside world, thus forcing this system to respond also to external stimuli.

When we talk about supervision over the exercise of judicial power, we are referring here in particular to its two aspects. The first concerns the supervision ensuring the unity of the decision-making activity of the courts, while the second relates to the statistical method of determining the duration of a litigation procedure.

26 See also the following and the last part of this chapter.

With regard to the supervision over the uniform exercise of judicial power, we believe that several entities should be involved in this type of supervision, both judicial authorities and bodies representing the executive power or *sui generis* entities. The decision-making activity of the highest judicial authorities ensures the uniformity of court decision-making at the highest level and with the highest degree of binding force. Whether it is the Supreme Court (be it the general or special judiciary, such as the administrative judiciary or the labour judiciary, etc.) or the Constitutional Court, their decision-making activity should demonstrate that legal opinions are unified. It should be the case that the decisions of these judicial authorities are bound by the force of legal reasoning to such an extent that the lower judicial authorities respect it unreservedly and deviate from it only if the facts of the case under review change or the relevant legislation has changed. In order to ensure uniformity in decision-making, the Constitutional Court or the Supreme Court itself is also bound by its own decision-making.

We believe that the uniformity of the decision-making activity of the courts can be ensured within the framework of the application practice itself, and thus within the decision-making activity of the court. It must be sufficiently consistent so that there are no unjustified differences in decisions in practice (in this view, it is not possible to speak of the exercise of supervision in the true sense, as it actually fulfils the basic role of the judiciary – the resolution of disputes).

In addition, however, there must be a mechanism for adopting opinions (legal conclusions), which do not necessarily have to be the result of the courts' own decision-making and whose task is to unify judicial case-law. The adoption of opinions can be considered as a less formal mechanism, the importance of which is also obvious. In our view, a court opinion represents the adoption of an opinion in relation to an issue which is either the subject of inconsistent decision-making at the level of the Supreme Court (unifying opinion) or which should proactively present the opinion of the judicial authority on a particular legal issue. The initiative to adopt such an opinion should arise from the exercise of supervision.

A characteristic feature of an opinion should therefore be that it is an internal act of the court, but it must be published. By publication we do not mean a publication in a form that is stipulated by law, but a publication in the sense that the opinion is available not only to the judiciary but also to the general public and that the general public is able to become acquainted with it.

The courts themselves should ensure the uniformity of decision-making. However, this responsibility cannot be assumed only by the court with the highest authority (the above-mentioned Constitutional Court or the Supreme Court), but it includes also the responsibility of all lower-level courts. Each court as such must ensure that its decision-making activity is uniform. The legal order should make it possible to create unified decision-making activity also in the lower-level courts. They must also be empowered to unify their decision-making on the basis of their opinions. It should be emphasised that such an opinion should always respect the opinions of the superior-level courts, and therefore its issuance is only possible where there is no opinion of the superior court.

The uniform decision-making activity of the courts should be overseen mainly by the president of the court (or otherwise called court representative responsible for the running of the court) in cooperation with the presidents of the colleges of the court (i.e. in the case of a court of general jurisdiction, these should be judges according to their professional profile, who are assigned to so-called colleges, which deal, for example, only with civil, commercial, labour, criminal, or administrative matters). The adoption of a unifying opinion must be the responsibility of the specific college. The adoption of the opinion should be the result of the inquiry work of the court itself. This is an internal process by which it is found that the decision-making activity of the court is not uniform. If such divergent decision-making persists, the court should be obliged to adopt a unifying opinion on the legal issue in question.

We have stated that proceedings which have resulted in the adoption of a unifying opinion could also be initiated by a body other than the court itself. Authorities that protect the public interest in judicial proceedings (such as the prosecution), that protect human rights (such as the ombudsman), or that administratively supervise the exercise of judicial powers (typically the Ministry of Justice or another public authority authorised to do so by law) should also be empowered in this area.

As regards the prosecutor's office or the ombudsman, they may, within the framework of their existing powers of scrutiny, conclude that the courts rule inconsistently and thus apply the law differently. For that reason, they should be entitled to bring an action before a court for a unifying opinion.

For some countries, although they do not fall under the Anglo-American legal culture, the decisions of some courts are legally binding and are published in a publication form reserved by law. An example is Slovakia, where the Constitutional Court has this position. According to the Constitution of the Slovak Republic and Act no. 314/2018 Coll. on the Constitutional Court of the Slovak Republic, decisions on the interpretation of legal regulations are published in the Collection of Laws as the official collection of legal regulations of the given country. This interpretation of the law is considered authentic and is legally binding.[27]

As regards the second aspect of supervision, this is supervision which should be based on the use of statistical methods to determine the duration of litigation. We believe that monitoring these statistics will help to determine the number of judges. In the case of a court where, on the basis of these methods, the length of the proceedings is disproportionately longer than other courts, this is necessarily an indication that the court has shortcomings in terms of the allocation of cases (for example, an uneven load on the court as such or on individual judges) or the number of judges is too low. This aspect of supervision should result from the internal supervision of the court. Jurisdiction for its exercise should be ensured primarily by the president of the court (or another designated person who is administratively at the head of the court), in cooperation with the relevant state administration body responsible for administrative supervision over the judiciary (typically the Ministry of Justice). Cooperation with this body should be primarily in the area of staffing of individual courts, and the outcome of administrative supervision should be:

a) The elimination of deficiencies related to the allocation of cases; or
b) Adopting a decision on the expansion of staff for the court.

Administrative supervision over non-decision-making activities.
Administrative supervision must also relate to activities which do not fall within the exercise of judicial power as such. This means supervision over activities other than decision-making. Here again, we believe that it should be a combination of supervision exercised by a representative of the judiciary (one of its bodies) and entities outside this structure (i.e. primarily executive bodies, but also other independent *sui generis* bodies). In this respect, we see the main direction in the supervision of compliance with the principles of judicial ethics.

Recommendation CM/Rec (2010) 12 of the Committee of Ministers of the Council of Europe to member states on judges' independence, efficiency and accountability of 17 November 2010 also states that the function of the judge should be performed in accordance with the ethical principles of professional

27 See Art. 128 of the Constitution of the Slovak Republic and Section 150 of Act no. 314/2018 Coll. on the Constitutional Court of the Slovak Republic; see also I. Macejková et al. Zákon o Ústavnom súde Slovenskej republiky. Komentár. Bratislava 2020, p. 1141 ff.

conduct. The principles of judicial ethics should be enshrined in the Code of Judicial Ethics and judges should be able to request the assistance of a body within the judiciary in the field of ethics. The Recommendation therefore provides for the establishment of a body to oversee the principles of judicial ethics. There is no doubt that it must be a collective body. This body should consist primarily of the judges themselves, but in our opinion, non-judges should also be members of this body, in order to ensure the widest possible consensus on the principles of judicial ethics.

The wording of the individual principles should be specific but with a degree of generality in order to provide sufficient guidance on how to behave in a particular situation. There is no doubt that judges must also be entitled to turn to this body with other questions that will help them to determine the appropriate ethical behaviour in a particular situation.

The text of the individual principles of judicial ethics must be based on the already mentioned Recommendation CM/Rec (2010) 12 of the Committee of Ministers of the Council of Europe. However, this is not the only source of inspiration. At the international level, we can also find other sources, including: the London Declaration of the European Network of Councils for the Judiciary (ENCJ) of 2010, the Magna Carta of Judges (Basic Principles) approved by the Consultative Council of European Judges (CCJE) of November 2010 and Opinion no. 3 (2002) of the Consultative Council of European Judges (CCJE) on the principles and rules governing the professional conduct of judges, their ethics, incompatible conduct and impartiality.

The principles of judicial ethics should be based on values such as independence, integrity, dignity, honour, impartiality, restraint, discretion, equal treatment, transparency, humanity or prudence.

There is no doubt that monitoring the observance of the principles of judicial ethics should be the primary responsibility of the body which drafted and adopted them. We see this supervision, especially at a general level, as generally supervising the compliance with these principles and issuing warnings if there are possible violations. In the event of a specific breach of the principles of judicial ethics, that body should also be empowered to bring an action before the competent disciplinary body. In our opinion, this body should not have the power to directly decide on disciplinary proceedings, but only to initiate it. We think that in this way a higher degree of independence in deciding on the merits of the matter will be ensured.

4. Administrative supervision and instance supervision

A distinction must be made between administrative supervision and instance supervision. Both these legal concepts perform different tasks and their use is not the same.

We mentioned that the aim of administrative supervision over the exercise of justice and over judges is, inter alia, to ensure the continuity of court proceedings. One of the preconditions for the continuity of court proceedings is the uniform case-law of the relevant judicial authorities. At the same time, the uniformity of the case-law is advantageous not only for the participants in the court proceedings but also for the judges themselves, as it enables them to formulate a decision in their case more quickly. Uniformity in decision-making is ensured by the predictability of legislation, but also by the predictability of the decision-making activity of judicial authorities.

The latter predictability of decision-making can be achieved in a number of ways, namely by publishing and promoting judicial decisions of fundamental importance, as well as by the aforementioned unifying opinions. In principle, the performance of these acts comes from within the judiciary as such.

This will be the main difference from instance supervision.

From the point of view of legal theory, instance supervision is a procedural concept and is performed by higher-ranking bodies over lower-level bodies, on the basis of a motion filed by an authorised person.[28] Instance supervision and its existence are derived from the idea that the application activities of the competent authorities may lead to errors which are reflected in the deficiencies of the acts issued. Even a defective act is capable of producing the relevant legal effects and, if it enters into force, unless it is amended or repealed, it must be complied with.[29]

Instance supervision within the judiciary can only be initiated on the basis of the procedural activity of the parties to the proceedings and the exercise of their right to appeal. It is irrelevant whether it is an ordinary remedy or an extraordinary remedy if, as a result of its application, there is a change in the jurisdiction to decide and the appeal will be decided by a superior court.

From the point of view of legal theory, we distinguish several principles of decision-making on an appeal. A distinction is made between the principle of appeal, review and cassation.[30] The principle of appeal gives the authority the

28 M. Kopecký. Správní právo. Obecná část. Praha 2019, p. 213.

29 P. Průcha, P. Správní právo. Obecná část. Brno 2007, pp. 368–369.

30 J. Vačok in M. Vrabko et al. Správne právo procesné. Všeobecná časť. Bratislava 2019, p. 131.

widest powers as to how the appeal can be decided, both in terms of the scope and aspects of the review, as well as possible decision.[31] The principle of appeal allows the body deciding on the appeal to rectify the decision itself and to decide on the merit itself. In doing so, it may deviate from the facts established by the first instance authority. The appeal is directed primarily against the shortcomings of the factual basis, but also against legal shortcomings. Depending on the outcome of the proceedings, the appellate body may confirm, amend or annul the contested decision.[32] This principle applies mainly in administrative proceedings[33] and not in judicial review, which is caused mainly by the fact that in administrative proceedings, in the instance review of a decision, the superior administrative body also deals with the factual correctness of the decision, i.e. its purposefulness, suitability, and effectiveness.[34] This is also supported by the case-law according to which, in administrative proceedings (as opposed to judicial), the appellate body is not bound by the facts found at first instance or by the evaluation opinion of the first-instance body.[35]

In court proceedings, we increasingly encounter the principle of review and the principle of cassation. The principle of review allows the authority deciding on the first-instance decision to change the decision under consideration, but only if the facts discovered remain unchanged.[36] However, if the law has been violated, then it must annul the decision and order a new hearing before the first-instance authority. The principle of cassation then means that the appellate body cannot change the contested decision but must annul it and return it to a new proceeding and decision.[37] As a rule, in such a case, the superior body will express in its decision a binding legal opinion on how the first-instance body should proceed in further proceedings.[38]

---

31 J. Škrobák. Preskúmanie neprávoplatných rozhodnutí vydaných v správnom konaní. Bratislava 2014, p. 145.

32 J. Sobihard. Správny poriadok. Komentár. Bratislava 2007, p. 231.

33 J. Škrobák. Preskúmanie neprávoplatných rozhodnutí vydaných v správnom konaní. Bratislava 2014, p. 145.

34 Cf. S. Košičiarová. Správne právo procesné. Všeobecná časť. Šamorín 2017, p. 246.

35 Decision of the Supreme Court of the Slovak Republic, file no. 4 Sž 74/2002 of 26 November 2002.

36 J. Vačok in M. Vrabko et al. Správne právo procesné. Všeobecná časť. Bratislava 2019, p. 131.

37 J. Sobihard. Správny poriadok. Komentár. Bratislava 2007, p. 231.

38 M. Kopecký. Správní právo. Obecná část. Praha 2019, p. 388.

The use of instance supervision is therefore possible if it is used directly by a party to the proceedings; instance supervision cannot be initiated on the court's own initiative. It is a process which is therefore dependent on the activity of an entity other than the court and whose rights are affected by a court decision.

Therefore, in our opinion, instance supervision is not administrative supervision, despite the fact that it also examines compliance with legal regulations, but in decision-making in a specific case, where the court must also take into account established decision-making practice.

Instance supervision can never interfere in the current decision-making activity of a particular court. This follows both from the point of view of time (instance supervision is carried out only when the case has already been decided) and also from the fact that the judge must be independent in his or her decision-making activity in every respect. If the instance supervision could interfere in the current decision-making activity of a judge, it would be a denial of his or her independence, which can be understood as a basic feature of the entire judiciary.

In our opinion, an inquiry within the constitutional judiciary or within the international judiciary cannot be perceived as instance supervision. In the case of the constitutional judiciary, it is basically scrutiny from the point of view of observance of the protection of the constitutionally guaranteed human rights and fundamental freedoms, i.e. constitutional conformity. In the case of scrutiny by international judicial institutions, it is often a matter of compliance with the international obligations of the state, again from the point of view of the protection of human rights and freedoms. In other words, in this case it is a matter of conformity with the international obligations of the state.

Although instance supervision is not administrative supervision, it can ultimately also help administrative supervision. As we have already mentioned, the application of instance supervision is, in principle, only possible where there is an entity which has appealed against a court decision. In the exercise of this right, a person may also argue for non-compliance with uniformity in the decision-making activity of the court, in particular non-compliance with the decision-making activity of the superior court. Also in this manner, there may be an indication of a different approach to decision-making in factually similar matters.

If such a situation arises, it is essential to analyse the situation and draw a proper conclusion as to whether the decision-making activity is in fact different or not. If the former proves to be true, then it is necessary to take steps that would lead to a unifying opinion. In the case of the Slovak Republic, an appeal filed this way (cassation appeal) would be decided by the so-called Grand Chamber. Pursuant to Section 22 of the Administrative Procedure Code, the

Supreme Court acts and decides on cassation appeals in a Grand Chamber composed of the President of the Chamber and six judges, if the Supreme Court Chamber has reached a legal opinion in its decision, which is different from the one already expressed in the decision of the Supreme Court, and the case was referred to the Grand Chamber for a decision, or if the Supreme Court Chamber again reached a legal opinion in its decision, which is different from the legal opinion of a public authority on the same legal issue, and referred the case to the Grand Chamber for a decision. The President of the Grand Chamber of the Supreme Court is the President of the Administrative College of the Supreme Court. The members of the Grand Chamber are the judges of the Chamber of the Supreme Court, which has referred the case to the Grand Chamber, and three judges appointed by the Supreme Court's work schedule. From the point of view of legal binding, special mention should also be made of Section 466 of the Administrative Procedure Code, according to which the legal opinion expressed in the decision of the Grand Chamber is binding for the Chambers of the Supreme Court. If the Chamber of the Supreme Court wishes to deviate from the legal opinion expressed in the decision of the Grand Chamber in its decision-making, it shall refer the case to the Grand Chamber for consideration and decision.

An interesting alternative also seems to be the possibility of using remedies in such a case, if the entity was not a party to the original court proceedings and its rights or obligations were not decided upon. However, such an alternative can only be accepted on the basis of law, i.e. only the law shall stipulate who and under what conditions is entitled to file an appeal and whether it may also be filed by a person whose rights or obligations have not been decided upon in the proceedings. The lodging of such an appeal must therefore be justified only in exceptional situations, and only very specific entities could have such a power, such as the Minister of Justice, the Attorney General or the Ombudsman. This power can never be in the hands of the judiciary, not even the self-governing bodies, because such a power would be contrary to maintaining the impartiality of the judiciary.

As far as the Minister of Justice is concerned, care must be taken not to grant him/her such a power, because it could be politically misused. In the case of the Ombudsman, in turn, it is questionable in whose favour he/she would file an appeal. In our view, such an appeal should be considered only for the protection of the public interest. However, in the case of the Ombudsman, the nature of the case would rather be to use the power for the benefit of a particular entity. Therefore, the Attorney General appears to be appropriate here as a (state) body that is independent and whose role is precisely to protect the public interest.

Here again, the legislation in the Slovak Republic, where the Attorney General has such authority, can serve as an example. Pursuant to Section 47 of the Administrative Procedure Code, the Attorney General is entitled to lodge a cassation appeal against a decision of an administrative court issued in proceedings in which the Attorney General was entitled to intervene but did not intervene, but may, in particular, propose the cassation appeal to be decided upon by the Grand Chamber of the Supreme Court. The reason is always that there is a different decision-making activity of administrative courts or a persistently different decision-making between administrative courts and public administration bodies.

The professional literature states that, thanks to this, it is possible to expect the unification of case-law, as well as its creation, through cassation appeals of the Attorney General (in the event that another party would not file a cassation appeal itself). The reason for the establishment of this legal concept is the effort to ensure predictable and equivalent decision-making in identical matters of administrative courts and, consequently, of public administration bodies.[39]

5. The relationship between administrative supervision and the disciplinary liability of judges

The disciplinary liability of judges is a necessary complement to the concept of the three divisions of state power. Its existence is a necessary precondition for building public confidence in the judiciary. However, according to the well-known question: "Who controls the controllers?," disciplinary liability must be seen as a legal institution that contributes to the transparency of the exercise of judicial power. Disciplinary liability must therefore not be seen as a scourge against judges, but as an awareness of one's own responsibility and the importance of the role that judges play in society.

Liability is generally perceived as the necessity of an entity bearing the adverse consequences of its own misconduct.[40] Disciplinary liability is then one of the types of liability that we classify as legal liability.[41] Since it is legal liability, it is a question of being responsible for the consequences of conduct which was contrary to the law.[42] Therefore, liability can only be attributed where there has been a breach of an obligation under the law.

---

39 J. Baricová et al. Správny súdny poriadok. Bratislava 2018, p. 330.

40 Cf. E. Ottová. Teória práva. Šamorín 2010, p. 283.

41 Cf. M. Vrabko et al. Správne právo hmotné. Všeobecná časť. Bratislava 2018, p. 196.

42 Cf. J. Boguszak, J. Čapek, A. Gerloch. Teorie práva. Praha 2003, p. 166.

Unlike other types of legal liability, disciplinary liability also shows certain peculiarities. First of all, it should be mentioned that the object of disciplinary liability is discipline. Discipline is the conscious submission to certain rules of conduct in a particular field, industry or human society. Discipline therefore has a necessary internal dimension and is linked to the internal regulations of a particular organisation. The subject of a disciplinary offence is therefore always special. It must have some specific relationship with the organisation whose internal regulations it is required to comply with. When defining disciplinary liability, it should also be noted that the features of the merits are usually defined not only in the law but also – on the basis of law – in internal regulations, which are often different disciplinary rules or codes of ethics.[43]

The rules for attributing liability must be set exactly. From the point of view of the substantive preconditions for liability, it must be clear under what conditions the judge is disciplinarily liable and for what action (or omission of action). It is inadmissible for these rules to be set at such a general level that it is not clear from them which action is inadmissible and which is not. In general, therefore, elements of an offence which are merely of a residual nature cannot be accepted. This is an example of such element of an offence which is fulfilled by a "breach of another obligation," i.e. other than that is expressively listed in the relevant article on offences. Alternatively, we can imagine the existence of such element of an offence, but only if it would precisely state the unlawful consequence which must occur in order for it to be fulfilled. For example, "breach of other obligations if they have reduced the weight of the judicial position."

Only in this way will the principle of *nullum crimen sine lege* and its individual aspects be fulfilled.

The legislation on disciplinary liability must also reflect the incentives able to initiate liability proceedings. There is no doubt that the question of authorised entities is an important procedural question to which the legislation should give a clear answer. It is possible to divide the authorised entities according to which ones can file a (non-binding) petition for discussion of the case and the entities that file a direct petition to initiate disciplinary proceedings, which must be properly dealt with by the competent body.

Disciplinary liability should be seen as a result of the application of additional supervisory tasks of the relevant entities, which we mentioned in the first part of this chapter. The exercise of administrative supervision on their part would be

43 Z. Hamuľáková, M. Horvat. Základy správneho práva trestného. Bratislava 2019, pp. 213–217.

incomplete if these entities did not have the opportunity to act also in the field of disciplinary liability. However, these entities can never have a decisive role.

The possibility of filing a motion to initiate disciplinary proceedings cannot be granted to everyone. This could mean overwhelming the entities deciding upon possible disciplinary offences. Careful consideration must therefore be given to whom this right is granted. In view of the above, we believe that this right should be assigned to Presidents of the Courts, Presidents of the Superior Courts, the President of the Supreme Court, but also to the Judicial Councils as representatives of the judiciary, which we listed as entities ensuring administrative supervision. In the first part of this chapter, we also mentioned that this right should also be granted to the body that oversees compliance with the ethical principles of professional conduct of judges. As it is also necessary for the judiciary to be open and not be a closed system, the possibility of filing a petition should also be granted, for example, to the Minister of Justice.

From a procedural point of view, it is also necessary to insist on maintaining a broad protection of the rights of the accused. It is clear that the accused must be acquainted with the nature of the act which he is accused of, must have sufficient time to prepare for the hearing of the case and must have the right to qualified legal representation.

It is open to consideration whether the issues of guilt in disciplinary proceedings will be dealt with by a specially defined branch of the judiciary (i.e. one of the courts operating within the state) composed only of judges or by a quasi-judicial body (disciplinary authority) whose members are both judges and non-judges (especially representatives of other legal professions, such as lawyers, prosecutors or academics). It is important that this body be independent and impartial and, if decision-making power is assigned to quasi-judicial bodies, that their decisions be subject to independent judicial review.

At the end of this section, it is necessary to emphasise that disciplinary liability should be taken as complementary to administrative supervision. Disciplinary liability is not precluded by administrative supervision, but, on the contrary, it complements it appropriately. Administrative supervision without the possibility of liability can be perceived as powerless, which will not help to ensure public confidence in the judiciary and its decisions.

However, given the unprecedented situation in which the Slovak Republic finds itself,[44] we would like to conclude with one partially related idea. We firmly

44 For better context, see many articles available at <https://spectator.sme.sk/t/42/corruption-scandals> depicting the charges pressed against many judges, prosecutors and politicians in Slovakia.

believe that in the event of a judge being charged with a criminal offence, it should be natural for that judge to have his or her term suspended temporarily. In the event that the judge himself refuses to suspend the performance of his duties until a decision on his charges has been validly made, the entities we have mentioned should also have the power to file a motion for such a suspension.

6. Conclusions

Based on the above ideas, we believe that in the end it is possible to proceed to the definition of the goal, functions and features of administrative supervision over the courts and judges.

The aim of administrative supervision over courts and judges is to ensure the continuity of court proceedings and their dignity, and to respect the principles of judicial ethics. The definition of this objective must always respect the principle of separation of the exercise of judicial power from the course of administrative supervision; administrative supervision must never interfere with the courts' own decision-making.

In the context of supervising the continuity of court proceedings, administrative supervision must be aimed primarily at ensuring the unification of decision-making practice, so as to avoid unjustified differences and discrepancies. Judicial case-law must be stable and must treat similar cases in the same way and dissimilar cases differently. In other words, there must not be a situation where the court considers the same situations differently. Supervision in this area should be carried out primarily by the courts themselves. The courts must proactively unify their own case-law on the basis of their own decision-making. The initiative for a unifying opinion should therefore come primarily from the judges themselves. Still, in this area, we must necessarily allow the initiative to come from entities other than only judges themselves.

The continuity of legal proceedings must also be the aim of administrative supervision. Here, too, the judicial authorities in particular must have a decisive say. On the basis of their own supervisory activities or even on the basis of an outside initiative, they must monitor whether the court proceedings are conducted within a reasonable time. If this is not the case, the judicial authorities, together with the administrative authorities (typically the Ministry of Justice), should use their supervisory activities to find out what was (is) the reason for the inaction or delays in the court proceedings. The solution here could be a personnel policy in the form of a more flexible staffing of the court (we mean not only new judges, but also assistant judges; or a solution involving so-called flying judges whose place of employment is not tied to a particular court but may, if necessary, be assigned to different courts of the same instance).

Supervision of the ethical exercise of judicial power should also be a very important goal of correct supervision. This objective must be manifested not only during the court proceedings but also outside the proceedings. Judges are obliged to behave in accordance with the principles of judicial ethics also "outside their job," i.e. outside their working hours. Adherence to the principles of judicial ethics in the form of dignity, honour, restraint or discretion helps to achieve a state of independence and impartiality of the judiciary in the eyes of the general public. They thus help to improve the overall image of the court in society. The definition of the principles of judicial ethics must be based on internationally recognised standards adapted to domestic realities; however, it can never deny them. As they will govern the conduct of judges, it is essential that a judicial self-government body (collective body) be responsible for their creation and updating. This body must be available to all judges, who can submit questions for a more detailed opinion in specific cases, and the replies of this body must be sufficiently specific. That body should also supervise compliance with the principles of judicial ethics, but should not have disciplinary authority over judges. However, it could initiate disciplinary proceedings.

In terms of the functions that administrative supervision over courts and judges should have, we believe that these functions should be: cognitive, comparative, analytical, reparative and repressive. Unlike the generally defined functions of control, we believe that the main difference should lie in the repressive function. We do not mean here the non-application of this function of administrative supervision, but rather its adjustment from the point of view of the authorised entity. While in general it is possible for a control body to also have powers of repression, we are of the opinion that in the area of judicial supervision, the repressive function should not be exercised by the same bodies that are responsible for administrative supervision. This follows from the fact that the exercise of judicial power must be separated from the exercise of the administrative and management activities of the court. Otherwise, the independence of the exercise of judicial power would be affected.

From the point of view of the features of administrative supervision, we believe that they should be the same as in the case of control. Administrative supervision over the exercise of judicial power and over judges must show features of objectiveness, professionalism, systematicity and timeliness.

In principle, we believe that administrative supervision should be distinguished from instance supervision, which performs different tasks and the basis for its use is different. Instance supervision as a procedural category can only be initiated by a party to the proceedings; instance supervision cannot be initiated by the judiciary alone. Nevertheless, instance supervision can also help with administrative supervision. Based on its use, supervisory authorities can learn about the need to unify the decision-making activities of courts and initiate appropriate supervisory processes to ensure this unity.

The disciplinary liability of judges is also a necessary complement to administrative supervision. In a legal state, the specific grounds for inferring disciplinary liability must be enshrined in law, both from the point of view of substantive law and procedural law. From the point of view of substantive law, disciplinary liability is specific in that rules of conduct, the violation of which may lead to disciplinary liability, can also be found in regulations of an internal nature, such as codes of ethics or disciplinary rules. What is subject to disciplinary action against judges must always be considered separately in relation to the legal culture of a specific country. There is no doubt, however, that this should include, in particular, shortcomings in the observance of ethics (ethical exercise of the judicial profession, as well as conduct outside of office), or observance and ensuring the continuity of court proceedings.

From a procedural point of view, it should be noted that disciplinary liability should be inferred on the basis of a proposal from the competent bodies authorised to do so. These should be, in particular, representatives of the judicial self-government, persons responsible for the administrative operation of the court and, finally, representatives of state power – in particular the Minister of Justice. However, the process itself must always be carried out independently and impartially in order to prevent abuse of this institute.

Therefore, disciplinary liability should be seen as a result of the performance of the supervisory tasks of the competent bodies.

References

Publications

Aristoteles, *Politika*, Praha: Petr Rezek, 1998.

Baricová, Jana, Marián Fečík, Marek Števček, and, Anita Filová, *Správny súdny poriadok*. Bratislava: C.H. Beck, 2018.

Boguszak, Jiří, Jiří Čapek, and, Aleš Gerloch, *Teorie práva*. Praha: ASPI 2003.

Cepek, Branislav et al., *Správne právo hmotné. Všeobecná časť*. Bratislava: Wolters Kluwer, 2018.

Hamuľáková, Zuzana, and, Matej Horvat, *Základy správneho práva trestného*, Bratislava: Wolters Kluwer, 2019.

Hendrych, Dušan, et al., *Správní právo. Obecná část*, Praha: C.H.Beck, 2009.

Kopecký, Martin, *Správní právo. Obecná část*, Praha: C.H.Beck, 2019.

Košičiarová, Soňa, *Správne právo procesné. Všeobecná časť*, Šamorín: Heuréka, 2017.

Macejková Ivetta et al. *Zákon o Ústavnom súde Slovenskej republiky. Komentár*. Bratislava: C.H. Beck, 2020.

Machajová, Jozefína et al, *Všeobecné správne právo*, Žilina: Eurokódex, 2009.

Motesquieu, Charles, *O duchu zákonů*. Plzeň: Aleš Čenek, 2003.

Ottová Eva, *Teória práva,* Šamorín: Heuréka, 2010.

Pekár, Bernard, *Kontrola vo verejnej správe v kontexte európskeho správneho práva*. Bratislava: Právnická fakulta UK, 2011.

Průcha, Petr, *Správní právo. Obecná část*. Brno: MU Brno – Doplněk Brno, 2007.

Prusák, Jozef. *Teória práva*. Bratislava: Vydavateľské oddelenie Právnickej fakulty Univerzity Komenského, 1999.

Seman, Tibor, Radomír Jakab, and Jozef Tekeli, *Správne právo hmotné. Všeobecná časť*. Košice: UPJŠ v Košiciach vydavateľstvo ŠafárikPress, 2020.

Škrobák, Ján, *Preskúmanie neprávoplatných rozhodnutí vydaných v správnom konaní*. Bratislava: Univerzita Komenského v Bratislave, Právnická fakulta, 2014.

Škultéty, Peter in: Škultéty, Peter et al. *Správne právo hmotné. Všeobecná časť*. Bratislava: Univerzita Komenského, 2005.

Sládeček, Vladimír, *Obecné správní právo*, Praha: ASPI, 2009.

Sobihard, Jozef, *Správny poriadok. Komentár*, Bratislava: Wolters Kluwer, 2007.

Tóthová, Katarína, et al. *Základy správneho práva hmotného*. Bratislava: Vydavateľské oddelenie Právnickej fakulty Univerzity Komenského, 1992.

Vačok, Juraj, in: Vrabko, Marian, et al, *Správne právo procesné. Všeobecná časť*, Bratislava: C.H.Beck, 2019

Vrabko, Marián et al. *Správne právo hmotné. Všeobecná časť*. Bratislava: C.H. Beck 2018.

Sources of law

Act no. 385/2000 Coll. on Judges.

the Administrative Procedure Code:

Act no. 106/1999 Coll. on Free Access to Information.

Act no. 357/2015 Coll. on financial control and audit.

Act no. 125/2006 Coll. on labour inspection.

Act no. 541/2004 Coll. on the Peaceful Use of Nuclear Energy (Atomic Act).
Act no. 10/1996 Coll. on control in state administration.
Act no. 10/1996 Coll. on control in state administration.
Act no. 357/2015 Coll. on financial control and audit.
Act no. 581/2004 Coll. on health insurance companies, health care supervision.
Act no. 357/2015 Coll. on financial control and audit.
the Constitution of the Slovak Republic:
Act no. 314/2018 Coll. on the Constitutional Court of the Slovak Republic.

Jurisprudence

Decision of the Supreme Court of the Slovak Republic, file no. 4 Sž 74/2002 of 26 November 2002.

Internet Sources

News on corruption in Slovakia, https://spectator.sme.sk/t/42/corruption-scandals (access date: 25.05.2021).

Martin Sunnqvist[1]

Public entities responsible for court administration and supervision over judges

Abstract: Public entities can be responsible for court administration and supervision over judges. This article provides an overview of this issue, using Sweden as the main example. The article contains a general discussion on what is understood by "supervision" and "public entities," how such a topic can be analysed, and how supervision can preferably be arranged so as to safeguard a high level of judicial independence, and, in turn, ensure impartiality. To guarantee impartiality and a fair trial within reasonable time, independence needs to go hand in hand with accountability. The Swedish development of supervision over courts and judges by governmental and parliamentary offices and administration through a public authority, namely the National Courts Administration, is discussed, and the need for reform is analysed. The Swedish institutions are also put in a wider European context, with reference to German, Italian, English and Danish examples.

Keywords: court administration, supervision, judicial councils, individual judicial independence, judicial impartiality

1. Varieties of supervision over courts and judges by public entities

The concepts "supervision" and "public entities" can mean many different things. To define the concepts more precisely, my point of departure is the definition of judicial accountability and court management elaborated by Francesco Contini and Richard Mohr. They have identified four types of judicial accountability, each with its own "forum" or "fora," which is an authority, an institution, or a group of stakeholders, etc., assessing the ways the judiciary works:

1. Legal accountability. This type of accountability includes the individual performance of judges; that formal procedures are adhered to, that the judge provides reasons for his or her decisions, etc. The assessments are made in relation to legal and ethical standards. The fora are disciplinary commissions,

1 Martin Sunnqvist, LL.D, Associate Professor of Legal History, Lund University (Sweden). Former District Judge, Malmö City Court. ORCID – 0000-0002-9952-9347.

other courts, and superior courts. The consequences can be personal, such as salary reductions or other disciplinary sanctions, or criticism.
2. Public accountability. This type could include possibly any affair related with the functioning of justice. The fora are media, organised groups, lobbies, researchers, individuals, etc. The values and principles that, for example, media campaigns are based on could, however, be at odds with legal rules, and contradictory views could be important at the same time.
3. Managerial accountability. This type includes both the individual performance of judges, and the performance of organisations such as courts, court divisions, etc. It includes control from ministries, court administrative authorities, chief judges etc. supervising that the judges work efficiently, based on statistical and economic approaches. The fora are court managers, ministries, and judicial councils. The consequences can be related to the allocation of resources to the court and to judicial remuneration.
4. Cooperative accountabilities. This type includes both the individual performance of judges, and the performance of organisations. The quality of decision-making is in focus. The fora are quality conferences and peer groups.[2]

One crucial factor in this context is how to balance independence and accountability, or rather, how accountability can be implemented without harming independence, or even in a way that strengthens independence.[3] Independence is not an end in itself, but a means to provide judicial assessments that are impartial and with regard to which the judge does not fear reprisals from the government or from other powerful entities.[4] At the same time, accountability is not an end in itself, but a means to – in the best of worlds – the same end, that is, independent and impartial judging.[5] Here, it is necessary to design procedures of accountability so that they do not put impartiality and independence at risk, but on the other hand also safeguard impartial and independent judging to the benefit of society. The overall aim is to safeguard the right of the individual citizen to a fair

2 F. Contini and R. Mohr, *Judicial Evaluation. Traditions, innovation and proposals for measuring the quality of court performance*, Saarbrücken: VDM Verlag, 2008, pp. 54–61.
3 F. Contini and R. Mohr, *Judicial…*, pp. 49–65.
4 M. Cappelletti, *Giudici irresponsabili? Studio comparativo sulla responsabilità dei giudici*, Milano: Giuffrè, 1988, pp. 19–23; M. Cappelletti, "'Who Watches the Watchmen?' A Comparative Study on Judicial Responsibility," *The American Journal of Comparative Law*, No. 1 (31), 1983, pp. 15–17.
5 Cf. F. Contini and R. Mohr, *Judicial…*, pp. 53 ff.

trial, including the right to a judgment in reasonable time – "justice delayed is justice denied."[6]

When I discuss "performance supervision over courts and judges," I will not discuss all the four aspects of judicial accountability. What is relevant here are the types of accountability managed by public entities, such as the legal accountability administered by disciplinary commissions and the managerial type of accountability administered by court managers, ministries, and judicial councils. Especially the latter type of accountability can be very different, depending on whether it is administered through the ministry, a national courts administration, or a judicial council where a majority of the members is elected from among the judges.

There is a difference, in terms of independence, depending on the organisational structure of court administration. Since not only office managers and judicial councils but also ministries are mentioned among the fora for managerial accountability, the latter may become political accountability. As Philip M. Langbroek et al. have written: "Delivering performance information to local court management is different from delivering performance information to a national court administration authority and to the political domain. Indeed, the latter's scope is much wider than managerial only, it is also political."[7]

The above four categories are not formally restricted to the national arena, but in practice the different types of accountability mainly work on a national level. To be sure, legal accountability through the European Court of Human Rights is important in this regard, especially when it comes to the right to a fair trial. When the European Court of Human Rights criticises parts of the legal procedures of a state, this criticism can also be indirectly aimed at judges who have not set national legal procedures aside to the benefit of the standards of a fair trial in accordance with art. 6 of the European Convention on Human Rights. Of course, researchers work internationally and assess the impartiality and independence of judges in their own and other countries, and judges can cooperate internationally in quality conferences and peer groups. When it comes to the managerial accountability, and the legal accountability through disciplinary commissions,

6 T. Sourdin, and N. Burstyner, "Justice Delayed is Justice Denied," *Victoria University Law and Justice Journal,* No. 1 (4), 2014, p. 46.

7 P.M. Langbroek, R.I. Dijkstra, K.B. Zadeh, Z. Türk, "Performance management of courts and judges: organisational and professional learning versus political accountabilities," in: *Handle with Care. Assessing and designing methods for evaluation and development of the quality of justice,* ed. by F. Contini, Bologna: IRSIG-CNR, 2017, p. 305.

these procedures are mainly national. On the other hand, there is cooperation between EU member states, presuming that the independence and impartiality of judges are on such a level that mutual trust in the legal procedures of other member states is possible.

Recent years have provided examples that the infringements of independence and impartiality in one member state are also relevant for consideration by the EU and judges in the other member states. This means that, in my opinion, a fifth category needs to be articulated:

5. International accountability. This type of accountability includes both the individual performance of judges and the performance of entire judiciaries. The principle of mutual trust presumes that a judge in one EU member state can trust the independence and impartiality of judges in other member states, but in exceptional circumstances, a judge can say that a colleague in another member state does not meet these criteria. The fora are, thus, judges in other countries and courts on the EU level. The consequences are brought to bear on a systemic level against court systems as a whole, since it is very difficult for judges in one country to use remedies against individual judges in another.

Examples of international accountability on an EU level can be found in partly different contexts. There are infringement actions which the Commission has brought before the Court of Justice in accordance with article 258 of the treaty of the functioning of the EU.[8] Then, there are the preliminary rulings from the Court of Justice at the request of a national court in another country, asking for guidelines about how to assess whether the principles of mutual recognition and mutual confidence need to be set aside in order to protect human rights[9] or the right to a fair trial.[10] And finally, there are the assessments by national courts of the independence and impartiality on an individual or systemic level of the judiciaries of another country.[11]

8 See the cases between the Commission and the Republic of Poland before the CJEU: C-192/18 (judgement 5.11.2019, ECLI:EU:C:2019:924), C-619/18 (judgement 24.06.2019, ECLI:EU:C:2019:531) and C-791/19 (pending).

9 CJEU Judgment 5.04.2016, Case C-404/15 and C-659/15 *Paul Aranyosi and Robert Căldăraru* (ECLI:EU:C:2016:198).

10 CJEU Judgment 25.07.2018, Case C-216/18 *PPU Minister for Justice and Equality* [LM] (ECLI:EU:C:2018:586).

11 See e.g. the judgment of the Supreme Court of Ireland, *Minister for Justice & Equality v. Celmer*, S:AP:IE:2018:000181, § 81, and the decision by a German Court of Appeal, Oberlandesgericht Karlsruhe, 17.02.2020, 301 AR 156/19.

It is problematic for one judge to assess the independence and impartiality of a colleague in another member state, and it is also problematic to discern between the true individual independence and impartiality of that judge, and the consequences for that judge, of changes made in national disciplinary or managerial procedures.[12] This is so especially if the principle "justice must not only be done, it must also be seen to be done"[13] is to be relevant also in this international assessment of independence and impartiality.

2. Supervision over courts and judges through a judicial council

Among the Council of Europe member states, most countries have a council for the judiciary that plays a role in the selection of judges, in disciplinary supervision, and/or in administration of the courts.[14]

According to articles 2 and 3 of the Universal Charter of the Judge, adopted by the central council of the International Association of Judges in 1999 and updated in 2017, a judicial council is defined as follows:

> In order to safeguard judicial independence a Council for the Judiciary, or another equivalent body, must be set up, save in countries where this independence is traditionally ensured by other means.
>
> The Council for the Judiciary must be completely independent of other State powers.
>
> It must be composed of a majority of judges elected by their peers, according to procedures ensuring their largest representation.
>
> The Council for the Judiciary can have members who are not judges, in order to represent the variety of civil society. In order to avoid any suspicion, such members cannot be politicians. They must have the same qualifications in terms of integrity, independence, impartiality and skills of judges. No member of the Government or of the Parliament can be at the same time member of the Council for the Judiciary.

---

12 Cf. also my article "The Changing Role of Nordic Courts," in: *Rethinking Nordic Courts*, ed. by L. Ervo, P. Letto-Vanamo and A. Nylund, Cham: Springer, 2021, pp. 167–183.

13 See e.g. judgements of ECtHR: *Delcourt v. Belgium*, 17.01.1970, No. 2689/65, § 31; *De Cubber v. Belgium*, 26.10.1984, No. 9186/80, § 26, and *Mežnarić v. Croatia*,15.07.2005, No. 71615/01, § 32. As regards the original version "justice should not only be done, but should manifestly and undoubtedly be seen to be done," see *R. v. Sussex Justices*, ex parte McCarthy ([1924] 1 KB 256, [1923] All ER Rep 233) per Lord Hewart C.J.

14 P. Langbroek et al., *Performance…*, p. 298.

> The Council for the Judiciary must be endowed with the largest powers in the fields of recruitment, training, appointment, promotion and discipline of judges.
>
> It must be foreseen that the Council can be consulted by the other State powers on all possible questions concerning judicial status and ethics, as well as on all subjects regarding the annual budget of Justice and the allocation of resources to the courts, on the organisation, functioning and public image of judicial institutions.[15]

Even though this document was adopted among judges themselves, the concept of a judicial council, and the demand that such a council should be organised in order to protect judicial independence, has been widely accepted outside of the judiciaries also, especially by different fora within the Council of Europe, such as its parliamentary assembly,[16] council of ministers[17] and Venice Commission.[18] The European Network of Councils for the Judiciary (ENCJ), co-funded by the EU, accepts as members only national institutions from EU member states which are independent of the executive and legislative branches, or are autonomous, and which ensure the final responsibility for supporting the judiciary in the independent delivery of justice.[19]

As regards the supervision of judges through court administration, some comparisons have, in recent years, been made between the German administration of courts and the Italian and English counterparts, respectively. One author, Martin Minkner, highlights the relationship between independence and accountability and cautions against such institutional independence where there is only independence and no checks and balances. In such a system, the institutional independence centralised in a judicial council can hamper the individual

15 Universal Charter of the Judge, adopted by the IAJ Central Council in Taiwan on November 17th, 1999, updated in Santiago de Chile on November 14th, 2017; https://www.iaj-uim.org/universal-charter-of-the-judge-2017/ (accesse date: 22.05.2021). See also Consultative Council of European Judges (CCJE) Opinion no. 10 (2007) to the attention of the Committee of Ministers of the Council of Europe on the Council for the Judiciary at the service of society.

16 Resolutions no. 1685 (2009) and 2040 (2015), www.assembly.coe.int (access date: 22.05.2021).

17 Recommendations Rec. (1994) 12 and Rec. (2010) 12, www.coe.int (access date: 22.05.2021).

18 See e.g. the opinion 16 January 2020 no. 977/2019, § 9, www.venice.coe.int (access date: 22.05.2021).

19 Article 6 (1), Statutes, Rules and Regulations of the International Not-For-Profit Association European Network of Councils for the Judiciary (i.n.p.a), https://www.encj.eu/statutes (access date: 22.05.2021).

independence of judges.[20] However, I do not agree with Minkner's somewhat critical attitude towards the documents pleading for judicial councils; in my view, albeit they are not binding, which Minkner repeatedly mentions,[21] they are adopted by such institutions and have such persuasive authority that they need to be taken into account and to be considered important. This is also the view of another author, Alexander von Bernstorff, who concludes that the documents are not binding, but he considers at least some of them important and persuasive when it comes to the development of legal standards on an international level.[22]

3. The Swedish example

In Sweden, the performance supervision over courts and judges is divided between several different bodies. I will first briefly discuss the legal accountability in terms of supervision over the individual performance of judges, for example the assessment of complaints that a judge did not adhere to correct formal procedures in a case. I will the discuss the National Courts Administration, and finally provide an example of how the supervisory and administrative functions interact.

3.1. The Parliamentary Ombudsman of Justice and the Chancellor of Justice

There are in Sweden two bodies with similar supervisory tasks in relation to judges: the Parliamentary Ombudsman of Justice (generally called *Justitieombudsmannen,* more formally *Riksdagens ombudsmän*),[23] and the Chancellor of Justice (*Justitiekanslern*).[24] There are four parliamentary ombudsmen, of which one is primarily responsible for supervision of courts. They are appointed by parliament. There is one chancellor of justice, appointed

---

20 M. Minkner, *Die Gerichtsverwaltung in Deutschland und Italien. Demokratie versus technische Legitimation,* Tübingen: Mohr Siebeck, 2015, pp. 772–775. Regarding Italy, see also M. Luminati, *Priester der Themis. Richterliches Selbstverständnins in Italien nach 1945,* Frankfurt am Main: Vittorio Klostermann, 2007.

21 M. Minkner, *Die Gerichtsverwaltung…*, pp. 32–38, 41, 431 and 707.

22 A. von Bernstorff, *Die Gerichtsverwaltung in Deutschland und England,* Berlin: Duncker & Humblot, 2018, pp. 32–66.

23 Instrument of Government Ch. 13 § 6; Riksdagsordningen (2014:801) Ch. 13 §§ 2–4; Lag (1986:765) med instruktion för Riksdagens ombudsmän.

24 Instrument of Government Ch. 12 § 1; Lagen (1975:1339) om justitiekanslerns tillsyn; Förordning (1975:1345) med instruktion för Justitiekanslern.

by the government. The ombudsmen and chancellor are lawyers, most often with experience as judges, law professors and/or senior governmental officials.

The ombudsmen and chancellor can both criticise judges, initiate disciplinary proceedings against them, and prosecute them. Prosecution takes places in the ordinary criminal courts, although with the court of appeal as court of first instance. Disciplinary proceedings take place in the Disciplinary Board for Higher Officials, with the possibility of an appeal to the Labour Court. Also chief judges and court presidents can initiate proceedings before the Disciplinary Board for Higher Officials. Both as regards disciplinary sanctions and punishments for official misconduct ("tjänstefel"), the independence of the judiciary calls for respect for judicial discretion, especially in matters of evidence or interpretation of the law. When it comes to breaches of formal rules of handling cases, or judgments obviously contradicting the law, disciplinary punishments can follow, especially in cases where judges have misinterpreted rules to the effect that an individual has been wrongfully held in detention.[25]

The functions of the Parliamentary Ombudsman of Justice and the Chancellor of Justice cannot be understood without knowledge of their respective histories. The office of the Chancellor of Justice is the oldest of the two and was established by King Charles XII in 1713 in order to check that public authorities followed laws and regulations and fulfilled their duties.[26] The office of the parliamentary ombudsman was established in 1809, when a new constitution was adopted. The office of the ombudsman was one of the parts of a compromise between the theory of the separation of powers, the need for checks and balances, and the will to restore a balance between king and parliament. Through the ombudsman, parliament got a way to control the workings of the administration, which belonged under the king.[27]

---

25 See e.g. AD (Labour Court Cases) 2014 No. 5, NJA (Supreme Court Cases) 2017, p. 842.

26 S. Rudholm, "Justitiekanslersämbetet 250 år," *Svensk Juristtidning*, No. 1, 1964, pp. 1–16; Statens Offentliga Utredningar (SOU) 1978:59, *JK-ämbetet. Översyn av justitiekanslerns arbetsuppgifter och statens tvistehandläggning*, pp. 35–37; SOU 1993:37, *Justitiekanslern. En översyn av justitiekanslerns arbetsuppgifter m.m.*, pp. 33–35; J. Ekroth, *JO-ämbetet. En offentligrättslig studie,* Stockholm: Stockholms universitet, 2001, pp. 40–45; see also the various articles in the anthology, *Justitiekanslern 300 år,* ed. by U. Göranson, Uppsala: Iustus 2013.

27 N. Bexelius, "JO-ämbetet 150 år," *Svensk Juristtidning,* No. 1, 1960, pp. 81–111; SOU 1965:64, *Riksdagens justitieombudsmän,* pp. 39–45; SOU 1975:23, *JO-ämbetet. Uppgifter och organisation,* pp. 35–38; SOU 1985:26, *JO-ämbetet. En översyn,* pp. 57–68; Ekroth, J., *JO-ämbetet…,* pp. 45–94; K. A. Borgström, *JO och tjänstemännen. En laghistorisk studie,* Uppsala: Iustus, 2003; H.-G. Axberger, "Justitieombudsmannen, tryckfriheten

During recent decades, there has been a discussion over whether both these offices ought to have the possibility to supervise the courts. The reason for scepticism has been that the Chancellor of Justice was also Prosecutor-General until 1948 and is still prosecutor in cases about the freedom of press and media, and that the Chancellor of Justice is also attorney-general.[28] Whilst the supervision of the Ombudsman of Justice is part of the checks and balances between parliament and the judiciary, there is reason to question why the Chancellor of Justice can both supervise the courts on behalf of the government and, as attorney-general, be a party before them on behalf of the government.[29] These discussions notwithstanding, the various tasks of this office have been retained.

3.2. The National Courts Administration

The National Courts Administration was established in 1975, and its organisation was structured in committee reports from 1971 and 1974.[30] Before that year, the administration of courts had been taken care of by the courts themselves and the Ministry of Justice. The court buildings and parts of the administration of district courts were financed through a specific tax, administered by the court. Part of the administration of the district courts was taken care of by the courts of appeal. The Supreme Court had a separate administrative office also responsible for preparing the cases for the justices.[31]

---

och maktdelningen," in: *Maktbalans och kontrollmakt. 1809 års händelser, idéer och författningsverk i ett tvåhundraårigt perspektiv*, ed. by M. Brundin and M. Isberg, Stockholm: Sveriges Riksdag, 2009, pp. 415–451; H.-G. Axberger, *JO – i riksdagens tjänst*, Visby: Eddy.se, 2014, pp. 11–36.

28 In SOU 1978:59, *JK-ämbetet. Översyn av justitiekanslerns arbetsuppgifter och statens tvistehandläggning*, pp. 125–126 it was suggested that a separate attorney-general's office ought to be established, but it came to nothing, see SOU 1993:37, *Justitiekanslern. En översyn av justitiekanslerns arbetsuppgifter m.m.*, p. 34, but the problem was once again addressed, see pp. 58–61, 130–133, 164 and 230.

29 See e.g. SOU 1994:99, *Domaren i Sverige inför framtiden – utgångspunkter för fortsatt utredningsarbete*, pp. 255–258; SOU 2007:69, *Bestämmelser om domstolarna i regeringsformen*, pp. 24–27 and M. Melin, "Svenska domstolars ställning och roll — om den långa resan på väg mot en tredje statsmakt," in: *Svea hovrätt 400 år*, ed. by F. Wersäll, J. Hirschfeldt, A. Eka, E. Fura, K.A. Modéer, Stockholm: Norstedts juridik, 2014, pp. 440.

30 SOU 1971:41 *Ny domstolsadministration*, and Ds Ju 1974:5 *Central, regional och lokal domstolsförvaltning m.m., betänkande avgivet av Domstolsstyrelseutredningen.*

31 See Code on Buildings, Ch. 26 § 4, and Code of Judicial Procedure Ch. 8 § 1, Law Code of 1734; SOU 1971:41 pp. 9–10, 15–25; SOU 1971:59 *Högsta domstolens kansli.*

In the 1970s, the system of the administrative courts was enlarged, so that a hierarchy of a Supreme Administrative Court, Administrative Courts of Appeal and Administrative Courts was established. A new constitution was adopted, which aimed at streamlining the organisation of the state and which did not focus especially on separation of powers and differences between courts of law and public authorities.[32] In this context, the idea of a National Courts Administration came to the surface.

Already in the decision of government setting up the committee, and then in greater detail in its report, some main reasons for establishing a National Courts Administration were highlighted. Administration could be centralised, and in that way the economy and the buildings of the courts could be handled more efficiently. That would make the administrative issues regarding staff and finances more uniform and cost-efficient. A need for computer systems was identified, both for the handling of cases and for the distribution of information about judgments and other decisions to various other authorities.[33]

The government went forward to parliament with a proposal for legislation.[34] The only question that caused debate was how the independence of judges ought to be mentioned in the governmental instruction to the National Courts Administration. The minister of justice had already on an early stage wanted to emphasise, even though he considered it self-evident, that the establishment of a National Courts Administration should not give rise to any infringements in the independence and integrity of the courts in their decision-making capacities. According to the minister, this did not mean, however, that the National Courts Administration could not use all the means available to rationalise the courts and make them more efficient.[35] The committee did not go much deeper into these issues, when it discussed matters of a more principled nature.[36] Among the courts which had given their views on the draft proposal, some argued that a National Courts Administration should only provide courts with services, whilst

32 Cf. M. Sunnqvist, "Domstolsliknande myndigheter och myndighetsliknande domstolar?," in: *Den svenska förvaltningsmodellen*, ed. by C. Peterson, Stockholm: Institutet för Rättshistorisk Forskning, 2020, pp. 234–255; G. Petrén, "Domstolarnas ställning enligt 1974 års regeringsform," *Svensk Juristtidning*, No. 1, 1975, pp. 1–14.

33 SOU 1971:41 pp. 9–13, 35–79.

34 Prop. 1974:149; bet. JuU 1975:1

35 SOU 1971:41 p. 11.

36 SOU 1971:41 pp. 29–34.

other accepted that the National Courts Administration also had a governing role in administrative issues.[37]

In the proposal to parliament, the minister of justice reiterated that the establishment of a National Courts Administration should not give rise to any infringements in the independence and integrity of the courts in their decision-making capacities. He acknowledged that one problematic issue was administrative decisions about the distribution of cases, which might interfere with judicial independence. The conclusion was, however, that the National Courts Administration should have a governing function. The minister stressed the *similarities* between the courts and the other branches of public administration.[38]

In parliament, the assessment of the proposal was positive, but with the caveat that further guarantees for the independence and integrity of the courts were needed. Parliament wanted to restrict the scope of the governing functions to matters that were clearly administrative. The justice committee stressed the *differences* between the courts and the other branches of public administration.[39] When the instruction for the National Courts Administration was enacted by the government, the governing function of the National Courts Administration was again wider in its scope.[40]

Gustaf Petrén (1917–1990), associate professor and justice of the Supreme Administrative Court, was very critical towards the way the National Courts Administration was established and the lack of clarity in the rules about the scope of the governing function of the National Courts Administration. He especially criticised the close connections between the National Courts Administration and a committee for proposals for judicial appointments. According to Petrén, the government had wanted to see judging as just any kind of public administration, whilst parliament had stressed the importance of guarantees for judicial independence and integrity.[41] Petrén concluded that what was established was "a central bureaucratic public authority with the task of largely directing

37 Prop. 1974:149 pp. 16–19.
38 Prop. 1974:149 pp. 27–30.
39 JuU 1975:1 pp. 13–16.
40 Förordning (1975:506) med instruktion för Domstolsverket.
41 G. Petrén, "Domstolsverket och domstolsväsendet – en studie i regeringsteknik," *Svensk Juristtidning*, No. 1, 1975, pp. 651–665.

the activity of the courts and of being a supervisory authority over the courts as regards the efficiency of their decision making."[42]

As has been mentioned, the National Courts Administration was established in 1975, and it exists to this day. Over the years, it has developed its activities into new areas whilst some matters have been taken away from it. Two director generals of the National Courts Administration, Barbro Thorblad (director general 2008–14) and Martin Holmgren (director general 2014–20), recently wrote an article about the development of the authority.[43] They highlighted that all issues concerning court budgets are handled by the National Courts Administration, including – since 2011 – individually decided salaries for judges. The authority decides, after a discussion with the president or chief judge of the relevant court, the salaries of newly appointed judges. The authority has, however, delegated to presidents and chief judges the responsibility to decide on new salaries for already appointed judges.[44] The salaries are, according to the policy of salaries made by the National Courts Administration, decided on the basis of criteria like the difficulty of the judge's tasks, the capacity to cooperate with other staff, the interest in developing their own and others' competences, etc. Of course, according to the policy, salaries may not be decided in a way that is a reaction to the way judges decide cases.[45]

Thorblad and Holmgren have discussed the fact that computerisation, information technology, and the way that information is communicated through the media and on social media, have been important issues in a way that could not have been foreseen when the National Courts Administration was established. The same can be said about issues relating to the security of court buildings. The authority has also worked with projects aimed at making the courts more efficient. In some respects, the authority has become more centralised; in 2006 the board of the authority was abolished and the director general became the sole head. At the same time, however, the National Courts Administration took the initiative to adopt more formalised ways of consultation between the authority and the court presidents and chief judges.[46] Some matters that were originally

---

42 G. Petrén, "Domstolsverket...," p. 652 ("ett centralbyråkratiskt ämbetsverk med uppgift att dirigera domstolsverksamheten i stora drag och vara tillsynsmyndighet över domstolarna vad gäller effektiviteten i deras dömande").

43 B. Thorblad, M. Holmgren, "Domstolsverket — från starten till våra dagar," *Svensk Juristtidning*, No. 1, 2018, pp. 16–35.

44 B. Thorblad, M. Holmgren, "Domstolsverket...," pp. 17–18.

45 *Lönepolicy för Sveriges Domstolar*, 26.10.2011.

46 B. Thorblad, M. Holmgren, "Domstolsverket...," pp. 19–22, 24–33.

part of the responsibilities of the National Courts Administration have been moved to more independent institutions. An independent Judges Proposals Board, with a majority of judges, was established in 2008, and its independence was further strengthened in 2010.[47] The training and education of judges was transferred to a semi-independent unit of the National Courts Administration in 2009.[48]

The article by Thorblad and Holmgren is partly hagiographic, to an extent that seems unnecessary even for two former director generals of the National Courts Administration. There is, in my view, a difference between the fact that a National Courts Administration might be necessary or at least beneficial when it comes to the coordination of, for example, court buildings and the structures for court computer systems, and the fact that the National Courts Administration could indeed be organised in a way that meets the standards of a judicial council. Thorblad and Holmgren also realise this difference and discuss various possible ways of reorganising the National Courts Administration to something more similar to a Judicial Council.[49]

In sum, the fact that the National Courts Administration, at least in large part, has worked with matters that have been necessary and relevant, does not mean that its constitutional status has been or is beneficial for judicial independence. Especially problematic in this regard are the individually determined salaries for judges, where the National Courts Administration can exert influence. Even though it should be borne in mind that Swedish public authorities benefit from a high degree of independence in their decision making – according to the instrument of government, public authorities are independent in their decision making in individual cases,[50] a rule which is the same as for the courts[51] – the risk lies in the fact that the director general is appointed by the government and that the risk of informal pressures cannot therefore be excluded. To be clear, I do

---

47 Lag (2010:1390) om utnämning av ordinarie domare (Statute on the appointment of ordinary judges) and Förordning (2010:1793) med instruktion för Domarnämnden (Ordinance with instruction for the Judges Proposals Board), which replaced Förordning (2008:427) med instruktion för Domarnämnden (Ordinance with instruction for the Judges Proposals Board).

48 B. Thorblad, M. Holmgren, "Domstolsverket…," pp. 22–24.

49 B. Thorblad, M. Holmgren, "Domstolsverket…," pp. 31–33; cf. also B. Thorblad, "Domaren, domstolschefen och Domstolsverket – ett arbetsgivarperspektiv," in: *Svea hovrät…*, pp. 365 ff.

50 Regeringsformen (Instrument of government) Ch. 12 § 2.

51 Regeringsformen (Instrument of government) Ch. 11 § 3.

not believe that there has been any political pressure in this regard so far, but the system is vulnerable as such. It is extremely hard to assess whether criteria like the difficulty of the judge's tasks, the capacity to cooperate with other staff, the interest in developing their own and others' competences, have been applied in a correct manner or whether undue influence has been exerted secretly.

Changes are, however, in the coming. Senior judges have again started to discuss the need for a more independent authority for the administration of the courts, especially with references to the recent dismantling of judicial independence in some European countries.[52] In 2018, parliament made it known to government that a commission ought to be appointed with the following tasks: to consider how to strengthen the independence of courts and judges in the long term, to consider constitutional amendments concerning the number and retirement age of supreme court justices, and to consider the organisation and role of the National Courts Administration, for example replacing it with an administration under a Judicial Council.[53] The commission was appointed in spring 2020, and it is chaired by the president of the Supreme Court, Anders Eka, and with representatives of all political parties as members.[54] We have yet to see exactly what the commission will suggest.

3.3. An example of supervision and administration

In order to explain how the supervision of judges and the administration of courts work in Sweden, I will discuss one example where these issues were assessed by the Ombudsman of Justice, at that time Mats Melin, later president of the Supreme Administrative Court.[55] The background was that cases had been severely delayed at one of the district courts. The Ombudsman of Justice investigated the matter and prosecuted one judge who was sentenced for official misconduct. The Ombudsman directed severe criticism against three other judges. Finally, the Ombudsman also investigated whether and in what way the chief

---

52 A. Eka, "Judicial Council – ett råd i tiden?," in: *Festskrift till Johan Hirschfeldt*, Uppsala: Iustus, 2008, pp. 95–105; F. Wersäll, "Domstolar och domare – tankar för framtiden," in: *Svea hovrät…*, pp. 233–237; M. Melin, *Svenska domstolars…*, pp. 437–440; F. Wersäll, "Ökad domarmakt och makten över domstolarna," *Svensk Juristtidning*, No. 1, 2017, pp. 6–8; M. Melin and S. Lindskog, "Domstolarnas oberoende behöver stärkas," *Svensk Juristtidning*, No. 5, 2017, pp. 353–355.

53 Bet. 2017/18:KU36.

54 Dir. Ju 2020:04, *Utredningen om förstärkt skydd för demokratin och domstolarnas oberoende (2020 års grundlagskommitté)*.

55 JO 2008/09 pp. 42–53.

judge could be held responsible for the delays. What was in focus was, thus, whether the chief judge had had a right and/or a duty to intervene in the way the judges handled their cases.

The Ombudsman observed that a chief judge cannot interfere with the independent decision making of a judge. A chief judge cannot order a judge to make certain decisions during the hearing of the case. Instead, the chief judge can discuss the case with the judge and give advice, as between any colleagues. The chief judge can also offer the judge relief in the distribution of cases – in that way, the judge keeps old cases already allotted to him or her but will not receive new cases for a certain period of time.[56]

The Ombudsman also discussed the possibility of taking cases away from a judge who was overloaded. In this context, the Ombudsman observed that any redistribution of cases would mean that the random allotment of cases to judges – which is of great importance for judicial independence – was set aside. The Ombudsman referred to the deliberations of a governmental committee which had discussed various issues about the governance of courts. The Ombudsman agreed with that committee that cases could have to be redistributed for objective reasons, such as if a judge suffered illness. In such cases, a chief judge could have both a right and a duty to redistribute cases, so that the parties will get a trial within reasonable time.[57] Later, rules have been adopted clarifying that only the court itself can regulate the distribution of cases among judges and that this should be done in an objective way, and that the way cases are distributed and redistributed needs to be specified in a clear set of rules.[58]

The Ombudsman observed that the workload at the district court at the time was heavy for all judges, including the chief judge, and that it could be difficult in such a situation to relieve one of the judges and add to the workload of the others. What could have been done, however, was to prioritise among the cases so that the cases that were already very delayed were decided first. The chief judge was criticised for his lack of control over old cases at his court.[59]

---

56 JO 2008/09 p. 47.

57 JO 2008/09 pp. 47–50; SOU 2009:99 *Domarutnämningar och domstolsledning. Frågor om utnämning av högre domare och om domstolschefens roll,* part A, pp. 261–265, 269–275.

58 Instrument of Government Ch. 11 § 3; Code of Judicial Procedure Ch. 4 § 11a: Act on General Administrative Courts (lag [1971:289 with subsequent amendments] om allmänna förvaltningsdomstolar) § 29.

59 JO 2008/09 pp. 51–53.

The example also highlights the difficulty of being a chief judge in such a situation. Even though the chief judge could have prioritised among the cases so that those already very delayed were decided first, lack of resources could be such that other cases would be delayed, and the chief judge could be criticised anyway. The chief judge has no powers in such a situation and can only try to negotiate with the National Courts Administration for more resources. If a judicial council were in charge of the National Courts Administration, at least a panel with a majority of judges would have to assess the situation at the court.

4. The Swedish example in the context of a comparison with some other countries

The Swedish example has illustrated some questions of principle as regards court administration and the supervision over judges. It is impossible for me to provide an overview over the ways the supervision and administration of courts is organised all over Europe. In different countries, the border between administration, supervision and the core area of independent judging can be drawn differently.[60] But I will use some information on a more principled level to be able to place the Swedish example in a European context. In that way, I will be able to discuss different types of public entities responsible for the administration of courts and supervision of judges.

Martin Minkner and Alexander von Bernstorff have compared the Italian and the English administration of courts to the German model. In Germany, there are no public entities responsible for court administration on a federal or state level. Court administration is taken care of by the ministries and by the courts themselves, through the court presidents, committees of judges, and all judges of

60 Cf. my example from JO 2008/09 p. 42, which can be compared with e.g. the view that the distribution of cases is a task of the court president as a manager of the distribution of work and "agent of the Ministry of Justice carrying out the State administration of the judiciary rather than as a member of the judiciary." Even though the combination of facts that the president reassigned the case to himself and subsequently decided the case infringed in the applicant company's right to have a hearing before a tribunal established by law, it could be discussed whether the distribution of cases is not in itself so close to the right to a fair trial that it is a judicial rather than an administrative task. See European Court of Human Rights, HUDOC, *DMD Group A.S. v. Slovakia*, 5.10.2010, no. 19334/03

a court in plenary, or by way of electing committees. There is no federal or state administrative authority for the courts.[61]

In Italy, there is a judicial council, the *Consiglio Superiore della Magistratura*, with members elected among judges and responsible for the administration of the courts, including disciplinary measures. This means that in Italy there is a central administrative authority for the courts, but it is characterised by the principle of *autogoverno*, self-government. The composition of the council is dominated by higher judges, and within the *Associazione Nazionale Magistrati*, the main organisation of judges, different associations of judges are formed, partly on a political basis. However, there is also a general inspectorate (*inspettorato generale*) by which the ministry of justice inspects the courts regularly. In order to secure the individual independence of judges, judges are promoted mainly on the basis of years in office; judges should fulfil their duties without hope of or fear for (*sine spe ac metu*) promotion.[62]

In England, there is an office called Her Majesty's Courts and Tribunals Service, which takes care of the administration of all courts except the Supreme Court. It has its origins in 1971 and has been adapted over the years to meet new needs and regulatory regimes. Since 2004, various agreements have been made between the Lord Chancellor, as representative of the executive, and the Lord Chief Justice, as representative of the judiciary, about how the courts administration should be arranged. Thus, both the executive and the judiciary have influence over the Courts and Tribunals Service. Also the disciplinary measures against judges outside the Supreme Court lie in the hands of the Lord Chancellor and the Lord Chief Justice through a Judicial Conduct Investigations Office.[63]

From a Nordic perspective, the Danish system is especially interesting. A judicial council, *Domstolsstyrelsen*, was organised in 1999, for the precise purpose of safeguarding judicial independence. *Domstolsstyrelsen* governs the administrative office. In the council, judges are in a majority – nominated by the Supreme Court, the two courts of appeal and the Danish associations of judges and judges under training – and there are representatives for advocates and other parts of society. Even though the courts and the judiciary were already considered independent, this should also be made symbolically clear.[64] Francesco Contini has

61 M. Minkner, *Die Gerichtsverwaltung…*, pp. 232–308; A. von Bernstorff, *Die Gerichtsverwaltung…*, pp. 115–212.

62 M. Minkner, *Die Gerichtsverwaltung…*, pp. 336–701.

63 A. von Bernstorff, *Die Gerichtsverwaltung…*, pp. 212–323.

64 J.P. Christensen, *Domstolene – den tredje statsmagt*, Århus: Magtudredningen, 2003, pp. 69–89.

provided an example of how the Danish auditor's office criticised the productivity of some district courts, and how this caused the judicial council to develop goals and introduce a reporting system which made the courts more efficient.[65]

Even though the examples that I have provided are few and brief, they might provide some context for an analysis of the Swedish public entities responsible for court administration and supervision over judges, and, thus, a basis for wider comparisons. Sweden is not unique in having a central entity responsible for the administration of courts; in that regard, Italy, England and Denmark are similar. But Sweden is unique, at least in this comparison, in having an administrative authority placed under the government. Even though the Swedish public authorities are relatively independent, compared to the authorities of other countries, there is a risk that the government exerts influence on the director general of the National Courts Administration, something which might also influence the courts and individual judges, since the administrative authority can interfere with their salaries.

In this respect, the Italian model with strong self-government is to be preferred, but it has other drawbacks. Minkner, for example, has – in a comparison with Germany – severely criticised the Italian court organisation for having too weak procedures for judicial accountability and too few incentives for judicial efficiency. He has, thus, argued that the principle of *autogoverno* is not a model to be followed in Germany, and that the guarantees for judicial independence there are already sufficient.[66] On a more general level, Minkner has concluded that it is difficult to strike the right balance between the independence of the judiciary and the democratic legitimacy of court administration.[67] In this context, reference could be made to the Danish *Domstolsstyrelsen,* which takes into account both the independence of judges and the interests of society at large.

Asking whether Germany could learn something from England, von Bernstorff has found that a central administrative authority could mean more efficient court administration, even though German federalism makes such a reform difficult. A more relevant model could be the English way of organising court administration and disciplinary measures through agreements between the executive and the judiciary through the Lord Chancellor and the Lord Chief Justice. This is a flexible solution, but it also requires that there should be a senior judge with the specific task of representing the judiciary in a legitimate way.[68]

65 F. Contini and R. Mohr, *Judicial…*, pp. 87–88.
66 M. Minkner, *Die Gerichtsverwaltung…*, pp. 736–775.
67 M. Minkner, *Die Gerichtsverwaltung…*, pp. 308–335.
68 A. von Bernstorff, *Die Gerichtsverwaltung…*, pp. 326–332.

The Swedish model with a parliamentary ombudsman acting in the framework of constitutional checks and balances seems to work fairly well, according to common opinion. The supervision by the Chancellor of Justice and the position of the National Courts Administration between the Government and the Courts are open to criticism. Nevertheless, one main reason why the system has worked fairly well and not been abused with flagrant encroachments into the area of judicial independence probably lies within Swedish legal culture. Legal culture can be said to form a layer under the day-to-day practices of law and provides legal actors with their pre-understanding (*Vorverständnis*).[69] As we have seen, the supervisory authorities are rather old, and originated as, or were made part of, the system of checks and balances that was introduced in Sweden in the early nineteenth century. Both they and the National Courts Administration are dominated by persons who have experience as judges. This does not make them reluctant to fulfil their duties in their new offices, but they have an understanding of the importance of judicial independence. This means, on the one hand, that the independence of the judiciary is strong on a legal cultural level, but, on the other hand, that the legislative and institutional structures are scattered and weak.

The National Courts Administration needs a reform. It is not likely that the German model would be chosen in Sweden, with administrative tasks again scattered over the different courts and the ministry of justice. The Italian model of *autogoverno* is similarly unlikely. The most likely reform is that the present National Courts Administration, or a new similar office, will be organised with a board of judges. This could be done in a similar way to that already chosen in Denmark, and which in Sweden has already been chosen for the Judges Proposals Board, even though the Danish model has an advantage in its broader representation of various groups of judges. If this could be done through an agreement between the executive and the judiciary, as in England, that would be an important step forward.

5. Concluding comments

When court administration and supervision over judges are to be designed, various factors need to be taken into account. The judiciary needs to be institutionally independent, and this can be secured through a judicial council. Italy has gone far in that respect, too far in the view of some, because the judiciary ought

---

69 See e.g. K. Tuori, "Towards a Multi-Layered View of Modern Law," in: *Justice, Morality and Society. A tribute to Aleksander Peczenik on the Occasion of his 60th Birthday 16 November 1997*, Lund: Juristförlaget, 1997, pp. 427–442.

not to become "a state within the state." However, it is not only a question about the independence of the courts or the judiciary; it must be done in such a way that the *individual* independence of judges is not threatened. The reasons for judicial independence must be kept in mind at all times, namely the right of citizens to a fair trial within a reasonable time by an impartial court.

When the Swedish Instrument of Government of 1809 was to be adopted, the Constitutional Committee summarised its main features in a report. Even though the constitution actually established a more complicated set of checks and balances, as for example the control function of the Parliamentary Ombudsman of Justice, these sentences have been much quoted in the Swedish constitutional debate. They summarise the principle of checks and balances in an eloquent way, which also captures some of the difficulties in promoting independence through accountability and *vice versa*:

> The committee has sought to shape an executive power, acting within fixed forms and united in its decision-making and implementing power, a legislative power, wisely slow to act but strong to resist, and a judicial power, independent under the laws but not autocratic over them. The committee has furthermore tried to structure these powers so that they check and restrain each other, without mixing them or granting the restraining function any power that belongs to the restrained function. The proposed constitution shall be based on these fundaments of the purposes of the different powers and their mutual balance.[70]

References

Publications

Axberger, Hans-Gunnar, *JO – i riksdagens tjänst*, Visby: Eddy.se, 2014.

---

70 "Utskottet har sökt att bilda en Styrande Magt, verksam inom bestämda former, med enhet i beslut och full kraft i medlen att dem utföra; En Lagstiftande Magt, visligt trög till verkning, men fast och stark till motstånd; En Domare-Magt, självständig under Lagarna, men ej självhärskande över dem. Det har vidare sökt att rikta dessa makter till inbördes bevakning, till inbördes återhåll, utan att dem sammanblanda, utan att lämna den återhållande något av den återhållnas verkningsförmåga. På dessa huvudgrunder av statskrafternas särskilda bestämmelser och ömsesidiga motvikt skall den statsförfattning vila, som utskottet föreslagit." Konstitutionsutskottets memorial i *Sveriges Konstitutionella Urkunder,* Stockholm: SNS, 1999, p. 184. Cf. O. Petersson, "The Swedish Constitution of 1809," in: *Contested Sovereignties. Government and Democracy in Middle Eastern and European Perspectives. Swedish Research Institute in Istanbul, Transactions, Vol. 19*, ed. by E. Özdalga and S. Persson, pp. 53–66.

Axberger, Hans-Gunnar, "Justitieombudsmannen, tryckfriheten och maktdelningen," in: *Maktbalans och kontrollmakt. 1809 års händelser, idéer och författningsverk i ett tvåhundraårigt perspektiv*, ed. by Margareta Brundin and Magnus Isberg, Stockholm: Sveriges Riksdag, 2009, pp. 415–451.

von Bernstorff, Alexander, *Die Gerichtsverwaltung in Deutschland und England*, Berlin: Duncker & Humblot, 2018.

Borgström, Katarina Alexius, *JO och tjänstemännen. En laghistorisk studie*, Uppsala: Iustus, 2003.

Cappelletti, Mauro, *Giudici irresponsabili? Studio comparativo sulla responsabilità dei giudici*, Milano: Giuffrè, 1988.

Cappelletti, Mauro, " 'Who Watches the Watchmen?' A Comparative Study on Judicial Responsibility," *The American Journal of Comparative Law*, No. 1 (31), 1983, pp. 1–62.

Christensen, Jens Peter, *Domstolene - den tredje statsmagt, Århus: Magtudredningen*, 2003.

Contini, Francesco, and Richard Mohr, *Judicial Evaluation. Traditions, innovation and proposals for measuring the quality of court performance*, Saarbrücken: VDM Verlag, 2008.

Eka, Anders, *Judicial Council - ett råd i tiden? in Festskrift till Johan Hirschfeldt*, Uppsala: Iustus, 2008.

Ekroth, Jesper, *JO-ämbetet. En offentligrättslig studie*, Stockholm: Stockholms universitet, 2001.

Justitiekanslern 300 år, ed. by Göranson, Ulf, Uppsala: Iustus 2013.

Langbroek, Philip, Rachel Dijkstra, Kyana Bozorg Zadeh, and Zübeyir Türk, "Performance management of courts and judges: organisational and professional learning versus political accountabilities," in: *Handle with Care. Assessing and designing methods for evaluation and development of the quality of justice*, ed. by Francesco Contini, Bologna: IRSIG-CNR, 2017, pp. 297–325.

Luminati, Michele, *Priester der Themis. Richterliches Selbstverständnins in Italien nach 1945*, Frankfurt am Main: Vittorio Klostermann, 2007.

Melin, Mats, and Stefan Lindskog, *Domstolarnas oberoende behöver stärkas*, Svensk Juristtidning, No. 5, 2017, pp. 345–355.

Minkner, Martin, *Die Gerichtsverwaltung in Deutschland und Italien. Demokratie versus technische Legitimation*, Tübingen: Mohr Siebeck, 2015.

Nils, Bexelius, *JO-ämbetet 150 år*, Svensk Juristtidning, No. 1, 1960, pp. 81–111.

Petersson, Olof, "The Swedish Constitution of 1809," in: *Contested Sovereignties. Government and Democracy in Middle Eastern and European Perspectives.*

Swedish Research Institute in Istanbul, Transactions, Vol. 19, ed. by Elisabeth Özdalga and Sune Persson, pp. 53–66.

Petrén, Gustaf, "Domstolsverket och domstolsväsendet - en studie i regeringsteknik," *Svensk Juristtidning*, No. 1, 1975, pp. 651–656.

Petrén, Gustaf, "Domstolarnas ställning enligt 1974 års regeringsform," *Svensk Juristtidning*, No. 1, 1975, pp. 1–14.

Rudholm, Sten, "Justitiekanslersämbetet 250 år," *Svensk Juristtidning*, No.1, 1964, pp. 1–16.

Sourdin, Tania, and Naomi Burstyner, "Justice Delayed is Justice Denied," *Victoria University Law and Justice Journal*, No. 1 (4), pp. 46–60.

Sunnqvist, Martin, "Domstolsliknande myndigheter och myndighetsliknande domstolar?" in *Den svenska förvaltningsmodellen*, ed. by Claes Peterson, Stockholm: Institutet för Rättshistorisk Forskning, 2020, pp. 234–255.

Sunnqvist, Martin, "The Changing Role of Nordic Courts," in: *Rethinking Nordic Courts*, ed. by Laura Ervo, Pia Letto-Vanamo and Anna Nylund, Cham: Springer, 2021.

Svea hovrätt 400 år, ed. by Fredrik Wersäll, Johan Hirschfeldt, Andres Eka, Elisabet Fura, Kjell A Modéer, Stockholm: Norstedts juridik, 2014.

Thorblad, Barbro, and Martin Holmgren, "Domstolsverket — från starten till våra dagar," *Svensk Juristtidning*, No. 1, 2018, pp. 16–35.

Tuori, Kaarlo, "Towards a Multi-Layered View of Modern Law," in: *Justice, Morality and Society. A tribute to Aleksander Peczenik on the Occasion of his 60th Birthday 16 November 1997*, 1997, pp. 427–442.

Wersäll, Fredrik, "Ökad domarmakt och makten över domstolarna," Svensk Juristtidning, No. 1, 2017, pp. 1–8.

Jurisprudence

Sweden

Decision of Labour Court of Sweden, 22.01.2014, AD 2014 No. 5.

Judgement of Supreme Court of Sweden, 17.11.2017, NJA 2017 p. 842.

European Court of Human Rights (ECtHR)

Judgement of ECtHR, 17.01.1970, *Delcourt v. Belgium*, No. 2689/65.

Judgement of ECtHR, 26.10.1984, *De Cubber v. Belgium*, No. 9186/80.

Judgement of ECtHR, 15.07.2005, *Mežnarić v. Croatia*, No. 71615/01.

Court of Justice of European Union (CJEU)

Judgement of CJEU, 5.04.2016, *Aranyosi and Căldăraru*, C-404/15 and C-659/15 (joined cases), ECLI:EU:C:2016:198.

Judgement of CJEU of 25.07.2018, C-216/18, *PPU Minister for Justice and Equality [LM]* ECLI:EU:C:2018:586.

Judgement of CJEU, 24.06.2019, *Commission v Poland*, C-619/18, ECLI:EU:C:2019:531.

Judgement of CJEU, 5.11.2019, *Commission v Poland*, C-192/18, ECLI:EU:C:2019:924.

Other

Decision by Court of Appeal of Karlsruhe, 17.02.2020, 301 AR 156/19.

Judgement of High Court of Justice of England, *R. v. Sussex Justices*, ex parte McCarthy ([1924] 1 KB 256, [1923] All ER Rep 233) per Lord Hewart C.J.

Judgement of the Supreme Court of Ireland, *Minister for Justice & Equality v. Celmer*, S:AP:IE:2018:000181.

Sources of law

Sweden

Code of Judicial Procedure, Law Code of the Realm, 1734.

Code of Judicial Procedure, Swedish Code of Statutes (SFS), 1942:740.

Instrument of Government, Swedish Code of Statutes (SFS), 1974:152.

Ordinance with instructions for the Chancellor of Justice, Swedish Code of Statutes (SFS), 1975:1345.

Ordinance with instructions for the National Courts Administration, Swedish Code of Statutes (SFS), 1975:506.

Ordinance with instruction for the Judges Proposals Board, Swedish Code of Statutes (SFS), 2008:427.

Ordinance with instruction for the Judges Proposals Board, Swedish Code of Statutes (SFS), 2010:1793.

Statute on General Administrative Courts, Swedish Code of Statutes (SFS), 1971:289.

Statute on the appointment of ordinary judges, Swedish Code of Statutes (SFS), 2010:1390.

Statute on the Chancellor of Justice's supervision, Swedish Code of Statutes (SFS), 1975:1339.

Statute with instructions for the Parliamentary Ombudsman, Swedish Code of Statutes (SFS), 1986:765.

The Riksdag Act, Swedish Code of Statutes (SFS), 2014:801.

European Sources of Law

Recommendation Rec. (1994)12 of The Committee of Ministers to Member States on the independence, efficiency and role of judges, rm.coe.int (access date: 22.05.2021).

Recommendation Rec. (2010) 12 of The Committee of Ministers to Member States on judges: independence, efficiency and responsibilities, rm.coe.int (access date: 22.05.2021).

Resolution no. 1685 (2009) *Allegations of politically motivated abuses of the criminal justice system in Council of Europe member states*, assembly.rm.coe.int (access date: 22.05.2021).

Resolution no. 2040 (2015) *Threats to the rule of law in Council of Europe member States: asserting the Parliamentary Assembly's authority*, assembly.rm.coe.int (access date: 22.05.2021).

Reports

Swedish Government Official (SOU) Reports

Bestämmelser om domstolarna i regeringsformen, Swedish Government Official Reports (SOU) 2007:69.

Domaren i Sverige inför framtiden – utgångspunkter för fortsatt utredningsarbete, Swedish Government Official Reports (SOU) 1994:99.

Domarutnämningar och domstolsledning. Frågor om utnämning av högre domare och om domstolschefens roll, Swedish Government Official Reports (SOU) 2009:99.

Högsta domstolens kansli, Swedish Government Official Reports (SOU) 1971:59.

Ny domstolsadministration, Swedish Government Official Reports (SOU) 1971:41.

Riksdagens justitieombudsmän, Swedish Government Official Reports (SOU) 1965:64.

JK-ämbetet. Översyn av justitiekanslerns arbetsuppgifter och statens tvistehandläggning, Swedish Government Official Reports (SOU) 1978:59.

JO-ämbetet. En översyn, Swedish Government Official Reports (SOU) 1985:26.

JO-ämbetet. Uppgifter och organisation, Swedish Government Official Reports (SOU) 1975:23.

Justitiekanslern. En översyn av justitiekanslerns arbetsuppgifter m.m., Swedish Government Official Reports (SOU) 1993:37.

Other reports and sources

Central, regional och lokal domstolsförvaltning m.m., betänkande avgivet av Domstolsstyrelseutredningen, Inquiry to the Judicial Council, Ds Ju 1974:5.

Consultative Council of European Judges (CCJE) Opinion no. 10 (2007) to the attention of the Committee of Ministers of the Council of Europe on the Council for the Judiciary at the service of society, https://rm.coe.int/168074779b (access date: 22.05.2021).

Documents of pending case C-791/19, Commission v Poland, ECLI:EU:C:2020:277

Justitieombudsmännens ämbetsberättelse, JO 2008/09.

Konstitutionsutskottets memorial i Sveriges Konstitutionella Urkunder, Stockholm: SNS, 1999

Kungl. Maj:ts proposition med förslag till organisation av den nya centralmyndigheten för domstolsväsendet m.m., Prop. 1974:149.

Lönepolicy för Sveriges Domstolar, 26.10.2011.

The opinion 16 January 2020 no. 977/2019, www.venice.coe.int (access date: 22.05.2021).

Utredningen om förstärkt skydd för demokratin och domstolarnas oberoende (2020 års grundlagskommitté), Inquiry into enhanced protection of democracy and the independence of the judiciary (2020 Constitutional Committee), Dir. Ju 2020:04.

Internet Sources

Universal Charter of the Judge, adopted by the IAJ Central Council in Taiwan on November 17th, 1999, updated in Santiago de Chile on November 14th, 2017; https://www.iaj-uim.org/universal-charter-of-the-judge-2017/ (access date: 22.05.2021).

Andrzej Skoczylas[1]

The organisation of the work of a judge and the activities of judicial administration bodies (comments from the viewpoint of the administrative judiciary)

Abstract: The aim of the paper is to present the characteristics of the judge's work from the perspective of the court's organisation and court administration tasks. The analysis is conducted on the basis of normative regulation concerning the Polish administrative courts issued by a judge of the Supreme Administrative Court. In addition to a presentation of the characteristics of the administrative courts as a separate branch of the judiciary, such phenomena as the allocation of cases and persons who cooperate with judges are presented. In the final remarks, a positive evaluation of the conditions for the organisation of the judge's individual workplace is formulated. However, the conclusion also proposes improvements for more a professional court organisation which would result in a better decision-making process. It therefore seems that judges should have more influence over the selection of the persons with whom they work.

Keywords: administrative judiciary, court authorities, allocation of cases, judge's assistants, court administration staff

1. Introduction

In the context of ensuring the proper work of judges and their independence, consideration should also be given to the impact of judicial administration bodies on the appropriate preparation of the court's auxiliary apparatus and the organisation of the work of judges.

In discussing the issues of the proper organisation of a judge's work, it should be pointed out that Article 178(2) of the Constitution of the Republic of Poland[2]

1 Andrzej Skoczylas, PhD, Professor of Law at Adam Mickiewicz University in Poznań, (Poland), The Supreme Administrative Court of Poland Judge. ORCID – 0000-0001-7951-7341.

2 The Constitution of the Republic of Poland of 2.4.1997 (Journal of Laws 1997, No. 78, item 483 with subsequent amendments, hereinafter referred to as the Constitution of the RP).

clearly states that judges shall be provided with working conditions and remuneration that correspond to the dignity of the office and the scope of their duties. In addition, in the exercise of their office judges are independent and subject only to the Constitution and statutes (Article 178(1) of the Constitution). It is stressed that "judges are the only group of public officials who are legally guaranteed appropriate working conditions and remuneration in the Polish Constitution."[3] The jurisprudence of the Constitutional Tribunal has indicated that it should be presumed that certain legal content may be extracted from each of the provisions of the Constitution of the Republic of Poland, including Article 178 Section 2, to the extent that "this provision requires that judges be provided with working conditions" and remuneration corresponding to, inter alia, "the dignity of the office." In the Tribunal's view, "it would be wrong to claim that Article 178 section 2 of the Constitution is merely a declaration and cannot be regarded as a norm of substantive law."[4] As Roman Hauser points out, "the systemic norm expressed in Article 178 section 2 of the Constitution is aimed at strengthening the position of the judiciary in the system of state bodies and guaranteeing to judges such working conditions and remuneration as are to serve the proper administration of justice."[5] According to the Constitutional Tribunal, "the dignity of the office means awareness of its value and respect for it, expressed both by its members and by outsiders, and more broadly by society as a whole."[6] One should agree with Michał Laskowski's view that "the dignity of the office is associated with a set of various factors relating to the place of work, its organisation, the provision of safety and assistance from others, the appropriate burden of tasks

3 Laskowski, M., "Warunki pracy sędziego a godność sprawowanego przez niego urzędu," in: Pozycja ustrojowa sędziego, ed. by Ryszard Piotrowski, Warszawa: LEX Wolters Kluwer, 2015, p. 70. Similarly, Roman Hauser, "Konstytucyjna zasada niezawisłości sędziowskiej," *Zeszyty Naukowe Sądownictwa Administracyjnego*, 2015, No. 1, p. 11.

4 Judgment of the Polish Constitutional Tribunal, 22.03.2000, P 12/98, OTK ZU 2000, No. 2, item 67. This decision is extensively discussed by Tuleja, P., "Realizacja zasady pierwszeństwa Konstytucji w orzecznictwie Trybunału Konstytucyjnego," in: *Stosowanie Konstytucji RP w świetle zasady jej nadrzędności (wybrane problemy)*, Kraków: Kantor Wydawniczy Zakamycze, 2003, https://sip.lex.pl/#/monograph/369135424/252312 (access date: 02 April 2020).

5 Hauser, R., "Konstytucyjna zasada niezawisłości sędziowskiej," *Zeszyty Naukowe Sądownictwa Administracyjnego*, 2015, No. 1, p. 11.

6 Judgment of the Polish Constitutional Tribunal, 12.12.2012, K 1/12, OTK ZU-A 2012, No. 11, item 134.

imposed on the judge and a set of other guarantees allowing judges to perform their functions with dignity."[7]

In this context, it should also be noted that the Polish Constitution adopts a judicial model consisting in separating two types of courts that are independent of each other – a division of the common and military courts (headed by the Supreme Court) and a separate division of administrative courts.[8]

The structure of the administrative courts is two-tier and includes voivodeship administrative courts (VAC) as courts of first instance, and the Supreme Administrative Court (SAC) as the court of second instance. Cases falling within the jurisdiction of the administrative courts are examined by voivodeship administrative courts in the first instance, while the Supreme Administrative Court supervises the activities of voivodeship administrative courts with respect to adjudication in accordance with the procedure set out in the statutes. In particular, the SAC considers appeals against the decisions of these courts, and it resolves disputes over competence and jurisdiction.

In Poland there are 16 administrative courts of first instance and one Supreme Administrative Court, which has its seat in Warsaw. The Supreme Administrative Court is divided into three chambers: Financial, Commercial and General Administrative.[9] Each chamber is headed by its president (who is also a

---

7 Laskowski, M., "Warunki pracy sędziego a godność sprawowanego przez niego urzędu," in: Pozycja ustrojowa sędziego, ed. by Ryszard Piotrowski, Warszawa: LEX Wolters Kluwer, 2015, p. 71.

8 Hauser, R., "U progu reformy sądownictwa administracyjnego," *Państwo i Prawo*, 2002, No. 11, p. 30.

9 The Chamber of Finance supervises the case-law of voivodeship administrative courts in matters of tax liabilities and other monetary performances, to which tax regulations apply, as well as the enforcement of monetary performances. The Economic Chamber supervises the decisions of voivodeship administrative courts in matters of business activity, the protection of industrial property, budget, foreign exchange, securities, banking, insurance, customs, prices and rights to perform certain activities or professions (including legal, e.g. attorneys-at-law, bailiffs, as well as refusal to present a candidate for the position notaries). The General Administrative Chamber, in turn, supervises the decisions of voivodeship administrative courts in other cases, and in particular in the field of construction and construction supervision, spatial development, water management, environmental protection, agriculture, forestry, employment (e.g. policemen, officers of special services), local government system, real estate management, privatisation of property, internal affairs – Skoczylas, A., "Administrative Proceedings and Judicial Review of Administration," in: *Handbook of Polish Law*, ed. by Wojciech Dajczak, Andrzej Szwarc, Paweł Wiliński, Warszawa – Bielsko-Biała: Park, 2011, pp. 382 ff.

vice-president of the SAC). The chambers are divided into departments (usually two or three), which are headed by appointed judges – heads of departments (sometimes they also have deputies).

Similarly, the administrative courts of first instance are divided into departments (created and abolished by the President of the Supreme Administrative Court). A department in the VAC is headed by the president or vice-president of the court or by a designated judge, i.e. the head of the department (Article 17 § 1 and 2 of the Law on the System of Administrative Courts).

2. The legal position of the judicial authorities

In the administrative judiciary, the functions of the judicial administration bodies are performed not only by typical judicial administration bodies[10] – that is, for example, by court presidents[11] (vice-presidents), heads of departments, but also, to some extent, by the college of judges of a given court.[12] In this context, attention should be paid to the specific structure of the system of administrative courts in Poland and the special role of its bodies, including the President of the Supreme Administrative Court, which results from the natural opposition of this court to the executive branch. A separate regulation of the system of administrative courts in Poland[13] is directly anchored in the Polish Constitution. Therefore, to the extent discussed above, provisions of the Law on the System of Administrative Courts and secondary legislation enacted on its basis are of fundamental importance, with the provisions of the law on the system of common courts[14] applying to a limited extent only.

---

10 Cf. Żurawik, A., *Ustrój sądownictwa w Polsce*, Warszawa: C.H. Beck, 2013, pp. 88 f.

11 It should be noted that in contrast to common courts, in administrative courts the court director is not a body of the court – cf. Article 21 of the Law on the System of Common Courts Act of 27.07.2001, Journal of Laws of 2019, item 52, with subsequent amendments (hereinafter: the LSCC) and Articles 19 and 31 of the LSAC.

12 Judgment of the Supreme Court, 22.2.2017, III KRS 2/17, LEX No 2271451. See also the judgment of the Supreme Administrative Court, 24.1.2014, I OSK 2037/13, publ. http://orzeczenia.nsa.gov.pl (access date: 02 April 2020); As the doctrine stresses, this body corresponds to the presidium of the court in some other legal systems – Szmulik, B., *Pozycja ustrojowa Sądu Najwyższego w Rzeczypospolitej Polskiej*. Warszawa: C.H. Beck, 2008, p. 276.

13 See Skoczylas, A.,"Kwestia zasadności odrębnej regulacji ustroju sądów administracyjnych w Polsce," *Iustitia – Kwartalnik Stowarzyszenia Sędziów Polskich*, 2011, No. 4, pp. 182–186.

14 Which results from the reference contained in Article 29(1) of the LSAC, whereas under Article 49 of the LSAC, the provisions on Supreme Court judges apply accordingly, and

This way of legal regulation stems from the fact that the administrative judiciary is to independently "protect the interests and public rights" of the individual, "and also the objectively existing rule of law."[15] As a consequence, this feature of the administrative judiciary also results in the supervision of the administrative activities of the courts being regulated by provisions that differ from those governing common courts of law. Pursuant to Article 12 of the Law on the System of Administrative Courts,[16] the administrative activities of administrative courts are supervised by the President of the Supreme Administrative Court.[17] This provision is equivalent to Article 9 of the Law on the System of Common Courts Act of 27 July 2001,[18] in the light of which the Minister of Justice exercises supreme supervision over administrative activities of common courts. Both these bodies perform "a similar role in individual branches of the judiciary, and neither of them may encroach upon the supervisory sphere exercised by the other body."[19] The President of the SAC is appointed by the President of the Republic of Poland for a 6-year term of office from among two candidates presented by the General Assembly of the SAC Judges. It is solely up to the President which of the two candidates is ultimately appointed.

The supervision of the President of the Supreme Administrative Court (SAC) over the administrative activities of courts concerns various matters connected with the creation of conditions for the efficient functioning of the courts. It includes, inter alia, organisational and human resources matters (e.g. the SAC President may: request the President of the Republic of Poland to create or abolish a first-instance court; appoint and dismiss the president of such a court; delegate first-instance court judges to adjudicate in another court; and determine the number of first-instance court judges and the number of vice-presidents), financial and technical-organisational matters (e.g., establishing office rules), as well as issues of supervision over the efficient functioning of the courts (e.g. by

---

only in cases not regulated by the Act, under Article 10(1) of the SC Act, the provisions of the LSCC. – see also Borkowski, J., in: B. Adamiak, J. Borkowski, *Metodyka pracy sędziego w sprawach administracyjnych*, Warszawa: Wolters Kluwer, 2009, p. 44.

15 Zimmermann, J., *Aksjomaty sądownictwa administracyjnego*, Warszawa: Wolters Kluwer 2020, p. 54.

16 Law on System of Administrative Courts, 25.7.2002 (Consolidated text: Journal of Laws of 2019, item 2161 with subsequent amendments, hereinafter the LSCC)

17 Judgment of the Supreme Administrative Court, 5.2.2008, I OSK 581/07, publ. http://orzeczenia.nsa.gov.pl (access date: 1.4.2021).

18 Consolidated text: Journal of Laws 2018, item 23, with subsequent amendments.

19 A. Żurawik, *Ustrój sądownictwa w Polsce*, Warszawa: C.H. Beck, 2013, p. 138.

visiting first-instance courts). As Aleksandra Puczko aptly observes, apart from the President of the Supreme Administrative Court and other persons holding managerial positions in the courts (including appointed judges), the supervision is also exercised by employees of the Supreme Administrative Court (especially employees of the Supreme Administrative Court's Judicial Decisions Bureau, the so-called supervision service), which means that it can be exercised even by persons not directly connected with adjudication.[20]

The supervision exercised in this way by the President of the Supreme Administrative Court includes examining the efficiency of proceedings in voivodeship administrative courts and in individual organisational units of these courts, as well as checking the observance of work culture and the dignity of the court by judges, court assessors, *court* referendaries, court assistants and officials, and other court employees. In the course of the inspection, the following matters are examined in particular: the workload of judges, in accordance with the number of new and resolved cases and the state of arrears; the efficiency of court proceedings, including preparation of hearings; and the performance of activities in the course of inter-instances proceedings (proceedings between the first and the second instances), including the timeliness of drafting reasons for judgments and performance of activities after the judgment has become final.

An extremely important aspect of the supervision exercised by the President of the Supreme Administrative Court, vice-presidents and other judges and employees is also the analysis of final court judgments in terms of assessing the level of uniformity of the case-law of administrative courts. It should be added that the SAC uses internal mechanisms to ensure the uniformity of administrative court judgments, and the main instrument of this type are the resolutions of the SAC (adopted, among others, at the request of the President of the SAC).[21] In

20 A. Puczko § 1, in: Commentary to the Regulation on the detailed procedure of exercising supervision over the administrative activity of voivodship administrative courts, in: Ustrój Naczelnego Sądu Administracyjnego. Komentarz. Warszawa: LexisNexis, 2013. Cf. also § 19 – 21 Regulation of the President of the Republic of Poland of 4 July 2020 – By-laws of the Supreme Administrative Court (Journal of Laws 2020, item 1202 with subsequent amendments).

21 The panels of administrative courts (VAC and SAC) are bound by resolutions (although, apart from cases where a specific legal question is presented, in a relative manner only), which means that if they do not share the position taken in a resolution, they should present the resulting legal question for resolution to the relevant extended panel of the SAC (seven judges, the entire Chamber or all SAC judges). However, they are already absolutely bound by the resolution issued following the initiation of this procedure, again clarifying the legal question that has arisen. To make matters simpler, it can be

addition, usually even before the commencement of a resolution procedure, the SAC's Judicial Decisions Bureau informs judges in the event of doubts or discrepancies in case-law, organises councils dedicated to specific issues and training sessions for judges and other court employees. Certain issues are also discussed during the conferences of SAC judges. These discussions shape the assumptions used for the interpretation of specific provisions, without violating the principle of independence, but indirectly influencing the line of jurisprudence, i.e. indicating proposals for a specific interpretation of particular provisions.[22] However, often, given the difficulties in reaching a consensus in these discussions and their non-binding nature, they can only play a limited role,[23] while the main task falls to the extended panels of the SAC (seven judges, the Chamber or all SAC judges), as already indicated above. In this respect, the exercise of supervision by the presidents of the courts of first instance, vice-presidents and heads of departments of these courts consists in analysing the case-law in terms of the level of its uniformity and signalling to the President of the Supreme Administrative Court any discrepancies which require clarification of legal regulations.

In this context, however, it should be stressed that one can generally agree with the view that since a judge is subject to the Constitution and to the statutes, the independence of a judge does not protect him or her against restrictions arising from the norms of law[24] – including those that define the supervisory

---

stated that the above procedure consists in breaking or approving the precedential nature of an SAC resolution. Of course, the interpretation discussed herein contained in SAC resolutions is binding only with respect to administrative courts, which means that it does not formally bind administrative bodies and parties and participants of administrative court proceedings. In practice, however, administrative bodies usually accept the legal view expressed in the SAC's resolution. This is primarily due to the concern about the fate of their decision in the event of an inspection as a result of bringing a legal remedy and, of course, about the authority of the SAC. Thus, even if SAC resolutions do not formally bind administrative bodies and citizens, they constitute actual precedents – not binding but having force.

22 Borkowski, J., "Przepisy postępowania cywilnego w procedurze sądu administracyjnego," in: *Księga Pamiątkowa ku czci Witolda Broniewicza*, ed. by A. Marciniak, Łódź: Wydawnictwo Uniwersytetu Łódzkiego, 1998, p. 54.

23 Świątkiewicz, J., *Naczelny Sąd Administracyjny. Komentarz do Ustawy*, Białystok: Prawo i Praktyka Gospodarcza, 1999, p. 23.

24 But only against all external pressures and influences exerted outside the current legal system – Gardocka, T., *Prejudycjalność w polskim procesie karnym*, Warszawa: Wydawnictwo Uniwersytetu Warszawskiego, 1987, p. 12 ff. and Hofmański, P., *Samodzielność jurysdykcyjna sądu karnego*, Katowice: Wydawnictwo Uniwersytetu Śląskiego, 1988, pp. 34 ff.

powers of the judicial administration bodies, since the laws define "simply the boundaries within which the court is independent."[25] Nevertheless, there is no doubt that under no circumstances may the judicial administration bodies be bound by administrative recommendations and orders that are incompatible with the constitutional principles of independence and the democratic state of law, even if they rest upon statutory provisions.

3. The allocation of cases to a judge

In the Polish administrative judicial system, a judge[26] has little influence on the allocation and timing of his/her cases. The head of the adjudicating department has basic competences in this respect. These issues are mainly regulated in secondary regulations[27] issued under the Law on the System of Administrative Courts Act of 25 July 2002.[28]

As a rule, cases brought before the administrative courts are heard at a hearing in the order in which they are received (unless a special provision requires that particular cases be heard out of sequence, e.g. in cases involving the granting of EU funds or access to public information,[29] or

25 Nowak, T., "Zasada niezależności sądu w systemie organów władzy państwowej i w ujęciu nowego ustawodawstwa karnoprocesowego," in: *Nowe prawo procesowe. Zagadnienia wybrane, Księga ku czci Prof. Wiesława Daszkiewicza*, ed. by T. Nowak, Poznań: Printer, 1999, pp. 73 ff.

26 Assistant judges have a status similar to that of judges.

27 See § 19–29 of the Regulation of the President of the Republic of Poland of 5 August 2015. Internal Office By-laws of Voivodeship Administrative Courts (Journal of Laws 2015, item 1177 with subsequent amendments) and § 25 – 30 of the Regulation of the President of the Republic of Poland of 4 July 2020 – By-laws of the Supreme Administrative Court (Journal of Laws 2020, item 1202 with subsequent amendments), as well as § 20 – 22 of the resolution of the General Assembly of Judges of the Supreme Administrative Court of 8 November 2010 on the office by-laws of the Supreme Administrative Court preceding these Regulations (M. P. of 2010, No. 86, item 1007 with subsequent amendments); see also the Regulation of the President of the Republic of Poland of 18 September 2003 on the detailed procedure of exercising supervision over administrative activities of voivodeship administrative courts (Journal of Laws 2003, No. 169, item 1645 with subsequent amendments).

28 Journal of Laws of 2018, item 2107, hereinafter referred to as the LSCC.

29 Normally such cases must be heard within 30 days of receipt of the file together with the response to the complaint made by the authority.

a party's request to speed up the hearing due to special circumstances is granted[30]).

In the courts of first instance, it is up to the heads of division to set the dates of court hearings (open and in camera heard by three-person panels) and to indicate the composition of individual panels (including their presidents and rapporteurs). They are also competent to draw the lots of panels to adjudicate on cases where legal provisions require them to do so (e.g. after a motion for exclusion of a judge has been accepted, and in a case brought by a motion for the resumption of proceedings).[31] Drawing a panel is intended to ensure "the randomness of the panel's selection, and thus its absolute impartiality."[32] To be sure, the Head of the Department does not have full discretion in appointing the judge rapporteur, as he/she appoints him/her in the subsequent cases brought before the court in the alphabetical order of the list of judges of the adjudicating department (this rule may be ignored if the subsequent cases may have been covered by a single complaint or are interrelated – including in substantive terms). In addition, if due to fortuitous reasons or legal impediments it is necessary to change the composition of the adjudicating panel, the president of the adjudicating department designates another judge in the alphabetical order of the list of judges of that department.

This means that a judge (as Judge-Rapporteur) may, in fact, only set the dates of sittings in camera for panels made up of a single judge, once the head of the department has appointed him/her as Judge-Rapporteur in a given case (but it is still up to the president of the department to supervise and control the efficiency of setting these dates).

In all cases, the Judge-Rapporteur appointed by the President is tasked, inter alia, with: issuing orders necessary for the efficient consideration of the case (e.g.

30 E.g. the application concerns the issue of consent to finance urgent medical treatment abroad.

31 In disciplinary cases of judges and assistant judges of administrative courts, it is the SAC college that determines the panel of the disciplinary court by drawing lots (from the list of SAC judges) – see Kuczyński, T. in: Małgorzata Masternak-Kubiak, Tadeusz Kuczyński, *Prawo o ustroju sądów administracyjnych, Komentarz*, Warszawa: WoltersKluwer, 2009, pp. 294–295 and Skoczylas, A., "Wpływ organów administracji wymiaru sprawiedliwości na postępowanie dyscyplinarne w sądownictwie administracyjnym," *Ruch Prawniczy Ekonomiczny i Socjologiczny* 2020, No. 1, pp. 57–69.

32 Ereciński, T., Gudowski, J., Iwulski, J., *Komentarz do prawa o ustroju sądów powszechnych i ustawy o Krajowej Radzie Sądownictwa*, ed. by J. Gudowski, Warszawa: LexisNexis, 2009, p. 514.

call for the power of attorney if it is incorrect); examining the motions of the parties filed in the course of the proceedings; deciding whether mediation is to take place; checking that his/her orders are executed by the secretariat in a timely and proper manner.

However, the president verifies the reasons for the postponement of hearings and the course of cases, as well as the timeliness of the drafting of reasons for judgments by judges.[33]

The president also performs ongoing oversight of the correctness and efficiency of the Secretariat's discharge of its duties and keeping office books, including a record of their verification at least once a quarter. He/she also issues appropriate orders in this respect.

The court's college, on the other hand, establishes the workload of judges in terms of the number of cases tried[34] and the rules of assigning cases to individual judges. This mainly takes into account: the judge's case-law specialisation; the scope of his/her duties unrelated to adjudication (e.g. presidents of courts and heads of departments usually adjudicate to a significantly reduced extent); and the obligation to ensure the efficiency of proceedings (and in particular the need to designate the longest-overdue cases to be tried first). Proper determination of the workload – appropriate to the organisation of the work of a given court and its human resources is one of the essential elements of the assurance of working

33 "Proper written motifs of the judgement allow the litigating parties to familiarise themselves with the manner of reasoning and argumentation in the process of controlling the legality of the contested decision; at the same time, they reduce the impression of the arbitrariness of the rendered decision, especially in cases where the judge is allowed discretion" – Wojciechowski, B., Zirk-Sadowski, M., "Justification as the limitation of the discretionary power of the administrative judge," in: *Discretionary Power of Public Administration Its Scope and Control*, ed. by L. Leszczyński, A. Szot, Frankfurt am Main: Peter Lang Edition, 2017, p. 147.

34 As in common courts in small VACs, a situation may occur where optimum results in terms of efficiency of proceedings are achieved while the number of cases handled is reduced. "In small units, it is then necessary to agree to the under-use of judges, usually temporary. The fact that they do not reach the limits set for a given category of cases should not be viewed negatively provided that the efficiency of proceedings is good. This should be included, in a way, in the operating costs of small units whose existence is justified by geographical considerations and public interest" – see Laskowski, M., "Warunki pracy sędziego a godność sprawowanego przez niego urzędu," in: Pozycja ustrojowa sędziego, ed. by R. Piotrowski, Warszawa: LEX Wolters Kluwer, 2015, pp. 77–78. In the administrative judiciary, however, there are attempts to ensure a balanced workload by, inter alia, voluntarily delegating judges to more busy courts or the SAC.

conditions corresponding to the dignity of the office provided for in Article 178 section 2 of the Polish Constitution.[35]

The college of judges also assigns judges (at the request of the President of the Court) to the individual adjudicating departments. In the case of the Supreme Administrative Court, on the other hand, it is the president of the chamber who sets the dates and compositions of panels for open and closed sittings for subsequent three-month periods, including open sittings in the Chamber as a whole or sittings of seven judges.[36] The head of a department or the judge-rapporteur may also set the dates of sittings in camera held with a single judge. On the other hand, the head in charge of the work of a SAC department assigns cases to specific judges (in accordance with the rules laid down by the SAC College) and, if necessary, draws panels of judges.

As in the courts of first instance, it is the College of the Supreme Administrative Court which, at the request of the President of the Court, assigns judges to Chambers (and a specific department in the Chamber) and sets out detailed rules for the assignment of cases to judges, taking into account their judicial specialisation and the scope of a judge's duties unrelated to adjudication. Where necessary, the SAC College makes changes to the allocation of judges to Chambers or departments and the rules for assigning cases to judges, but these are rather rare instances. It should be born in mind that during a competition procedure, candidates for the post of SAC judge in a particular Chamber, and therefore changes in this respect should be treated as exceptional situations justified by specific circumstances, such as a change in the material jurisdiction of a particular Chamber and the consequent need to ensure that judges specialising in a particular type of case adjudicate there.

However, when discussing the competences of court presidents and heads of adjudicating departments, it should be remembered that it is first and foremost

---

35 Wiliński, P., Karlik, P., in: Konstytucja RP, Vol. II, Komentarz do art. 87–243, ed. by M. Safian, L. Bosek, Warszawa: C.H. Beck, 2016, p. 1038.

36 It is different, for example, in the Supreme Court (see § 83–85 of the Regulation of the President of the Republic of Poland of 29 March 2018 – By-laws of the Supreme Court, Journal of Laws 2018, item 660 with subsequent amendments), where the president of the adjudicating panel is automatically the oldest judge of the Supreme Court appointed to the adjudicating panel, unless the members of the adjudicating panel who are judges elect another presiding judge from among themselves. It is for the presiding judge to appoint a rapporteur from among the members of the panel, unless the members of the adjudicating panel elect another rapporteur from among themselves. The presiding judge also issues an order setting the date of a hearing or sitting.

judges who have been entrusted with the function of internal management under certain terms and conditions.[37] The special systemic position of the administrative judiciary and its bodies also allows them to perform tasks in the area of judicial administration related indirectly to the adjudicating activity of the courts, including in this regard. There should therefore be no doubt that a judge who performs the administrative function of the president of a court or the head of a department may, for example, sit on the bench in a case in which he or she has performed important administrative activities (i.e. if he or she appointed himself or herself to the bench). According to the ECtHR's decisions, the participation of a judge in activities of a procedural or administrative nature that are not related to the outcome of the case, but which are intended to organise the course of proceedings, is not sufficient to call into question his/her impartiality.[38] In addition, both the president as a judge and the other judges are independent in the exercise of their judicial office and are subject only to the statutes, which cannot, however, preclude them from fulfilling their tasks in the area of judicial administration.[39]

4. Persons cooperating with the judge

In order to increase the speed with which cases are dealt with in the administrative courts, in addition to typically administrative staff (e.g. court clerks in court secretariats), numerous judge's assistants[40] and court referendaries have been recruited (performing their duties mainly in mediation proceedings and exemption from court costs). Assistants and court clerks are mainly recruited through a competition to select the best employees (i.e. the selection board recommends the recruitment of specific individuals).[41] A judge has no direct influence on the selection (assignment) of his/her assistants, court clerks or other employees of the administrative courts – decisions in this respect are taken by the presidents

37 Cf. the dissenting opinion (votum separatum) of Czeszejko-Sochacki, Z., judge of the Polish Constitutional Tribunal, to the judgment of the Polish Constitutional Tribunal, 21.10.1998, No. K. 24/98; quoted in: Oniszczuk J., *Konstytucja Rzeczypospolitej Polskiej w orzecznictwie Trybunału Konstytucyjnego*, Kraków: Zakamycze, 2000, p. 202 ff.

38 Ruling of ECtHR, 23.04.2002, *Jerzy Tartak v. Poland*, No. 46015/99, LEX No 52957.

39 Cf. the reasons for the judgment of the Polish Constitutional Tribunal, 21.10.1998, K 24/98, OTK 1998, No. 6, item 97.

40 See Wajda, D., "Status prawny asystenta sędziego," *Przegląd Sądowy*, 2006, No. 3, pp. 48–66.

41 See Stasiak, R., Chojnowska, Z., "Ocena pracowników sądowych," in: *Sprawny sąd. Zbiór dobrych praktyk*, ed. by Ł. Bojarski, Warszawa: C.H. Beck, 2004, p. 21.

of the courts (presidents of chambers in the Supreme Administrative Court) and heads of adjudicating departments.

This is particularly important in the case of assistants of judges who, as highly qualified lawyers,[42] have the task of preparing draft judgments and justifications for them and dealing with judicial administration issues.[43] As one assistant usually works with one judge (exceptionally with two judges),[44] the right choice, mutual understanding and trust between them are very important. My practice (both as a first- and second-instance judge and as an assistant) has shown that the assistant's support is a great help to the judge in preparing cases for hearing as well as drafting orders and justifications for court judgments.[45] It is particularly important to be able to use the aid of an assistant for work performed by a judge at sittings held in camera.[46] It should be noted that the principle of automatic replacement of absent persons has been implemented in the case of court clerks (in particular, recording clerks) and assistants. Each list of tasks and responsibilities, and in particular the schedule of court hearings, includes information on the replacements, which is necessary to ensure continuity and harmony in the

---

42 In the Supreme Court, assistants to judges may be judges of common or military courts delegated to assist a *Supreme Court* judge – *see § 69* of the Regulation of the President of the Republic of Poland of 29 March 2018 – By-laws of the Supreme Court, Journal of Laws 2018, item 660, with subsequent amendments. *Such a possibility is not provided for in the Supreme Administrative Court.*

43 Cf. Gonera, K.,"Status prawny asystentów sędziów," in: *Zatrudnianie pracowników sądów z perspektywy prawa pracy i zarządzania*, ed. by A. Rycak, LEX 2020, publ. https://sip.lex.pl/#/monograph/369307153/256865 (access date: 27.3.2020).

44 This is different in the Supreme Court, where a judge's assistant cannot assist more than one judge (see § 70 Regulation of the President of the Republic of Poland, 29.03.2018 – By-laws of the Supreme Court, Journal of Laws 2018, item 660 with subsequent amendments). See also Szmulik, B., *Pozycja ustrojowa Sądu Najwyższego w Rzeczypospolitej Polskiej*, Warszawa: C.H. Beck, 2008, pp. 277–278.

45 Assistants' high qualifications mean that they usually have no problems with drafting reasons for judgments (especially in uncomplicated cases), and as a rule they prepare the so-called historical part of the reasons (i.e. in administrative courts a description of the current state of the case and the positions of the parties) – see Konczewski, T., "Sporządzenie projektów uzasadnień orzeczeń przez asystenta sędziego," in: *Sprawny sąd. Zbiór dobrych praktyk*, ed. by Ł. Bojarski, Warszawa: C.H. Beck, 2004, p. 51. See also Rzucidło-Grochowska, I., "`Część historyczna` uzasadnienia orzeczenia sądowego," in: *Uzasadnienia decyzji stosowania prawa*, ed. by I. Rzucidło-Grochowska, M. Grochowski, Warszawa: Wolters Kluwer 2015, pp. 170–199.

46 Cf. Machura-Szczęsna, J., "Praktyczne aspekty pracy asystentów sędziów," in: *Sprawny sąd. Zbiór dobrych praktyk*, ed. by Ł. Bojarski, Warszawa: C.H. Beck, 2004, p. 47.

work of the judicial administration, without causing a paralysis due, for example, to illness or planned leave.[47]

Once an assistant is assigned to a given department and certain tasks or activities are assigned to him/her, the competent head (president) of the department or a person authorised by the head of the department indicated by the president (in the Supreme Administrative Court, by the president of the chamber) discusses with him/her the requirements for the performance of the assigned duties and informs about the applicable rules for periodic evaluation of assistants. The assessment of an assistant in the Supreme Administrative Court (the criteria are formulated in an order of the President of the SAC[48]) is performed by the president of the department at least once every 12 months. The judges with whom the assistant has cooperated have some influence on this evaluation. In fact, the head of the department attaches the opinion of each of the judges with whom the assistant has worked to the assistants' evaluation sheet.

This assessment is based on the following criteria:

1) quality, i.e. an appropriate standard of professionalism,[49] including: a) knowledge and skills (including: knowledge of the regulations necessary for the proper performance of the assigned tasks; the ability to apply legal regulations; recognition of the essence of the problem); b) conscientiousness and diligence (including objective and impartial recognition of circumstances and making decisions on the basis of available documents and verified information); and c) independence (including the ability to independently search for and obtain information, formulate conclusions and propose solutions in order to effectively perform the assigned tasks; the ability to independently analyse facts and regulations),
2) timely performance of tasks and effective use of time, including: a) effective planning and organisation of work (including proper prioritisation of activities and effective use of working time); and b) work discipline (including timely performance of tasks; taking action without undue delay; reliability),

47 Ziółkowska, A., Gronkiewicz, A., *Organizacja pracy biurowej w administracji*, Katowice: Forma studio, 2014, p. 43.

48 Ordinance of the President of the Supreme Administrative Court (SAC) No. 29 of 8.9.2016 on the periodic evaluation of a judge's assistants at the Supreme Administrative Court.

49 Therefore, these are general standards of good administration relating to clerical staff – see Princ, M., *Standardy dobrej administracji w prawie administracyjnym*, Poznań: Wydawnictwo Naukowe UAM, 2017, p. 289 ff.

3) culture in the office (this means standards of good behaviour including personal and work organisation culture, i.e.: dealing with respect with the public and co-workers; appropriate dress and choosing the right style and language of expression in the workplace; creating a positive working atmosphere; ability to work in a team),
4) professional development (including focusing on the development of professional qualifications, readiness to learn, improving professional qualifications, striving to improve the manner in which tasks are performed).

The assistant has the right to file an objection with the President of the Chamber to the assessment received. The president may uphold the assessment or modify it. Before taking a decision, the President of the Chamber may request additional explanations from the assistant or the president of the department.

It should be noted that an extensive system of assistants' training has been set up in the administrative judiciary (in fact, it rather resembles post-graduate studies than typical training), which ends with an examination. Adequate seniority and positive evaluations determine the possibility of promotion to the position of senior assistant.

5. Final remarks

Generally speaking, administrative courts provide judges with good conditions for the organisation of their individual workplace, because:

a) usually, very good work conditions are provided (perhaps with the exception of the Voivodeship Administrative Court in Warsaw) – the judges have rooms for work and meetings at their disposal (individual or for two judges).
b) appropriate equipment is provided (judges have desktop and laptop computers and appropriate software – some of the court records are also kept in electronic form).
c) the judges of the administrative courts also receive appropriate remuneration.
d) a professional assistant is assigned to assist the judge.

The working conditions of a judge of an administrative court are therefore adequate to the dignity of the judge's office and the scope of his/her duties.[50] However, there is no doubt that, as in other branches of the judiciary, *judges at*

50 The CT's jurisprudence points out that in a "democratic state of law, a well-functioning justice system is a guarantee and condition for the functioning of the rule of law. The legislator assumes that the justice system will function properly when the working conditions of judges and their remuneration are adequate to the dignity of the judge's

the administrative courts are subject to significant internal pressure (exerted by department heads and court presidents as part of administrative supervision) to resolve cases efficiently and quickly.[51] However, this state of affairs, which is linked to the imposition of *appropriate* adjudication limits on *judges*, is difficult to assess negatively, because according to Article 45 section 1 of the Constitution of the Republic of Poland,[52] everyone has the right to have their case considered in court proceedings without undue delay,[53] i.e. within a reasonable time.[54] From this viewpoint, when talking about the working conditions of a judge, one should first and foremost have in mind creating organisational freedom of action for the

---

office and the scope of his/her duties" – judgment of the Polish Constitutional Tribunal, 4.10.2000, P 8/00, OTK 2000, No. 6, item 189, LEX No. 44839.

51 Łazarska, A., "Czy pensum sędziowskie narusza niezawisłość sędziowską?," *Krajowa Rada Sądownictwa*, 2016, No. 4, pp. 43–48.

52 The right to a fair trial (literally: the right to court) provided for in this provision consists of three inseparable elements – the right of access to court, the right to a properly formed court procedure and the right to a court decision – Wyrzykowski, M., in: *Zasady podstawowe polskiej konstytucji*, ed. by W. Sokolewicz, Warszawa: Wydawnictwo Sejmowe, 1998, p. 82.

53 It is emphasised that although the elements of the right to a court, regulated in this provision of the Constitution, "are generally accepted and their introduction does not pose difficulties," due to "factors of an organisational and functional nature" the issue of the right to "have the case considered without undue delay" raises serious problems – W. Skrzydło, *Konstytucja Rzeczypospolitej Polskiej, Komentarz*, Kraków: Zakamycze, 1998, p. 44.

54 A reasonable period of time is also referred to in Article 6 section 1 first sentence of the Convention for the Protection of Human Rights and Fundamental Freedoms done at Rome on 4 November 1950, Journal of Laws 1993, No. 61, item 284 with subsequent amendments. However, the limitation of the scope of application of Article 6(1) of the Convention to civil and criminal cases results in the fact that the said regulation does not apply to a significant part of cases pending before the administrative courts, which in the light of the case-law of the European Court of Human Rights (ECtHR) are considered to belong "exclusively to the field of public law which does not cover rights and obligations of a civil nature," see the judgment of ECtHR, 9.12.1994, *Schouten and Meldrum v. Netherlands*, No. 19005/91, 19006/91, LEX No. 80505 and judgment of the ECtHR, 28.06.1978, *König v. Germany*, No. 6232/73, LEX No 80802 judgment of ECtHR, 15.6.2004, *Piekara v. Poland*, No. 77741/01, LEX No 122542; See judgment of the ECtHR, 23.7.2002 as regards the relationship between the concept of "criminal prosecution" within the meaning of Article 6 of the Convention and the classification of proceedings concerning administrative sanctions (tax surcharges), Judgment of ECtHR, 23.7.2002, *Janosevic v. Sweden*, No 34619/97, LEX No. 75486; Judgment of ECtHR, 11.12.2001, *Fuchs v. Poland*, No 33870/96, LEX No. 49866.

judge, as the judge should focus on the administration of justice in specific cases. This means that secondary activities of an administrative nature should be taken over by the court secretariats and judges' assistants,[55] which would increase the number of cases dealt with by the judge. It must be emphasised that hiring auxiliary staff "means that the judges are no longer overburdened with less important, sometimes merely administrative issues and may focus on their core functions" – i.e. the "judge as a manager of the trial."[56]

The fact that judges have little influence over the decision-making process of the secretariats or the administration office should therefore be seen as a negative phenomenon. In fact, the judge can only, for example, ask those responsible to explain the reasons for not implementing his/her orders and submit observations (remarks) and complaints to the competent judicial administration bodies. However, without having a direct influence on the choice of his/her own assistant, the judge is responsible for his/her actions (e.g. if the assistant does not deliver the reasons prepared and signed by the judge for their recording and dispatch, the judge will be responsible for the failure to comply with the deadline). It therefore seems that judges should have more influence over the selection of the persons with whom they work.[57]

References

Publications

Borkowski, Janusz, "Przepisy postępowania cywilnego w procedurze sądu administracyjnego," in: *Księga Pamiątkowa ku czci Witolda Broniewicza*, ed. by A. Marciniak, Łódź: Wydawnictwo Uniwersytetu Łódzkiego, 1998, pp. 45–56.

Adamiak Barbara, Janusz Borkowski, *Metodyka pracy sędziego w sprawach administracyjnych*, Warszawa: Wolters Kluwer, 2009.

55 Wiliński, P., Karlik, P., in: Konstytucja RP, Vol. II, Komentarz do art. 87–243, ed. by M. Safian, L. Bosek, Warszawa: C.H. Beck, 2016, pp. 1037–1038.

56 Skoczylas, A., Swora, M., "Administrative judiciary in Poland in search for fairness and efficiency – an overview," *Transylvanian Review of Administrative Sciences* 2007, No. 19 E, pp. 124–125.

57 For instance, in granting assistants awards for exceptionally conscientious work, or in the evaluation of the assistant as his/her direct superior – cf. Stasiak, R., Chojnowska, Z., "Ocena pracowników sądowych," in: *Sprawny sąd. Zbiór dobrych praktyk*, ed. by Ł. Bojarski, Warszawa: C.H. Beck, 2004, p. 22.

Czeszejko-Sochacki, Zdzisław, judge of the Polish Constitutional Tribunal, to the judgment of the Polish Constitutional Tribunal, 21.10.1998, No. K. 24/98. Quoted in: Oniszczuk, Jerzy, *Konstytucja Rzeczypospolitej Polskiej w orzecznictwie Trybunału Konstytucyjnego*, Kraków: Zakamycze, 2000.

Ereciński, Tadeusz, Gudowski, Jacek, Iwulski, Józef, *Komentarz do prawa o ustroju sądów powszechnych i ustawy o Krajowej Radzie Sądownictwa*, ed. by J. Gudowski, Warszawa: LexisNexis, 2009.

Gardocka, Teresa, *Prejudycjalność w polskim procesie karnym*, Warszawa: Wydawnictwo Uniwersytetu Warszawskiego, 1987.

Hauser, Roman, "U progu reformy sądownictwa administracyjnego," *Państwo i Prawo*, 2002, No. 11, pp. 28–43.

Hauser, Roman, "Konstytucyjna zasada niezawisłości sędziowskiej," *Zeszyty Naukowe Sądownictwa Administracyjnego*, 2015, No. 1, pp. 9–22.

Hofmański, Piotr, *Samodzielność jurysdykcyjna sądu karnego*, Katowice: Wydawnictwo Uniwersytetu Śląskiego, 1988.

Konczewski, Tomasz, "Sporządzenie projektów uzasadnień orzeczeń przez asystenta sędziego," in: *Sprawny sąd. Zbiór dobrych praktyk*, ed. by Łukasz Bojarski, Warszawa: C.H. Beck, 2004, pp. 51–52.

Małgorzata Masternak-Kubiak, Tadeusz Kuczyński, *Prawo o ustroju sądów administracyjnych, Komentarz*, Warszawa: WoltersKluwer, 2009.

Laskowski, Michał, "Warunki pracy sędziego a godność sprawowanego przez niego urzędu," in: *Pozycja ustrojowa sędziego*, ed. by Ryszard Piotrowski, Warszawa: LEX Wolters Kluwer, 2015, pp. 66–83.

Łazarska, A., "Czy pensum sędziowskie narusza niezawisłość sędziowską?," *Krajowa Rada Sądownictwa*, 2016, No. 4, pp. 43–48.

Machura-Szczęsna, Jolanta, "Praktyczne aspekty pracy asystentów sędziów," in: *Sprawny sąd. Zbiór dobrych praktyk*, ed. by Ł. Bojarski, Warszawa: C.H. Beck, 2004, pp. 45–50.

Nowak, Tadeusz, "Zasada niezależności sądu w systemie organów władzy państwowej i w ujęciu nowego ustawodawstwa karnoprocesowego," in: *Nowe prawo procesowe. Zagadnienia wybrane, Księga ku czci Prof. Wiesława Daszkiewicza*, ed. by Tadeusz Nowak, Poznań: Printer, 1999, pp. 69–76.

Princ, Marcin, *Standardy dobrej administracji w prawie administracyjnym*, Poznań: Wydawnictwo Naukowe UAM, 2017.

Puczko, Aleksandra, § 1 in: Commentary to the Regulation on the detailed procedure of exercising supervision over the administrative activity of voivodship administrative courts, in: Ustrój Naczelnego Sądu Administracyjnego. Komentarz. Warszawa: LexisNexis, 2013.

Rzucidło-Grochowska, Iwona, "'Część historyczna' uzasadnienia orzeczenia sądowego," in: *Uzasadnienia decyzji stosowania prawa*, ed. by Iwona Rzucidło-Grochowska, Mateusz Grochowski, Warszawa: Wolters Kluwer 2015, pp. 170–199.

Skoczylas, Andrzej, "Administrative Proceedings and Judicial Review of Administration," in: *Handbook of Polish Law*, ed. by Wojciech Dajczak, Andrzej Szwarc, Paweł Wiliński, Warszawa - Bielsko-Biała: Park, 2011, pp. 381–402.

Skoczylas, Andrzej, "Kwestia zasadności odrębnej regulacji ustroju sądów administracyjnych w Polsce," *Iustitia - Kwartalnik Stowarzyszenia Sędziów Polskich*, 2011, No. 4, pp. 182–186.

Skoczylas, Andrzej, Swora, Mariusz, "Administrative judiciary in Poland in search for fairness and efficiency - an overview," *Transylvanian Review of Administrative Sciences* 2007, No. 19 E, pp. 38–54.

Skoczylas, Andrzej, "Wpływ organów administracji wymiaru sprawiedliwości na postępowanie dyscyplinarne w sądownictwie administracyjnym," *Ruch Prawniczy Ekonomiczny i Socjologiczny* 2020, No. 1, pp. 57–69.

Skrzydło, Wiesław, *Konstytucja Rzeczypospolitej Polskiej, Komentarz*, Kraków: Zakamycze, 1998.

Stasiak, Ryszarda, Chojnowska, Zofia, "Ocena pracowników sądowych," in: *Sprawny sąd. Zbiór dobrych praktyk*, ed. by Łukasz Bojarski, Warszawa: C.H. Beck, 2004.

Szmulik, Bogumił, *Pozycja ustrojowa Sądu Najwyższego w Rzeczypospolitej Polskiej*. Warszawa: C.H. Beck, 2008.

Świątkiewicz, Jerzy, *Naczelny Sąd Administracyjny. Komentarz do Ustawy*, Białystok: Prawo i Praktyka Gospodarcza, 1999.

Wajda, Dominik, "Status prawny asystenta sędziego," *Przegląd Sądowy*, 2006, No 3, pp. 208–220.

Wiliński, Paweł, Karlik, Piotr, in: Konstytucja RP, Vol. II, Komentarz do art. 87–243, ed. by Marek Safian, Leszek Bosek, Warszawa: C.H. Beck, 2016.

Wojciechowski, Bartosz, Zirk-Sadowski, Marek, "Justification as the limitation of the discretionary power of the administrative judge," in: *Discretionary Power of Public Administration Its Scope and Control*, ed. by Leszek Leszczyński, Adam Szot, Frankfurt am Main: Peter Lang Edition, 2017, pp. 137–150.

Wyrzykowski, Mirosław, in: *Zasady podstawowe polskiej konstytucji*, ed. by Wojciech Sokolewicz, Warszawa: Wydawnictwo Sejmowe, 1998, pp. 80–83.

Zimmermann, Jan, *Aksjomaty sądownictwa administracyjnego*, Warszawa: Wolters Kluwer 2020.

Ziółkowska, Agnieszka, Gronkiewicz, Anna, *Organizacja pracy biurowej w administracji*, Katowice: Forma studio, 2014.

Żurawik, Artur, *Ustrój sądownictwa w Polsce*, Warszawa: C.H. Beck, 2013.

Jurisprudence

European Court of Human Rights

Judgment of the ECtHR, 28.6.1978, *König v. Germany*, No. 6232/73, LEX No. 80802.

Judgment of ECtHR, 9.12.1994, *Schouten and Meldrum v. Netherlands*, No. 19005/91, 19006/91, LEX No. 80505.

Ruling of ECtHR, 23.04.2002, *Jerzy Tartak v. Poland*, No. 46015/99, LEX No. 52957.

Judgment of ECtHR, 11.12.2001, *Fuchs v. Poland*, No 33870/96, LEX No. 49866.

Judgment of ECtHR, 23.7.2002, *Janosevic v. Sweden*, No 34619/97, LEX No. 75486.

judgment of ECtHR, 15.6.2004, *Piekara v. Poland*, No 77741/01, LEX No. 122542.

Polish Constitutional Tribunal

Judgment of the Polish Constitutional Tribunal, 21.10.1998, K 24/98, OTK 1998, No. 6, item 97.

Judgment of the Polish Constitutional Tribunal, 22.3.2000, P 12/98, OTK ZU 2000, No. 2, item 67.

Judgment of the Polish Constitutional Tribunal, 12.12.2012, K 1/12, OTK ZU-A 2012, No. 11, item 134.

Polish Supreme Court

Judgment of the Supreme Court, 22.2.2017, III KRS 2/17, LEX No 2271451.

Sources of law

The Constitution of the Republic of Poland of 2.4.1997, Journal of Laws 1997, No. 78, item 483 with subsequent amendments.

Law on the System of Common Courts Act of 27.07.2001, Journal of Laws of 2019, item 52, with subsequent amendments.

Regulation of the President of the Republic of Poland, 29.3.2018 – By-laws of the Supreme Court, Journal of Laws, item 660, with subsequent amendments.

Internet sources

Gonera, Katarzyna, "Status prawny asystentów sędziów," in: *Zatrudnianie pracowników sądów z perspektywy prawa pracy i zarządzania*, ed. by Artur Rycak, publ. https://sip.lex.pl/#/monograph/369307153/256865 (access date: 27.03.2020).

Tuleja, Piotr, "Realizacja zasady pierwszeństwa Konstytucji w orzecznictwie Trybunału Konstytucyjnego," in: *Stosowanie Konstytucji RP w świetle zasady jej nadrzędności (wybrane problemy)*, Kraków: Kantor Wydawniczy Zakamycze, 2003, publ. https://sip.lex.pl/#/monograph/369135424/252312 (access date: 2.04.2020).

Judgment of the Supreme Administrative Court, 24.01.2014, I OSK 2037/13, publ. http://orzeczenia.nsa.gov.pl (access date: 2.04.2020).

Andrzej Paduch[1]

Supervision over a court as a tool to protect the right to have a court case heard within a reasonable time

Abstract: The timeframe for court hearings is a vital aspect of the right to a fair trial. On the level of international law it was formulated in art. 6 sec. 1 ECHR. The right to a have a case heard within a reasonable time means constant court's activities to eventually adjudicate in the case. States introduces necessary regulations to secure it. There are two types of such legal measures: supervisory measures, which focus on disciplinary consequences for judges, and complaint measures, which consist of various forms of compensation claims. There are different measures in different countries. Moreover, the mixed instrument, in which the complaint impacts not only pecuniary but also disciplinary consequences, is in use in some countries. The measures referring to court timeframes are a significant part of supervision over courts, which should not be limited to disciplinary matters only, but should also, if necessary, be applied to protect the individual against the damage caused by the excessive length of the proceedings.

Keywords: right to a fair trial, supervision over courts, disciplinary measures, complaint measures, court proceedings, delay in court proceedings

1. Introduction

The right to a fair trial fulfils its role not only if it involves the right of the individual to take legal action but also if the case is to be resolved within a certain time frame.[2] A court trial is associated with legal uncertainty: by initiating a court dispute, a party seeks to objectify certain rights or obligations. This uncertainty, by its very nature, must be temporary and exist for as short a time as possible. The uncertain duration of court procedures makes the right to a fair trial incomplete and reduces litigation to a lengthy discussion, which is purely

---

1 Andrzej Paduch, PhD, Adam Mickiewicz University in Poznań, (Poland). ORCID – 0000-0002-0033-011X.

2 Z. Kmieciak, *Postepowanie administracyjne i sądowoadministracyjne a prawo europejskie*, Warszawa: Wolters Kluwer, 2010, p. 102, A. Zieliński, "Postępowanie przed NSA w świetle prawa do sprawiedliwego procesu sądowego," *Państwo i Prawo*, No. 7 (569), 1992, p. 15.

cognitive. Thus, the unreasonable exceeding of the timeframe of hearing a case must be regarded as a substantial violation of the right to a fair trial. From this perspective, the question of the duration of a hearing should also be considered as falling under the supervision over court activities.

The thesis of this study is as follows: the right to have a case heard within a reasonable time, established in international law, should be secured by the measures of court supervision provided for in domestic law systems. The instruments of supervision in this field may be of different types. They include, firstly, the disciplinary supervision over the court or judge examining the case, and secondly – the compensation due as a result of lengthy case examination. The study addresses the issue of measures in court proceedings that concern rights and obligations derived from public law. Counteracting violations in this category of cases should be considered as particularly important. A quick decision on the public-law rights or obligation of an individual (i.e. a building permit, an administrative penalty, or awarding a specific benefit under social assistance) is of key importance for the assessment of the state's efficiency as such. However, the presented comments also apply to other categories of court disputes, in particular – civil disputes.

The analysis of the issue is carried out with the use of dogmatic-legal and comparative methods, consisting in the analysis of the provisions of international law, in particular the European Convention of Human Rights (ECHR),[3] and selected legal regulations of European countries. This is complemented by reference to the jurisprudence of the European Court of Human Rights (ECtHR), as well as the research work of the European Commission for the Efficiency of Justice (CEPEJ)[4] and the doctrine. The structure of the study is as follows: first the issues of international law are analysed, then consideration turns to the problem of legal instruments that guarantee the party the possibility to initiate extensive supervision over court proceedings, in the context of its possible excessive length, and finally selected examples of regulations functioning in practice are provided.

3 Convention for the Protection of Human Rights and Fundamental Freedom, Rome, 4.11.1950, English version available on website www.conventions.coe.int (access date: 10.12.2020).

4 The above-mentioned reports are available online on the website https://www.coe.int/en/web/cepej/country-profiles (access date: 6.01.2021).

2. Timeframes of court cases in international law

At the outset, it is necessary to acknowledge that the issue of the speed of the court hearings is not a new phenomenon. The problem of excessively long court proceedings and the negative impact of this phenomenon was first noticed in Roman Law, when a Latin maxim *in diem vivere in lege sunt detestabilis* (Eng.: delays in justice are hateful) was formulated. Today the phrase "justice delayed is justice denied" is used to describe the problem.[5] The concept of quick court proceedings may be considered not only as an ethical or professional matter, but primarily as a part of the foundations of the rule law. For this reason the issue of the right to a hearing within a reasonable time is regulated at the level of international law.

From the European perspective, the ECHR is of the greatest importance, as well as – albeit in a complementary scope – the Charter of Fundamental Rights of The European Union (hereinafter: the Charter).[6] The question of the timeframe of a court hearing has also been a subject of some analysis made by CEPEJ.

The provision of article 6 sec. 1 ECHR provides that everyone has the right to a fair and public hearing within a reasonable time by an independent and impartial tribunal established by law. Thus, the indicated provision establishes the obligation of the signatory to the ECHR to guarantee to individuals that court cases are heard within a reasonable time. Two doubts arise in connection with this provision. Firstly, does the discussed provision also apply to administrative court cases, and secondly, what exactly is the examination of a case "within a reasonable time"? Referring to the first question, it should be noted that the provision of article 6 sec. 1 of the ECHR relates directly to a civil or criminal court trial. However, it also seems to apply to proceedings in the field of administrative court cases. Such a conclusion stems from the extensive jurisprudence of the ECtHR.[7] The Court recognises the broad meaning of the rights and obligations of a civil nature, recognising as them also those resulting from the public law of a state.[8] The ECtHR assumes that the subject of such cases is, in fact, the rights or

---

5 T. Sourdin and N. Burstyner, *Justice Delayed is Justice Denied* (January 24, 2016), SSRN, https://poseidon01.ssrn.com (access date: 9.01.2021).

6 Official Journal "C," 26.10.2012, pp. 391–407.

7 The jurisprudence is presented in detail in *Guide of the ECtHR on the application of article 6 – Right to a fair trial (civil limb)*, Strasbourg 2020, www.echr.coe.int (access date: 19.11.2020) and in the study by F. Edel, *The length of civil and criminal proceedings in the case-law of the European Court of Human Right*, Strasbourg: Council of Europe Publishing, 2007, pp. 7 ff.

8 *Guide...*, p. 12. See also judgements of ECtHR: *Georgiadis v. Greece*, 29.05.1997, No. 21522/93, § 34, *Airey v. Ireland*, 9.10.1979, No. 6289/73, § 21, *Gorzkowski v. Poland*,

obligations of private entities. For this reason, the ECtHR includes them in the category of civil matters.

Therefore, as rights and obligations of a civil law nature, the ECtHR recognises permits of various types (e.g. for the sale of land, running a private clinic, building permits, permits to perform a specific profession or serve alcoholic beverages[9]) or revocations (this also applies to disciplinary proceedings undertaken by professional self-government bodies, under which special obligations are imposed on members of the professional self-government, e.g. a disciplinary penalty, or their professional rights are limited, e.g. the right to exercise their profession[10]). Moreover, in one of its judgments the ECtHR explicitly stated that a case concerning an action to cancel an administrative decision violating the party's rights is also a case in which civil rights and obligations are adjudicated.[11] Therefore, there can be no doubt that requirements regarding the length of the trial also apply to litigation concerning rights or obligations of a public law nature, regardless of where they are located doctrinally or normatively in national law.[12]

The second issue is the problem of what constitutes a "reasonable time" for hearing the case. The provision of article 6 sec. 1 of the ECHR does not define this term. A linguistic interpretation indicates that it means the examination of a case in which the activities of the proceedings are undertaken continuously, i.e. there are only necessary and reasonable breaks between individual activities.[13] The ECtHR has repeatedly stated that the concept of a hearing within a reasonable time should be understood as one in which there is no delay, threatening

19.11.2020, No. 65546/13, § 8, *König v. Federal Republic of Germany*, 28.06.1978, No. 6232/73, § 90.

9 Judgements of ECtHR: *Aldo and Jean-Baptiste Zanatta v. France*, 28.03.2000, No. 38042/97, § 22–26, *Allan Jacobsson v. Sweden*, 25.10.1989, No. 10842/84, § 72–74, *Skärby v. Sweden*, 28.06.1990, No. 12258/86, § 26–30, *Tre Traktörer Aktiebolag v. Sweden*, 7.07.1989, No. 10873/84, § 43–44, *Feldbrugge v. the Netherlands*, 29.05.1986, No. 8562/79, § 26–40, *König v. the Federal Republic of Germany*, 28.06.1978, No. 6232/73, § 98 – see *Guide…*, p. 13. See also F. Edel, *The Length…*, pp. 8–9.

10 *Guide…*, p. 13, judgements of ECtHR: *Benthem v. The Netherlands*, 23.10.1985, No. 8848/80, § 36, *Le Compte van Leuven and De Meyere v. Belgium*, 23.06.1981, No. 6878/75, *Philis v. Greece (No. 2)*, 27.06.1997, No. 19773/92§ 45, *Tre Traktörer Aktiebolag v. Sweden*, 7.07.1989, No. 10873/84, § 43–44.

11 Judgement of ECtHR, *The Geouffre de la Pradelle v. France*, 16.12.1992, No. 12964/87.

12 It has to be highlighted that in some matters, such as foreigners or financial cases, the ECtHR refuses to include them in the scope of article 6 – cf. *Guide…*, p. 18.

13 The ECtHR made this point in its judgement *Beaumartin v. France*, 24.11.1994, No. 15287/89, § 33.

the effectiveness and credibility of the proceedings.[14] It should be noted that the ECtHR emphasises the effect of delays on the party's opinion about the procedural law being unfair, partial and ineffective.[15] The problem of a reasonable time for hearing a case should therefore refer not only to its simple, calendar-based approach but also to the continuity of the actions of the case being examined, expressed in the ongoing analysis and response by court-to-court documents, efficient organisation of its proceedings, and finally in the fast and complete issuance of justified judgements.

At the same time, the ECtHR indicates that the "reasonable time" should be counted from the first action that directly aims at launching the proceedings, e.g. bringing an action to the competent court.[16] However, if the precondition for the initiation of court proceedings is that the case is handled by an administrative authority, the time at which the case is examined by the administrative authorities should be counted towards the duration of the court case.[17] Therefore, in administrative court cases, which are usually of a verificatory nature in relation to previous administrative acts or activities, the problem of the duration of the proceedings is of substantial importance. While for professionals such as attorneys or judges administrative proceedings and subsequent court proceedings are separate matters, for lay persons it is just one and the same case. For the same reason, the reasonable time limit for a case hearing may not be subject to any kind of limitation, such as a specific instance or certain incidental issues.[18] It is also obvious that the court hearing the appeal cannot be responsible for the slowness of the authority which issued the appealed decision. However, the action taken in such a case cannot be oblivious to the prior failure to ensure timely proceedings.

---

14 *Guide…*, p. 82, judgements of ECtHR: *H. v. France*, 24.10.1989, No. 10073/82, § 58, *Katte Klitsche de la Grange v. Italy*, 27.10.1994, No. 12539/86 § 61, *Keaney v. Ireland*, 30.04.2020, No. 72060/17, § 86.

15 Judgements of ECtHR: *Scordino v. Italy*, 29.03.2006, No. 36813/97, § 224, *Martins Moreira v. Portugal*, 26.10.1988, No. 11371/85, § 44.

16 Cf. *Guide…*, p. 82, F. Edel, *The Length…*, p. 19, judgements of ECtHR: *Styranowski v. Poland*, 30.10.1998, No. 28616/95, § 45–46, *Poiss v. Austria*, 23.04.1987, No. 9816/82, *Bock v. Germany*, 29.03.1989, No. 11118/84, *Kirinčič v. Croatia*, 30.07.2020, No. 31386/17, § 73, *Bognár v. Hungary*, 20.10.2020, No. 75757/14, § 25.

17 Judgements of ECtHR: *König v. Germany*, 28.06.1978, No. 6232/73, § 98, *X. v. France*, 31.03.1992, No. 18020/91, § 31, *Bognár v. Hungary*, 20.10.2020, No. 75757/14, § 25.

18 Judgements of ECtHR: *Pretto and Others v. Italy*, 8.12.1983, No. 7984/77, § 37.

Moreover, the ECtHR points out that it is not possible to establish a single, reasonable time for all cases to be settled.[19] Therefore, when determining a reasonable time for hearing a case, one should refer to the circumstances of a specific case, taking into account factual or legal complexity, the multiplicity of entities, the behaviour of the complainant, expressed in the conscientious fulfilment of procedural obligations, the actions of the relevant authorities (bodies examining the case) in terms of the organisation and course of court sessions, the order of activities, or the importance of the subject of the dispute.[20] Regional or local conditions are also important. Both the doctrine and CEPEJ reports note that a "reasonable time" in one place (court, region) is not necessarily reasonable in another.[21] At the same time, it should be emphasised once again that in the case of administrative court proceedings, one should also take into account the complex nature of the administrative court case. When assessing the time of its examination, one should also take into account administrative proceedings preceding court actions.

On a marginal note, it should be mentioned that the right to have a case heard within a reasonable time has also been regulated in the Charter, which obviously

19 Cf. *Guide…*, p. 83.

20 Cf. judgements of ECtHR: *Parinov v. Ukraine*, 10.12.2020, No. 48398/17, § 59, *Hadobás v. Hungary*, 10.12.2020, No. 3686/20, § 6, *Melnikov v. Ukraine*, 22.10.2020, No. 66753/11, § 39, *Mirjana Marić v. Croatia*, 30.07.2020, No. 9849/15, § 89, *Satakunnan Markkinapörssi Oy and Satamedia Oy v. Finland*, 27.06.2017, No. 931/13, § 214, *Kisházi and others v. Hungary*, 22.10.2020, No. 28814/19, § 39, *Comingersoll S.A. v. Portugal*, 6.04.2000, No. 35382/97, § 19, *Keaney v. Ireland*, 30.04.2020, No. 72060/17, § 85, 89, 90, *Katte Klitsche de la Grange v. Italy*, 27.10.1994, No. 12539/86, § 55, *H. v. The United Kingdom*, 8.07.1987, No. 9580/81, § 72, *Humen v. Poland*, 15.10.1999, No. 26614/95, § 63, *Wiesinger v. Austria*, 30.10.1991, No. 11796/85, § 57, *Vernillo v. France*, 20.02.1991, No. 11889/85, § 34, *Frydlender v. France*, 27.06.2000, No. 30979/96, § 43, *Obermeier v. Austria*, 28.06.1990, No. 11761/85, § 72, *Pretto and Others v. Italy*, 8.12.1983, No. 7984/77, § 37, *Buchholz v. Germany*, 6.05.1981, No. 7759/77, § 49, *A. and Others v. Denmark*, 8.02.1996, No. 20826/92, § 78 – 81, *Politikin v. Poland*, 27.04.2004, No. 68930/01, § 32, *Grigoryan v. Armenia*, 10.07.2012, No. 3627/06, § 127. This aspect was highlighted in the CEPEJ Report by N. Rubotham, I. Borzova, *The Role of Parties and Practitioners in Avoiding or Reducing Delay in Disposal of Court Proceedings*, Strasbourg 2018, https://rm.coe.int (access date: 10.12.2020). See also F. Edel, *The Length…*, pp. 34 ff.

21 See CEPEJ Report by M. Fabri, P. Langbroek, *Delay in Court Proceedings: A Preliminary Inquiry into the Relation Between the Demands of the Reasonable Time Requirements of Article 6, 1 ECHR and Their Consequences for Judges and Judicial Administration in the Civil Criminal and Administrative Justice Chain*, Strasbourg 2003, https://rm.coe.int (access date: 10.12.2020) and the literature cited therein.

has a limited scope in comparison to the ECHR.[22] For this reason, it should be assumed that the Charter, in this field, is rather an introduction of the Council of Europe's regulations regarding the right to a fair trial to EU law.[23] On the basis of the Charter, the doctrine highlighted the importance of the timeframe of the proceedings in the context of legal remedy. The lengthy court proceedings make the remedy ineffective since it may contribute to the alleged violation itself.[24] Therefore, Member States are obliged to guarantee certain legal measures to counteract this kind of contribution. This leads to the conclusion that the basis of international legal standards in the context of the ECHR right to have a case heard within a reasonable time are plain and standardised.

3. Typology of measures of supervision

The right to have a case heard within a reasonable time is regulated not only internationally but also – and perhaps primarily – in the domestic legal systems. International law does not indicate the way in which this issue should be regulated by a particular state.[25] However, the general importance of such clear

22 The provision of article 51 sec. 1 of the Charter states that the provisions of the Charter apply to the Member States only in so far as they implement EU law.

23 Such a combination of two legal orders is an example of a phenomenon characteristic of contemporary law systems – their multicentricity. The multi-level nature of regulations enacted by various authorities or organisations leads to the formation of the legal system as a kind of mosaic in which the jurisprudence of one legal act affects another. For more on this, see E. Łętowska, "Multicentryczność współczesnego systemu prawa i jej konsekwencje," *Państwo i Prawo*, No. 4 (710) 2005, pp. 3 ff., Z. Kmieciak, *Postępowanie…*, p. 24 ff, A. Wróbel, "Autonomia proceduralna państw członkowskich. Zasada efektywności i zasada efektywnej ochrony sądowej w prawie Unii Europejskiej," *Ruch Prawniczy, Ekonomiczny i Socjologiczny*, No. 67 (1), 2005, p. 35 ff.

24 W. Piątek, "The right to an effective remedy in European Law: significance, content and interaction," *China-EU Law Journal*, No. 6, 2019, p. 171.

25 F. Edel, *The Length…*, p. 14 and the case-law cited therein, in particular the judgement of ECtHR, *Johnston and others v. Ireland*, 18.12.1986, No. 9697/82, § 77. It seems that regulating this issue in the ECHR would be contrary to the principle of procedural autonomy of states – *lex fori processualis*. According to this concept, the way procedural law is shaped at the national level is left to the free regulation of the state and is not of interest to international law, except for fundamental issues – see K. Przybyłowski, *Prawo prywatne międzynarodowe. Część ogólna*, Warszawa 1935, p. 184, quoted in: J. Jodłowski, "Zasady przewodnie polskiego międzynarodowego prawa procesowego cywilnego," in: *Księga pamiątkowa ku czci Prof. Kamila Stefki*, ed. by W. Berutowicz, J. Jodłowski, J. Fiema, W. Siedlecki, E. Wengerek, Warszawa-Wrocław: Państwowe Wydawnictwo Naukowe, 1967, pp. 119–145, W. Grunsky, "Lex

regulations is recognised in ECHR judgements themselves.[26] A popular solution is to establish the right to have a case heard within a reasonable time at a constitutional level.[27] However, no such obligation arises from international law.

The mere declaration of this right being stipulated in law does not guarantee that it will be respected in each individual case. In addition to its explicit (or implicit) normative approach, it therefore seems necessary to develop instruments which guarantee its execution. The literature and jurisprudence indicate two basic directions of state activity in this area. The first concerns introducing "soft" regulations into national legal systems. Their purpose is to eliminate those factors that cause delays in settling cases.[28] In particular, this involves enacting a law that favours the active role of the court, judge and participants in the proceedings. The CEPEJ noted that there are important aspects, such as the definition of the objectives of the procedure, an indication of the methods of its implementation, current information about the state of affairs – including through information systems and the training of judges.[29]

However, these mechanisms are not always sufficient. Hence, it is necessary to take the second direction: the introduction of "hard" instruments, that is, supervision over the activity of courts in the scope of hearing cases without undue delay. These instruments, in a way, force the court or judge to take action in a case so that there is no delay in considering the case. From the theoretical viewpoint, it should be assumed that the discussed instruments, due to their

---

fori und Verfahrensrecht," *Zeitschrift fur Zivilprozesss*, No. 89 (3), 1976, p. 241. Having analysed the freedom of domestic regulation in the field of the right to a fair trial under EU law, W. Piątek came to the conclusion that it is justified by the different legal traditions, culture and experience of each country – see W. Piątek, *The right…*, p. 170.

26 See judgement of ECtHR, *Keaney v. Ireland*, 30.04.2020, No. 72060/17, § 109.

27 See e.g. article 45 sec. 1 of the Constitution of Republic of Poland or article 48 sec. 2 of the Constitution of Republic of Slovakia. An interesting Swedish solution should be mentioned – § 19 of the Form of Government Act of 28.02.1974 states that no law or other normative act may enter into force that is contrary to the obligations of Sweden, resulting from the European Convention for the Protection of Human Rights and Fundamental Freedoms. In this approach, it seems that the right to a hearing within a reasonable time has been incorporated into the domestic legal order of Sweden in a specific blanket manner. A similar solution is also provided for in the Constitution of Germany (Article 25 of Basic Law for The Federal Republic of Germany), with reference to the general principles of international law.

28 F. Edel, *The Length…*, p. 16.

29 See M. Fabri, P. Langbroek, *Delay…*, and the literature mentioned therein.

features, take one of two theoretical forms: a supervisory instrument or a complaint instrument.

The use of a supervisory instrument consists in introducing into the legal system of the state the specific powers of judicial authorities. That includes access to the files of the supervised courts, participation in activities undertaken by these courts, requests from courts or judges for explanations or for the removal of deficiencies identified by the supervisory authority. In this approach, supervision is structured vertically, i.e. a higher court or other supervisory body controls a lower court, e.g. by carrying out an inspection or obliging it to provide specific information on the status of a case or actions taken in a given case. Supervisory activities may be undertaken in any case in which the supervising authority becomes aware of any irregularities, unreliability or lawfulness of the court's activity. Therefore, actions will be taken ex officio and will not depend on the submission of a complaint in this regard by the party. It should be noted that, of course, there is no prohibition of applying by a party or other entity (e.g. MPs intervening or journalists) for specific supervisory actions – they are, however, only initiators for the ex officio activity of a supervisor.

On the other hand, the complaint instrument consists in granting an individual (the party) the right to lodge a complaint with a supervisory court or other authority for not hearing the case within a reasonable time. The court hearing the complaint then examines the duration of the proceedings and, if it finds that the case was protracted, orders the supervised court to act immediately and issues appropriate recommendations. A judgement on excessive length, depending on the legal system, may also contain a preliminary ruling for a party to subsequently seek damages or compensation, or which awards it already.

The complaint is therefore of a dual nature. On the one hand, it is an instrument of supervision – it leads to the order to take specific actions in a specific case – but, on the other hand, the procedure is initiated at the request of a party. This means that the supervisory authority is obliged to take actions, unlike in the case of supervisory instruments in which information from a party may be ignored. The complaint instrument therefore consists in giving a party the right to initiate supervision of a specific court case. Moreover, due to the fact that the party initiates the complaint procedure, it should receive back full information on the examination of its complaint, or even be able to appeal against the decision issued in this manner, if it is unfavourable.

A particularly important role of a complaint about the excessive length of court proceedings is expressed in the fact that it protects not only the individual interest (which is expressed in granting the party the initiative in supervision and the possibility of receiving compensation for damages caused by prolonged court proceedings), but also the general interest. A complaint about the excessive length of court proceedings allows for verification of whether a given judge or judges of a given court undertake the hearings of cases, how quickly they proceed, and with what effect. Therefore, the supervisory nature of a complaint results in many cases in a more efficient verification of judges and the organisation of the work of courts – supervision is performed not as part of periodical inspections but following a signal about irregularities from a direct entity.[30] Moreover, the systemic aspect of the complaint instrument is to be noticed. The delays at a certain stage in cases of the same type should be a reason to introduce appropriate changes in the law, aimed at removing the causes of such delays. In particular, the important role of complaints about the excessive length of proceedings is thus also expressed in the fact that it allows a catalogue of delays to be constructed, to examine their causes and, if those causes are systemic in nature – to remove them.

The above-mentioned measures may be graphically described, as below (Fig. 1):

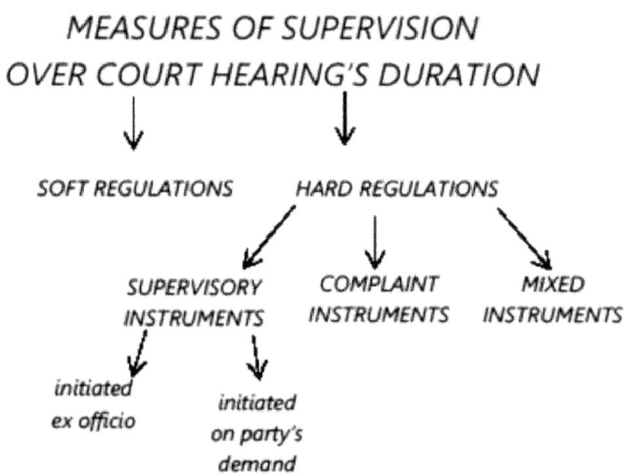

Fig. 1. A graphic presentation of measures of supervision over a court hearing's duration

30 Obviously this does not exclude introduction of regulations in the field of ex officio supervision.

4. Examples of measures

As indicated above, the right of a party to have the case heard within a reasonable time is one of the foundations of the right to a fair trial. One of the guarantees that this right will be respected is ex officio supervision over the courts, another is to grant a party the right to bring a complaint about the excessive length of the proceedings. The regulations in this area adopted in various legal systems can be divided into several models.

The first type of adopted regulation emphasises the supervisory nature of a complaint about the excessive length of proceedings. In this model, the party is entitled to file a complaint which initiates supervisory activities over the court or judge conducting the case. However, these activities may also be undertaken ex officio, in the event that the competent court or authority becomes aware of the violation of the party's right. As a result of examining the complaint, supervisory or disciplinary measures are taken by the court or judge.

An example of this type of legislation is found in Danish law. It is included in the Danish code of judicial procedure – Administration of Justice Act (*Retsplejeloven*).[31] The procedure has been uniformly regulated in relation to various court proceedings, and the discussed regulation concerns in particular, and not only, the length of court proceedings. Paragraph 48 of the Code of Judicial Procedure provides for the judge's liability for such neglect of duties which does not constitute a breach of criminal law, as well as for improper or indecent behaviour. The basis of that liability may therefore be many different events, including, in particular, the excessive length of court proceedings.[32] The category of violation of a party's right to a hearing within a reasonable time has not, however, been explicitly separated. There is no doubt, however, that lengthy handling of a case should be regarded as a neglect of judicial duties. The consequence of that negligence is the imposition by the president of the court or the immediate superior court (§ 1a p. 3 and 4 and § 48 Administration of Justice Act) of a specific disciplinary sanction on the judge – a warning. What is extremely

31 Official Journal of Law, 12.12.2014.

32 It must be highlighted that the question of hearing a case in a reasonable time is one of the main goals of court proceedings in Nordic countries – see C.S. Petersen, *A Comparative Perspective on Recent Nordic Reforms of Civil Justice*, in: *The Future of Civil Litigation: Access to Courts and Court-Annexed Mediation in the Nordic Countries*, ed. by L. Ervo and A. Nylund, Cham Heidelberg New York Dordrecht London: Springer, 2014, p. 9 ff.

important is that these actions can be taken not only as a result of a complaint brought by a party to the proceedings but also ex officio.

The second solution emphasises the compensatory nature of the complaint. In this case a party, by bringing a complaint about the length of the proceedings, may claim compensation for the damage caused by the delay in examining the case. An example of the above is the regulation introduced to German law by the Act on Legal Redress for Excessive Length of Court Proceedings and of Criminal Investigation Proceedings of 24 November 2011 (*Gesetz über den Rechtsschutz bei überlangen Gerichtsverfahren und strafrechtlichen Ermittlungsverfahren*)[33] which amended The Law on The System of Courts (*Gerichstsfersassungsgesetz*, GVG).[34] These provisions also apply to administrative court proceedings pursuant to § 173 of The Act on Administrative Courts Proceedings (*Verwaltungsgerichtsordnung*, VwGO).[35]

The regulations provide for the following structure: a party who has found itself "at a disadvantage" as a result of prolonged court proceedings may apply for damages to be awarded itself. It is a flat-rate amount of EUR 1,200 for each year of delay. In exceptional cases, this amount may be increased or decreased. Importantly, the procedure is initiated at the request of a party, submitted not more than once every six months. At the same time, the court hearing the complaint has the power to refrain from considering the length complaint until the end of the proceedings in which the excessive length is alleged to have occurred (§ 201 (3) GVG).

Thus, the German legal system directly refers to the category of excessive length of proceedings as a negative procedural occurrence that entitles the party to be awarded compensation. The discussed regulation of the GVG provide for a specific action for payment in connection with the violation of the party's right to hear the case within a reasonable time. The action is therefore compensatory in nature. Whether the excessive length of the proceedings has occurred is considered by taking into account the complexity of the case, the importance of the subject of the dispute, and the conduct of participants and third parties in the case.[36] Importantly, the German model adopts the concept of a "set of cases" already present in the ECHR: excessive length of proceedings is therefore not

33 Official Journal of Law, 2.12.2011, p. 2302.
34 Official Journal of Law, 9.05.1975, p. 1077, with subsequent amendments.
35 Official Journal of Law, 21.01.1960, p. 17 with subsequent amendments.
36 See the judgement of the Regional Social Court in Hamburg (*Landessozialgericht Hamburg*) Urt. v. 30.10.2014, Az.: L 1 SF 16/13 ESV.

so much related to the proceedings in a given instance or at a given stage of the case, but more broadly in relation to the entire period during which a given case is considered (§ 198 (6) GVG). This regulation is supplemented by the provision according to which the complaint may be granted only if the circumstances of the case indicate that it will not be completed within a reasonable time (§ 198 (3) GVG). It therefore excludes those cases where an award of damages could be made solely because the legal proceedings are long, but for reasons other than violation of the party's right to have the case heard within a reasonable time.

A compensatory complaint model was also introduced in other countries – for example in Italy (Act No 89/2001, the so-called Pinto Act[37]). The Italian model provides that a party is entitled to file a complaint where the case has not been dealt with within a reasonable time. The Act stipulates that a reasonable period covers the examination of the case within 3 years at first instance and 2 years at second instance (Article 2 (2) bis Pinto Act). When assessing whether the case was lengthy, the applicant's behaviour is also taken under consideration (Article 2 of the Pinto Act). The amount of compensation is determined separately for each case. However, the Act indicates that it should not be lower than EUR 400 or higher than EUR 800 for each year of excessive length of the litigation (Article 2-bis Pinto Act).

The third model of the adopted solutions should also be mentioned. This is the mixed model, which combines compensatory and supervisory measures. An example of such regulations is the Polish Act of 17 June 2004 on a complaint about the violation of a party's right to have a case heard in preparatory proceedings conducted or supervised by a prosecutor and in court proceedings without undue delay.[38] The complaint has been uniformly regulated in court proceedings (civil, criminal and administrative court) and criminal preliminary investigations.[39] The assumption of the act in terms of administrative court proceedings is as follows: if the entity (for instance, in administrative court

37 Act of 24.03.2001 – Provision of equitable reparation in case of violation of the reasonable term of the trial and modification of article 375 of the code of civil procedure No. 89/2001, Official Journal of Law of Italy, 3.04.2001, No. 78. For more on the Italian model, see G. Esposito, S. Lanau, S. Pompe, *Judicial System Reform in Italy – A Key to Growth*, International Monetary Fund Working Paper 2014/14/32, https://www.imf.org/external/pubs/ft/wp/2014/ wp1432.pdf (access date: 8.12.2020).

38 Official Journal of Law 2018, item 75 with subsequent amendments.

39 Moreover, these provisions will also be applied in the event of excessive length of proceedings relating to the enforcement of a court judgment (article 1 (2) of the Act).

proceedings it is the complainant and a participant with the rights of a party[40]) believes that the right to have a case heard within a reasonable time has been violated, may file a complaint. The complainant may demand: a sole declaration of violation of the right and recommendations as to the further hearing of the case. Additionally a lump-sum compensation may be awarded (article 3 (6) and article 12 of the Act).

The regulation thus pursues two goals. Firstly, it enables the supervision of a specific case pending before a court. Secondly, it is a specific, simplified procedure for awarding compensation for damages caused by lengthy court proceedings. A specific safeguard for the efficiency of the procedure in question is the deadline provided for in the act for considering a complaint: it should be examined within two months of receiving the complaint (article 11 of the Act). The complaint is examined by the court superior to the court before which the proceedings are pending (article 4 (1) of the Act). In the above-mentioned administrative court proceedings, complaints are examined by the Supreme Administrative Court (article 4 (3) of the Act).

A similar regulation was introduced to Croatian law. According to article 27 of the Court Act,[41] a party is entitled to file an application to the superior court for protection of the right to a hearing within a reasonable time. The application is decided in an urgent procedure that lasts no longer than six months. If the superior court decides positively on the merits of the application, the timeframe for hearing the case is settled and the party is granted compensation. It has to be highlighted that although the compensation is paid by a Republic of Croatia, the judge who heard the case can also be required to pay the compensation, if the excessive length occurred due to the intention or gross negligence of the judge (Article 106 (3) of the Act).

The regulations presented above are based on the fact that the issue of whether or not there has been a violation of a party's right to have a case heard within a reasonable time is decided either by the court or another body superior to the court, or the judge hearing the case. However, in European legal systems there is another type of regulation. It emphasises the constitutional origin of the right to have a case heard within a reasonable time. In this approach, the complaint is examined by the constitutional court. An example is the regulation in the law

40 See article 32 of the Act of 30.08.2002 on Administrative Court Proceedings, Official Journal of Law 2019, item 2325 with subsequent amendments.

41 Courts Act, Journal of Law No. 150/05 with subsequent amendments.

of Slovakia. According to article 127 paragraph 1 of the Slovak Constitution,[42] the Constitutional Court adjudicates on complaints from natural persons or legal persons if they alleged violation of their fundamental rights or freedoms, or human rights and fundamental freedoms arising from an international agreement that the Slovak Republic has ratified and announced in the manner prescribed by law, if the rights and freedoms are not resolved by another court. If the violation of the rights or freedoms referred to in paragraph 1 arose as a result of an omission, the Constitutional Court may order that whoever violated this right or freedom must act in the case (Article 127 (2), second sentence, of the Slovak Constitution). The Constitutional Court may, in its ruling admitting the complaint, grant to the person whose rights specified in paragraph 1 have been violated, appropriate financial compensation (article 127 (3) of the Slovak Constitution). The Slovak regulation therefore entrusts the Constitutional Court to rule on the excessive length of proceedings. Therefore, the competence to hear disputes of the type in question is placed high.

5. Conclusions

The above research leads to the following conclusions: first, the right to a court hearing within a reasonable time is one of the fundaments of the right to a fair trial. Only when court cases are heard without any delays is this right itself guaranteed. Court proceedings that extend beyond the necessary time are negative phenomenon for both economic and social reasons. They also undermine confidence in the judiciary and state as such.

Secondly, the problem of delays in proceedings as a violation of a party's right to a fair trial is already recognised in international law. The right to a have a case heard within a reasonable time has already been recognised under the ECHR and the Charter. Thus, this right should be treated as having a strong normative, as well as axiological, basis in European domestic legal orders. International law regulation of this right enforces the introduction of solutions to national legal systems that ensure fast and efficient justice. Such regulations must also include provisions on the supervision of the speed and efficiency of court proceedings.

Third, supervision over the speed and efficiency of court proceedings can be regulated in many ways. An analysis of regulation adopted in various European countries leads to the conclusion that it tends to take one of three models: the

42 Act of 1.09.1992 with subsequent amendments, based on translation by K. Skotnicki, Konstytucja Republiki Słowackiej, http://biblioteka.sejm.gov.pl/wp-content/uploads/2016/11/Slowacja_pol_010711.pdf (access date: 10.12.2020).

model of supervisory activities, the model of complaints, or the mixed model. The first model stipulates that the duration of the proceedings is subject to supervision with regard to the correctness of the actions taken by a court or judge. Any shortcomings in a specific case may result in an order for the matter to be settled immediately. Moreover, they may lead to specific disciplinary consequences against the judge hearing the case. Thus, the instruments of supervision over the exercise of the party's right to have a case heard within a reasonable time are aimed at bringing a specific case to examination, and are therefore instruments operating "forwards." This model is present in Danish court law.

The second model is the model of complaints. It was adopted in Germany and Italy. Here, in case of subjective excessive length of the proceedings, the party is entitled to bring a specific complaint, which initiates a separate court procedure. In this procedure it is examined whether the right of the party to have the case heard within a reasonable time has been violated and whether the party has suffered damage and – if so – compensation is awarded. The goal of this model is compensation, and the complaint itself is in fact a specific payment lawsuit based on the length of the proceedings.

The third solution is called the mixed model. Its goal is, on the one hand, the efficient settlement of the pending court case, and, on the other hand, awarding the claimant to the proceedings. Thus, the construction of the procedure is based on a complaint of the party, which initiates the hybrid procedure consisting of disciplinary, supervision and compensation measures. In this case, if the complaint is filed, the supervising court analyses whether the right to have a case heard within a reasonable time was violated and, if so, orders that action be taken in the case within a specified period and awards compensation to the complainant. Hence, there are two different measures undertaken. This mixed model was adopted in the Polish and Croatian legal systems.

In conclusion, it has to be highlighted that there is no doubt that the solutions adopted constitute significant guarantees for the case to be examined within a reasonable time. Regulations in which supervision is exercised ex officio, usually the supervisory activities model, do not require any activity by the party – it can therefore be assumed that in this model such supervision activities are undertaken on a permanent, continuous basis and in relation to all matters. In such cases, judges must take into account that each of their cases may become the subject of an analysis by the supervisory authority in terms of the timeliness of the actions taken. In turn, the party may focus on conducting the dispute that has already been initiated, i.e. presenting the appropriate argumentation or evidence and is not required to be active in any way in order to initiate supervisory measures.

Still, the positive aspects of the model of compensation and the mixed model should be noted. The initiative to lodge a complaint is left to the complainant. The question of excess in the length of the procedure is rather subjective at the beginning of the supervisory activity. Therefore, the supervision may be launched even when the authority responsible for this supervision remains passive. It is this feature of the models in question which is their undoubted advantage. Those models also take into account the compensatory consequences of excessive length of proceedings.

The comparison of the extracted models does not lead to clear conclusions as to which of them should be given priority or which of them should be assessed as better or more effective in controlling the length of court procedures. It seems that each of them should be related to the legal system in which it was introduced and the specificity of the circumstances in which it was decided to adopt it (for example, the Polish and Italian solutions were introduced in the face of enormous public and international criticism as to the excessive length of court proceedings in these countries). Undoubtedly, solutions aimed at increasing the efficiency of supervision over court proceedings – especially in relation to proceedings before administrative courts – are very much needed and the resources of national instruments in this area should be increased.

References

Publications

Jodłowski, Jerzy, "Zasady przewodnie polskiego międzynarodowego prawa procesowego cywilnego," in: *Księga pamiątkowa ku czci Prof. Kamila Stefki*, ed. by Włodzimierz Berutowicz, Józef Jodłowski, Józef Fiema, Władysław Siedlecki, and Edmund Wengerek, Warszawa-Wrocław: Państwowe Wydawnictwo Naukowe 1967, pp. 119–145.

Edel, Frédéric, *The Length of Civil And Criminal Proceedings In The Case-law of The European Court of Human Right*, Strasbourg: Council of Europe Publishing, 2007.

Grunsky, Wolfgang, "Lex fori und Verfahrensrecht," *Zeitschrift fur Zivilprozesss*, No. 89 (3), 1976, pp. 241–259.

Kmieciak, Zbigniew, *Postepowanie administracyjne i sądowoadministracyjne a prawo europejskie*, Warszawa: Wolters Kluwer, 2010.

Łętowska, Ewa, "Multicentryczność współczesnego systemu prawa i jej konsekwencje," *Państwo i Prawo*, No. 4 (710), 2005, pp. 3–10.

Petersen, Clement Salung, "A Comparative Perspective on Recent Nordic Reforms of Civil Justice," in: *The Future of Civil Litigation: Access to Courts and Court-Annexed Mediation in the Nordic Countries*, ed. by Laura Ervo and Anna Nylund Cham Heidelberg New York Dordrecht London: Springer, 2014, pp. 9–29.

Piątek, Wojciech, "The right to an effective remedy in European Law: significance, content and interaction," *China-EU Law Journal*, No. 6, 2019, pp. 163–174.

Sourdin, Tania, and Naomi Burstyner, *Justice Delayed is Justice Denied* (January 24, 2016), SSRN, https://poseidon01.ssrn.com (access date: 9.01.2021), pp. 46–60.

Wróbel, Andrzej, "Autonomia proceduralna państw członkowskich. Zasada efektywności i zasada efektywnej ochrony sądowej w prawie Unii Europejskiej," *Ruch Prawniczy, Ekonomiczny i Socjologiczny*, No. 67 (1), 2005, pp. 35–58.

Zieliński, Adam, "Postępowanie przed NSA w świetle prawa do sprawiedliwego procesu sądowego," *Państwo i Prawo*, No. 7 (569), 1992, pp. 15–26.

Jurisprudence

ECtHR

The judgement of ECtHR, 28.06.1978, *König v. Federal Republic of Germany*, No. 6232/73.

The judgement of ECtHR, 9.10.1979, *Airey v. Ireland*, No. 6289/73.

The judgement of ECtHR, 6.05.1981, *Buchholz v. Germany*, No. 7759/77.

The judgement of ECtHR, 23.06.1981, *Le Compte Van Leuven and De Meyere v. Belgium*, No. 6878/75.

The judgement of ECtHR, 8.12.1983, *Pretto and Others v. Italy*, No. 7984/77.

The judgement of ECtHR, 23.10.1985, *Benthem v. The Netherlands*, No. 8848/80.

The judgement of ECtHR, 29.05.1986, *Feldbrugge v. the Netherlands*, No. 8562/79.

The judgement of ECtHR, 18.12.1986, *Johnston and others v. Ireland*, No. 9697/82.

The judgement of ECtHR, 23.04.1987, *Poiss v. Austria*, No. 9816/82.

The judgement of ECtHR, 8.07.1987, *H. v. The United Kingdom*, No. 9580/81.

The judgement of ECtHR, 26.10.1988, *Martins Moreira v. Portugal*, No. 11371/85.

The judgement of ECtHR, 29.03.1989, *Bock v. Germany*, No. 11118/84.

The judgement of ECtHR, 7.07.1989, *Tre Traktörer Aktiebolag v. Sweden*, No. 10873/84.

The judgement of ECtHR, 25.10.1989, *Allan Jacobsson v. Sweden*, No. 10842/84.

The judgement of ECtHR, 24.10.1989, *H. v. France*, No. 10073/82.

The judgement of ECtHR, 28.06.1990, *Obermeier v. Austria*, No. 11761/85.

The judgement of ECtHR, 28.06.1990, *Skärby v. Sweden*, No. 12258/86.

The judgement of ECtHR, 20.02.1991, *Vernillo v. France*, No. 11889/85.

The judgement of ECtHR, 30.10.1991, *Wiesinger v. Austria*, No. 11796/85.

The judgement of ECtHR, 31.03.1992, *X. v. France*, 31.03.1992, No. 18020/91.

The judgement of ECtHR, 16.12.1992, *The Geouffre de la Pradelle v. France*, No. 1296/87.

The judgement of ECtHR, 27.10.1994, *Katte Klitsche de la Grange v. Italy*, No. 12539/86.

The judgement of ECtHR, 24.11.1994, *Beaumartin v. France*, No. 15287/89.

The judgement of ECtHR, 8.02.1996, *A. and Others v. Denmark*, No. 20826/92.

The judgement of ECtHR, 29.05.1997, *Georgiadis v. Greece*, No. 21522/93.

The judgement of ECtHR, 27.06.1997, *Philis v. Greece (No. 2)*, No. 19773/92.

The judgement of ECtHR, 30.10.1998, *Styranowski v. Poland*, No. 28616/95.

The judgement of ECtHR, 15.10.1999, *Humen v. Poland*, No. 26614/95.

The judgement of ECtHR, 28.03.2000, *Aldo and Jean-Baptiste Zanatta v. France*, No. 38042/97.

The judgement of ECtHR, 6.04.2000, *Comingersoll S.A. v. Portugal*, No. 35382/97.

The judgement of ECtHR, 27.06.2000, *Frydlender v. France*, No. 30979/96.

The judgement of ECtHR, 27.04.2004, *Politikin v. Poland*, No. 68930/01.

The judgement of ECtHR, 29.03.2006, *Scordino v. Italy*, No. 36813/97.

The judgement of ECtHR, 10.07.2012, *Grigoryan v. Armenia*, No. 3627/06.

The judgement of ECtHR, 29.11.2016, *Lupeni Greek Catholic Parish and others v. Romania*, No.76943/11.

The judgement of ECtHR, 27.06.2017, *Satakunnan Markkinapörssi Oy and Satamedia Oy v. Finland*, No. 931/13.

The judgement of ECtHR, 30.04.2020, *Keaney v. Ireland*, No. 72060/17.

The judgement of ECtHR, 30.07.2020, *Kirinčič and others v. Croatia*, No. 31386/17.

The judgement of ECtHR, 30.07.2020, *Mirjana Marić v. Croatia*, No. 9849/15.

The judgement of ECtHR, 20.10.2020, *Bognár v. Hungary*, No. 75757/14.
The judgement of ECtHR, 22.10.2020, *Kisházi and others v. Hungary*, No. 28814/19.
The judgement of ECtHR, 22.10.2020, *Melnikov v. Ukraine*, No. 66753/11.
The judgement of ECtHR, 19.11.2020, *Gorzkowski v. Poland*, No. 65546/13.
The judgement of ECtHR, 10.12.2020, *Hadobas v. Hungary*, No. 3686/20.
The judgement of ECtHR, 10.12.2020, *Parinov v. Ukraine*, No. 48398/17.
The judgement of ECtHR, 10.12.2020, *Sakhanenko v. Ukraine*, No. 9749/11.

Other

Judgement of Regional Social Court in Hamburg, Urt. v. 30.10.2014, Az.: L 1 SF 16/13 ESV.

Sources of law

International

Charter of Fundamental Rights of The European Union, Official Journal "C," 26.10.2012, pp. 391–407.

Convention for the Protection of Human Rights and Fundamental Freedom, Rome, 4.11.1950, (English version available on website www.conventions.coe.int; access date: 10.12.2020).

Croatia

Courts Act, Journal of Law No. 150/05 with subsequent amendments.

Denmark

Administration of Justice Act, Official Journal of Law, 12.12.2014.

Germany

The Code of Judicial Procedure, Official Journal of Law, 9.05.1975, item 1077, with subsequent amendments.

Law on legal protection in the event of lengthy court proceedings and criminal investigations, Official Journal of Law, 2.12.2011, item 2302.

Administrative Court Code, Official Journal of Law, 21.01.1960, item 17 with subsequent amendments.

Italy

Act of 24.03.2001 – Provision of equitable reparation in case of violation of the reasonable term of the trial and modification of article 375 of the code of civil procedure No. 89/2001, Official Journal of Law, 3.04.2001, No. 78.

Poland

Act of 17.06.2004 on a complaint for violation of a party's right to hear a case in preparatory proceedings conducted by the prosecutor's office or under the supervision of the prosecutor and in court proceedings without undue delay, Official Journal of Law 2018, item 75 with subsequent amendments.

The Act of 30.08.2002 – Law on proceedings before administrative courts, Official Journal of Law 2019, item 2325 with subsequent amendments.

Constitution of the Republic of Poland of 2.04.1997, Official Journal of Law 1997, No. 78, item 483 with subsequent amendments.

Slovakia

Constitution of Republic of Slovakia of 1.09.1992, Official Journal of Law No. 460/1992.

Sweden

The Form of Government Act of 28.02.1974, Swedish Code of Statutes (SFS), 2011:109.

Translations of legal documents

Dembiński, Krzysztof, and Marian Grzybowski, *Konstytucja Królestwa Szwecji*, http://biblioteka.sejm.gov.pl/wp-content/uploads/2016/04/Szwecja_pol_010711.pdf (access date: 9.01.2021).

Skotnicki, Krzysztof, *Konstytucja Republiki Słowackiej*, http://biblioteka.sejm.gov.pl/wp-content/uploads/2016/11/Slowacja_pol_010711.pdf (access date: 9.01.2021).

Reports and Analyses

Fabri, Marco, and Philip Langbroek, *Delay in Court Proceedings: A Preliminary Inquiry into the Relation Between The Demands of The Reasonable Time Requirements of Article 6, 1 ECHR and Their Consequences For Judges and Judicial Administration in the Civil Criminal and Administrative Justice Chain*, Strasbourg 2003, https://rm.coe.int/1680747b67 (access date: 10.01.2020).

Rubotham, Noel, and Ivana Borzova, *The role of parties and practitioners in avoiding or reducing delay in disposal of court proceedings*, Strasbourg 2018, https://rm.coe.int/09000016808ccb9e (access date: 10.12.2020).

Guide of the ECtHR on the application of article 6 – Right to a fair trial (civil limb), www.echr.coe.int (access date: 10.12.2020).

Esposito, Gianluca, Lanau, Sergi, and Sebastiaan Pompe, *Judicial System Reform in Italy – A Key to Growth*, International Monetary Fund Working Paper 2014/14/32, https://www.imf.org/external/pubs/ft/wp/2014/ wp1432.pdf (access date: 8.12.2020).

Igor Gontarz[1]

Electronic case distribution as a measure enhancing neutrality in the assignment of cases

Abstract: The aim of this paper is to consider the pros and cons of the electronic case distribution system used in some European countries. The article demonstrates that this solution enhances the internal independence of judges, as it limits the influence of the president of the division. Nevertheless, the automation causes specific problems due to the algorithm's opacity with regard to the main assumptions underlying the regulation – randomness and equal caseload – which may negatively affect the efficiency of court operations. The issues considered are: the non-transparency of the software source code, a necessity of maintaining the system's flexibility by considering the judge's specialisation and the risk of inequality of caseload due to the complexity of cases. The analysis is organised around the requirements stipulated in article 6 (1) of the European Convention of Human Rights. It is conducted in the comparative context of chosen European case distribution systems.

Keywords: European Convention on Human Rights, case management, transparency, objectivity, randomness, equal caseload, efficiency of court operations, internal independence

1. Introduction

In 2017, the Polish Parliament enacted an amendment of the Law on the system of Ordinary Courts, by which it introduced an electronic case distribution system.[2] On the basis of this statue, the competence to assign cases to judges was taken from the presidential judge and partially automated. Specific rules on that matter were issued by the Minister of Justice, who – on the same legal basis – introduced the principle of random panel composition. A possible breach of the statutory delegation led to the discussion on the separation of powers, the independence of judges and limits of ministerial supervision over the courts.[3]

---

1 Igor Gontarz, PhD Student, Adam Mickiewicz University in Poznań, (Poland). ORCID – 0000-0002-6138-1244.

2 Law amending the Law on the system of ordinary courts and certain other laws of 12.07.2017 (Journal of Laws 2017, item 1452).

3 See, inter alia, P. Rygiel, "Losowy przydział spraw cywilnych w sądzie drugiej instancji," *Przegląd Sądowy*, No. 2, 2019, pp. 39–56, A. Łazarska, *Niezawisłość sędziowska i jej gwarancje w procesie cywilnym*, Warszawa: Wolters Kluwer, 2018 and M. Pytlewska,

These circumstances are a great occasion to assess the assumptions of electronic case distribution in a comparative context and try to consider arguments that are for and against introducing electronic case distribution systems to the courts. The preliminary thesis is that the introduction of electronic case distribution enhances courts' independence, as it limits the influence of the president of the division. Furthermore, it is aimed at ensuring the equality of caseload and assumes complete randomness, which definitely has a positive influence on impartiality. Although, systems of this kind meet some criticism on the grounds of efficiency, they have some safeguards to assure flexibility in the case of excessive caseload or specialisation. This may explain why many countries still prefer to distribute cases in the traditional way.

2. Requirements deriving from art. 6(1) ECHR

Clear rules on case distribution and panel composition play a crucial role in enhancing the transparency of the court and the objectivity of the case outcome. The significance of this issue has been stressed many times by the European Court of Human Rights (hereinafter: "the ECtHR") in the case-law related to art. 6(1) of the European Convention of Human Rights (hereinafter: "the ECHR"), which states "...everyone is entitled to a fair and public hearing within a reasonable time by an independent and impartial tribunal established by law." In the European context of this contribution, attention should be drawn to the few remarks regarding requirements deriving from the regulation.

In the case-law related to case distribution and panel composition, the ECtHR highlights significance of the independence, the impartiality and the legality of the tribunal. Firstly, the ECtHR observes that the requirement of "tribunal established by law" covers not only the legal basis for the very existence of a tribunal but also the composition of the bench in each case,[4] thus art. 6(1) ECHR requires the bench to be composed according to the established law. Furthermore, ECtHR explains, "it is not the role of the Court to assess whether there were valid grounds for the domestic authorities to (re)assign a case to a particular judge or court, the Court must be satisfied that such (re)assignment was compatible

---

"System Losowego Przydziału Spraw jako gwarancja bezstronnego prawa do sądu w kontekście zaleceń Unii Europejskiej," *Prawo w Działaniu. Sprawy Cywilne,* No. 40, 2019, pp. 265–280. DOI: 10.32041/pwd.4008.

4 Judgement of ECtHR, 9.7.2001, *Posokhov v. Russia*, No. 63486/00, § 39. Quoted in: M. A. Nowicki, *Wokół Konwencji Europejskiej. Komentarz do Europejskiej Konwencji Praw Człowieka*, Warszawa: Wolters Kluwer, 2017, pp. 531 ff.

with Article 6 § 1, and, in particular, with its requirements of independence and impartiality."[5] Finally, the requirements of judicial independence and legal certainty for the rule of law call for particular clarity of the rules applied in any one case, and for clear safeguards to ensure objectivity and transparency, and, above all, to avoid any appearance of arbitrariness in the assignment of particular cases to judges.[6]

Similar requirements are formulated in the constitutions of European countries, some of which directly express a subjective right to a judge.[7] In the *Comments on European standards as regards the independence of the judicial system* A. Nussberger indicates, "The guarantee [right to the lawful judge – I.G.] can be understood in two different ways. Either it is related only to the court as a whole or it is related also to the individual judge dealing with the case." In her opinion "Experience shows that the latter understanding of the 'right to the lawful judge' should be promoted."[8]

The examples of the more "individual" approach are the Constitutions of Spain, Belgium, Germany and Slovenia.[9] The Constitution of Poland establishes the "general" right to a court, stating that "Everyone shall have the right to a fair and public hearing of his case, without undue delay, before a competent, impartial and independent court."[10] In the opinion of some commentators, this provision embraces also the right to a lawful judge, as the "Competent court" referred to in art. 45 sec. 1 of the Constitution, means not only competent case distribution between courts (in the external aspect) but also competent case allocation between judges (in the internal aspect).[11] Behind such an interpretation are the

5 Judgement of ECtHR, 8.7.2008, *Sutyagin v. Russia*, No. 30024/02, § 87. Quoted in: M. A. Nowicki, *Wokół Konwencji…*, pp. 531 ff.

6 Judgement of ECtHR 5.10.2010, *DMD Group a.s. v. Słowacja*, No. 19334/03, § 66. Quoted in: M. A. Nowicki, *Wokół Konwencji…*, pp. 531 ff.

7 For more detailed discussion, see: *European Commission for Democracy Through Law (Venice Commission). Comments on European Standards as Regards the Independence of The Judicial System: Judges* by Ms Angelika Nussberger (Substitute Member, Germany), Strasbourg, 5 December 2008, pp. 2 ff.

8 *European Commission for Democracy…*, p. 3.

9 According to the Constitution of Spain, "Likewise, all persons have the right of access to the ordinary judge predetermined by law…." Similarly, according to the Constitution of Belgium: "No one can be separated, unwillingly, from the judge that the law has assigned to him." Art. 101 of The Constitution of Germany: "(1) Extraordinary courts shall not be allowed. No one may be removed from the jurisdiction of his lawful judge."

10 The Constitution of the Republic of Poland of 2.4.1997 (Journal of Laws 1997, No. 78, item 483 with subsequent amendments).

11 A. Łazarska, *Niezawisłość sędziowska…*, p. 539.

mechanisms leading to breaches of internal independence of a judge (e. g. taking the case away from a judge unwilling to follow one's orders, exposing to disciplinary penalties by assigning a lot of complex cases in order to cause overload), which were experienced in the past.[12]

The requirements of transparency, objectivity and avoidance of arbitrariness may be associated with the concept of the neutral assignment of cases. P. Butler defined the latter as "systems designed to counter the risk of panel packing and the risks associated with the perception that panel packing may have occurred or may occur in the future." By the term "panel packing" the author means the "deliberate allocation of one or more judges to a judicial panel in order to achieve a particular outcome (…)."[13] As manipulation may be achieved mainly by the administrator in charge of allocating judges to panels, judicial systems seek to clearly separate his administrative competences from the sphere of independent decision-making (e.g. limiting arbitrariness). The term "panel packing" will also be used in this narrow meaning in this paper.

P. Butler indicates four instrumental functions of the neutral assignment of cases in respect to the rule of law:

> First, it protects courts from intervention when searching for truth and justice (…) Second, neutral assignment of cases is conducive to public confidence in the impartiality and independence of the judiciary. Third, the neutral case assignment guarantees that everyone has the same chance of getting a judge favorable to his or her cause (…) and fourth, since the judiciary performs a very important task in upholding basic rights and freedoms it is vital that panel selection processes be robust to ensure that those rights are not compromised.[14]

It should thus be noted that the neutral system of case distribution serves significant functions that uphold the rule of law. Requirements regarding this issue are well-grounded in art. 6(1) ECHR, as it establishes the right to a hearing before "an independent and impartial tribunal established by law." Compliance with the ECHR thus requires transparent, objective and previously enacted rules on case assignment, enabling manipulation to be avoided. A similar requirement may be found in some of the European domestic law systems, which express a right to a judge or a more general right to court, considered as a source of the same

12 A. Łazarska, *Niezawisłość sędziowska…*, pp. 539–540.

13 P. Butler, "The Assignment of Cases to Judges," *New Zealand Journal of Public and International Law*, No. 1(1), 2003, p. 85.

14 P. Butler, "The Assignment of Cases…," p. 87.

guarantees. The Polish legal order is an example of the latter solution, which is less promoted by the Venice Commission.

3. The main assumptions behind electronic case distribution

From the analysis of the various legal systems, it may be observed that the common purpose of implementing electronic case distribution system in the courts is to limit the influence of the president of the division and strengthen the judges' independence. There are two main assumptions, sometimes enacted as principles governing the procedure of case assignment, namely the principles of randomness and equal (or balanced) caseload. It is difficult to realise both of them simultaneously, as randomness is a value affecting judges' impartiality, whereas a balanced caseload is the basis of court efficiency.[15]

The abovementioned principles are the essence of the new distribution system in Poland.[16] Before the amendment of the Polish Law on Ordinary Courts, objectivity was assured by following alphabetical order of judges in each division. The case was assigned to the appropriate division of the court according to the internal legal act, called the "division of activities," assigned with a number and associated with a judge on the basis of a list in a secretariat.[17] Importantly, the president of the division had a lot of discretion and could change the assignment, taking into account the caseload of a judge or the complexity of the case.[18] In a fact, there was no strict control, neither over his activity nor the actual causes of his/her decisions. Therefore, during the legislative process, it was argued that the president's influence on judges may be less significant after depriving him of the competence to distribute cases.[19]

The same rationale was behind introducing electronic case distribution to the Georgian judicial system, in respect to which, according to the report issued by

15 M. Fabri, P.M. Langbroek, "Is There a Right Judge for Each Case? A Comparative Study of Case Assignment in Six European Countries," *European Journal of Legal Studies*, No. 2(1), 2007, p. 19.

16 See art. 47a § 1 and § 2 of the Act from 27th of July 2001 – Law on the system of ordinary courts, Consolidated text – Journal of Laws 2020, item 2072 and § 43 para. 1 of the Regulation of the Minister of Justice of 18.6.2019 – Rules of procedure of ordinary courts (Journal of Laws 2019, item 1141).

17 M. Pytlewska, "System Losowego Przydziału…," p. 266.

18 P. Rygiel, "Losowy przydział…," p. 40.

19 A. Machnikowska, *O niezawisłości sędziów i niezależności sądów w trudnych czasach. Wymiar sprawiedliwości w pułapce sprawności*, Warszawa: Wolters Kluwer, 2018, pp. 341–342.

the Georgian Democracy Initiative, "well-founded misgivings regarding manipulation by court presidents in assigning cases to judges were raised on numerous occasions during examination of high-profile cases by certain judges."[20] As in Poland, in Georgia cases are currently assigned to judges following the principles of random distribution and equal caseload in order to create a transparent and influence-free system.[21] However, the president of court is empowered, inter alia, to determine the percentage indicator of the caseload for certain cases (to prevent delays in administration of justice) or to prepare a shift schedule for judges on duty.[22] It is worth mentioning that in some courts (Tbilisi City Court and Court of Appeals) presidents are additionally empowered to unilaterally allocate judges to adjudicate on certain cases in a narrow specialisation (created to lower a large caseload).[23]

Likewise, in respect to the Slovenian case distribution system, the doctrine indicates that the allocation of cases using computer algorithms and public annual schedules guarantee that "nobody can tamper with the random case assignment to judges."[24] The court presidents still monitor the performance of the court and set productivity and timeframe targets for their court by presenting a proposal for an annual work program, but they are not allowed to interfere with the judge in the decision making on cases.[25] The president's right to order the reassignment of a case may be regarded as discretional competence, if he establishes that the undue delay in decision making is due to excessive workload or the judge's extended absence.[26]

To round out the picture of electronic case allocation in Europe, in Switzerland judges are electronically allocated to cases in e.g. The Federal Administrative Court (FAC), The Cantonal Supreme Court in Graubünden and the Cantonal Supreme Court in Neuchatel.[27] The FAC uses a specially designed software

---

20 Georgian Democracy Initiative, *Legal and Technical Analysis of the New System of Case Distribution in General Courts*, p. 5.

21 *Legal and Technical Analysis…*, p. 8.

22 *Legal and Technical Analysis…*, pp. 8–9, 16.

23 *Legal and Technical Analysis…*, p. 15.

24 N. Betetto, "Slovenia," in: *Courts in Evolving societies. Sino-European Dialogue between Judges and Academics*, ed. R. Aarli and A. Sanders, Leiden: Brill Nijhoff, 2021, p. 51.

25 N. Betetto, "Slovenia," in: *Courts in Evolving societies…*, p. 52.

26 N. Betetto, "Slovenia," in: *Courts in Evolving societies…*, p. 52.

27 An interesting fact might be also that there are also electronic systems of criminal legal aid assignment (e.g. in New Zealand). On the Ministry of Justice website detailed description of the process and some reports with data on the number of assignments to concrete attorneys may be found.

application called Bandlimat, which guarantees the impartial distribution of work among the available judges with the help of a random generation algorithm.[28]

Outside Europe, in China cases are assigned to judges via a computer system, which is to prevent corruption.[29] As the Chinese doctrine indicates "The Chief Justice in the court has no possibility to influence court decisions by hand-picking a particular judge for the management of a singular case."[30] Nevertheless, a result of the latter is under the control of a senior judge – a mandatory supervisor.[31] Electronic case distribution also operates in the USA, with a balance between impartiality and efficiency that is similar to the European model.[32]

It should be noted then that two main assumptions underpinning electronic case assignment are randomness and balanced caseload. The distribution is organised around those principles both inside and outside Europe. The goal is to limit the competences of the administrator in charge of allocating cases to panels (mainly the president of the division), however for reasons of efficiency, presidents are empowered to lower the caseload of a certain judge, influence the choice of judges into specialised units within a division, or to reallocate cases in specific circumstances.

4. Other systems of case distribution

The possible breaches noted in Polish scholarship were behind the new regulation on case assignment, the act that was aimed at enhancing the transparency of the process, assuring equal and just caseload and guaranteeing impartiality of

---

See: https://www.justice.govt.nz/about/lawyers-and-service-providers/legal-aid-lawyers/criminal-legal-aid-assignments-information-and-criminal-case-reports/

28 *FOURTH EVALUATION ROUND. Corruption prevention in respect of Members of Parliament, Judges and Prosecutors. EVALUATION REPORT SWITZERLAND.* Adopted by GRECO at its 74th Plenary Meeting (Strasbourg, 28 November – 2 December 2016), pp. 32 ff.

29 R. Aarli, "China," in: *Courts in Evolving societies…*, p. 26.

30 R. Aarli, "China," in: *Courts in Evolving societies…*, p. 26.

31 R. Aarli, "China," in: *Courts in Evolving societies…*, p. 27.

32 P. Butler, "The Assignment of Cases…," p. 30. For example, the most recent monograph on case management from the Federal Judicial Center notes that in the Fourth Circuit, "active judges are randomly assigned to argument panels by a computer program." See: L. Hooper, D. Miletich, and A. Levy, *Case Management Procedures in the Federal Courts of Appeals,* 2nd edition, Washington: Federal Judicial Center 2011, p. 99.

the proceedings.[33] In the justification of the new internal Rules of Court,[34] the Minister of Justice made reference to the Council of Europe's Recommendation CM/Rec (2010)12 on independence, efficiency and responsibilities of judges, according to which "The allocation of cases within a court should follow objective pre-established criteria in order to safeguard the right to an independent and impartial judge."[35]

In the explanatory memorandum to the Recommendation, automatic (or electronic) case distribution is mentioned in the not exhaustive catalogue of the solutions that fulfil the requirement of pre-established criteria, next to the drawing of lots, distribution in accordance with alphabetical order of the names of judges, and the sharing out of cases among judges by decision of court Presidents.[36] The European Committee on Legal Co-operation (CDCJ) remarks later "What is important is that the actual distribution is not subject to external or internal influence and is not designed to benefit any of the parties (…) Caseload and overburdening are valid reasons for the distribution or removal of cases provided such decisions are taken on the basis of objective criteria."[37]

It follows that electronic case distribution is just one of the various options to enhance the internal transparency of the court. Distribution may also be performed by a decision of the court president if he cannot influence the judge or act in favour of any of the parties. The president of the court may decide upon distribution, however the criteria taken into consideration must be pre-established and objective, so as to avoid arbitrariness.

Assigning cases in accordance with the alphabetical list of judges is the method employed in the Polish administrative courts of both instances. In the courts of the first instance, the main competences in this respect are in the hands of the head of division, who indicates the composition of individual panels and draws

---

33 A. Wleklińska in: *Prawo o ustroju sądów powszechnych. Komentarz, 3rd edition*, ed. I. Hayduk-Hawrylak, B. Kołecki, A. Wleklińska, Warszawa: C.H. Beck, 2018, pp. 135–136, nb. 1.

34 Explanatory statement to Rules of Minister of Justice of 4.12.2017 r. amending Rules of procedure of ordinary courts, p. 34. Quoted in: and M. Pytlewska, *System Losowego…*, supra note nb. 20.

35 *Recommendation CM/Rec (2010)12 adopted by the Committee of Ministers of the Council of Europe on 17 November 2010 and explanatory memorandum*, point nb 24.

36 *Draft Recommendation CM/Rec (2010) of the Committee of Ministers to member states on judges: independence, efficiency and responsibilities – Explanatory Memorandum*, point nb. 32.

37 Draft Recommendation CM/Rec (2010) …, point nb. 32.

the lots of panels to adjudicate on cases when it is required by law. A judge-rapporteur is assigned according to the alphabetical order,[38] and this is to ensure the impartiality of the panel. If it is necessary to change the composition of the adjudicating panel, the president repeats the same procedure and designates another judge on the basis of the list.[39]

In England and Wales, the criterion of distribution is the necessary expertise[40] (in the domain of law, such as family or planning law). Competences are formally entrusted to the head of the court, however the assignment is made by a listing officer, who is supposed to follow the listing policies set up by judges.[41] In contrast, in Germany, the assignment of cases to the different chambers or senate courts is undertaken according to a "case assignment plan" (Geschäftsverteilun gsplan).[42] It is the consequence of the previously discussed constitutional rule of the lawful judge which is interpreted as "a demand that the judge or the chamber or senate of judges deciding each case are predetermined even before the case arrives at the court."[43] The plan is decided by the Präsidium, whose members are elected by judges and "neither court president nor the ministries of justice have disciplinary or supervisory competence with respect to the judges and their work."[44]

With respect to discretionary competences, the system which operates in the lower Norwegian courts might be regarded as the most liberal one. Cases are assigned there by the Chief Justice on the basis of criteria such as experience and qualifications (so it is non-random).[45] According to R. Aarli and W.E. Arntzen, the acceptance of a non-transparent system of case assignment by the judges and the parties "reflects the high trust in the Norwegian court system in general."[46] Thus, it is enough that a judge holds sole responsibility for the management

38 See: § 23 para. 2 Regulation of the President of Poland of 5.08.2015 – Rules of procedure of voivodeship administrative courts (Journals of Laws 2015, item 1177) and § 42 para. 2 Regulation of the President of Poland of 4.07.2020 – Rules of procedure of Supreme Administrative Court (Journal of Laws 2020, item 1202).

39 See more in this book in: A. Skoczylas, "The organisation of the work of a judge and the activities of judicial administration bodies (comments from the viewpoint of the administrative judiciary)."

40 R. Aikens, "UK – England and Wales," in: *Courts in Evolving societies…*, p. 66.

41 M. Fabri, P.M. Langbroek, "Is There a Right Judge for Each Case?...," pp. 13 ff.

42 R. Gaier, A. Sanders, "Germany," in: *Courts in Evolving societies…*, p. 39.

43 R. Gaier, A. Sanders, "Germany," in: *Courts in Evolving societies…*, p. 39.

44 R. Gaier, A. Sanders, "Germany," in: *Courts in Evolving societies…*, p. 39.

45 R. Aarli, W. E. Arntzen, "Norway," in: *Courts in Evolving societies…*, p. 78.

46 R. Aarli, W. E. Arntzen, "Norway," in: *Courts in Evolving societies…*, p. 79.

of a case with no possibility of interference by the Chief Justice.[47] Such non-transparency would be impossible in Poland – a country with significantly low levels of trust placed in the courts.[48]

It follows that electronic case distribution is one of the systems that supports the neutrality of the panel. It should be observed that all of the abovementioned systems meet the requirements of Recommendation in its basic assumptions. One could ask whether it was necessary to introduce automatic case distribution in Poland if the previous system met the standards mentioned in the Recommendation. It should be noted that the intention of the Polish legislator was to enhance the level of the internal independence of the judges. If the latter is the main goal, the electronic case distribution guarantees one of the highest levels of neutrality among all of the mentioned solutions.[49] The role of the president of a division is very limited, as he has only few competences to influence the outcome of a draw.

5. Specific problems associated with electronic case distribution

Despite the abovementioned advantages, electronic case distribution also faces some criticism. This is connected with the opacity of an algorithm or the inflexibility of the system, which may be the reason for inefficiency in the court's operation. Considering arguments for and against electronic case distribution, attention should be focused on a few of those issues, in the context of the requirements deriving from the art. 6(1) ECHR.

5.1 The algorithm's opacity in the context of transparency

One of the problems connected with electronic case distribution systems, as the automated decision-making systems (hereinafter: "ADM") applied to court

47 R. Aarli, W. E. Arntzen, "Norway," in: *Courts in Evolving societies…*, p. 79.

48 The level of trust in the courts in Poland is significantly lower than approximate level of trust in the rest of EU countries (35 % of trust declarations to 51 % approximately, and 58 % of non-trust declarations to 45 % approximately). See: B. Kociołowicz-Wiśniewska, B. Pilitowski, *Ocena polskiego sądownictwa w świetle badań Vol. 2. Bilans efektów reform wymiaru sprawiedliwości w latach 2017–2019*, Toruń: Fundacja Court Watch Polska, 2019, p. 22.

49 Electronic assignment of cases is in some of the analysis considered as "the most transparent method of assigning cases to judges" (in the cited contribution – among the American appellate courts). P. Butler, "The Assignment of Cases…," p. 32.

operation, is the opacity of the algorithm that the system is based on. If the proprietor of the software does not provide access to the source code, it is impossible to scrutinise the way it works. It goes without saying that lack of control over the case distribution causes a risk of manipulation and unauthorised influence on the composition of a panel adjudicating a case. This leads to a question concerning the real transparency of the electronic case distribution system. If there is no way to scrutinise the software, which is the core of the system, should be the latter called "transparent"?

These doubts are becoming crucial in the context of the unequal caseload established in few of the Polish courts under scrutiny.[50] In that case, what are the ways of executing principles of randomness and equal caseload at the level of software? According to the Polish regulation, the electronic case distribution system (in Poland: "System of Random Case Assignment") is based on a number generation algorithm. Besides this general definition, detailed information about its functioning comes from court practice and the Ministry of Justice's explanations,[51] which are not sufficient to provide a full image of the software. It follows that the algorithm on which the system is based may differ from the regulation and declarations. In his famous book *Code and Other Laws of Cyberspace*, L. Lessig expressed this opacity in a short phrase – "code is law."[52] In saying this, he meant that the practical functioning of the system may be at least a bit different than it ought to be according to the law, so the crucial factor is whether the details of the regulation are coded effectively.[53] This relation entails there is a risk of mistakes in the source code of the software, which cannot be discovered. The computer programs, including the regulating code, are proprietary, so only the proprietor has exclusive authority to regulate free of legal or constitutional

50 Such a conclusion was reached after an audit of the District Court in Toruń. See: https://torun.so.gov.pl/container//sprawozdanie.pdf. Inequality has been observed also by the presidents of division during the audit of the Supreme Audit Office, See: https://www.nik.gov.pl/kontrole/wyniki-kontroli-nik/pobierz,lwr~p_19_038_202002111434591581428099~id1~01,typ,kj.pdf (access date: 10.04.2020).

51 See: https://torun.so.gov.pl/container//sprawozdanie.pdf (access date: 10.04.2020).

52 L. Lessig, *Code and Other Laws of Cyberspace*, New York: Basic Books, 1999. Quoted in: G. Moody, *Code is law: why software openness and algorithmic transparency are vital for privacy*, 10.02.2021 https://www.privateinternetaccess.com/blog/code-is-law-why-software-openness-and-algorithmic-transparency-are-vital-for-privacy/ (access date: 10.04.2020).

53 This explanation comes from a blog post on that subject written by G. Moody, who writes "these are the details of how software is coded effectively that create laws on their own, separate from traditional ones." See: G. Moody, *Code is law…*

scrutiny.[54] And the latter is indispensable when it comes to the algorithms used in courts, deciding who will adjudicate a case. Lack of external control over the IT system may lower the trust in the whole case distribution procedure, making it less transparent than a traditional system (with the role of a president of a division or a court clerk).

In the case-law of the Polish Supreme Administrative Court, the source code of an algorithm is not treated as public information, so the Ministry of Justice refuses to provide access to it.[55] It goes without saying that this non-transparency makes it impossible to find out what detailed assumptions are underlying the software, and whether they comply with the principles of randomness and equal caseload. A similar opinion is expressed towards the other ADM systems applied in the courts.[56] This rationale may be behind the future changes in thinking about the System of Random Case Assignment in administrative courts.[57] It follows that the transparency of the electronic case distribution procedure depends on the availability of the algorithm's source code to the public, and this is one of a few points that has to be taken into consideration by the lawmaker considering the introduction of this solution.

5.2 The specialisation of judges in the context of court efficiency

The other problem associated with automated case assignment is its inflexibility, which is not a problem in systems where the president of a division has a more

---

54 H. H. Perritt Jr., "Lawrence Lessig, Code and Other Laws of Cyberspace," *Connecticut Law Review*, No. 3(32), 2000, p. 1064.

55 Judgment of Supreme Administrative Court, 27.02.2014, I OSK 2014/13, publ. http://orzeczenia.nsa.gov.pl.

56 The Algorithm Watch in the Automating Society Report 2020 indicated that "The message for policy-makers couldn't be clearer. If we truly want to make the most of their potential, while at the same time respecting human rights and democracy, the time to step up, make those systems transparent, and put ADM wrongs right, is now." See: *Automating Society Report 2020*, October 2020, Bertelsmann Stiftung. Available online at https://automatingsociety.algorithmwatch.org (access date: 10.04.2020).

57 At the moment of preparing this contribution, there is still no final judgement in a case concerning the "public" character of the SRCS's (in Polish: "SLPS") source code. The Supreme Administrative Court will decide a case under the reference number "II SAB/Wa 502/18." The international organisation called ARTICLE 19 takes part in the proceedings. For more detailed discussion, see: K. Izdebski, *Jawność przydzielania sędziów do postępowań. Ważne zwycięstwo, ale droga do jawności jeszcze daleka*, 22.12.2020, https://epf.org.pl/pl/2020/12/22/jawnosc-przydzielania-sedziow-do-postepowan-wazne-zwyciestwo-ale-droga-do-jawnosci-jeszcze-daleka/ (access date: 10.04.2020).

significant role. From the ECHR it follows that rules on case distribution should be organised in a way that allows courts to operate efficiently and enables judgement to be received in a reasonable time (art. 6(1) ECHR). One of the factors which supports achieving that goal is the flexibility of the system, understood as assigning cases in accordance with the judge's availability, experience and specialisation. Including all of these factors in the draw, limits the group of possible judges to compose a panel, which then affects its randomness.

The specialisation of judges is a crucial factor influencing the efficiency of proceedings. The growing volume of cases and the complexity of regulations created on the European and national levels broadens the scope of material that has to be taken into consideration in the process of dealing with a case.[58] In effect, lawyers (including judges) have to specialise in a chosen area of knowledge, with its specific problems.[59] This finds confirmation in the words of P. Butler, who indicates that "Judges' specialist experience and understanding of the particular field can cut down hearing time and costs for litigants. They can also produce a better-quality decision through the right questions being asked, thus reducing the likelihood of a further appeal."[60] At the same time, however, there is impartiality, supported by principles of randomness and equal caseload.

The value that is supported more strongly depends on the judicial system. According to the analysis of M. Fabri and P. M. Langbroek, "the highest priority" in European countries is assigned to the balanced caseload among judges.[61] Further, the authors indicate that "other aspects are relevant such as specialisation or judicial continuity in dealing with a case, but they are specific for each country and are related to the way in which local case assignment processes work."[62] "Balanced caseload" that the authors mention does not mean absolutely equal, as it is inefficient to maintain a system whose task is to distribute cases regardless of any other factors. The same argument is also put forward in the

58 W. Kluth, "Die Rolle des Richters in der Verwaltungsgerichtsbarkeit vor dem Hintergrund ihres Funktionswandels," in: *Entwicklungen im Verwaltungsprozessrecht*. W. Kluth, K. Rennert (Hrsg.), Halle–Leipzig: Universitätsverlag Halle-Wittenberg, 2009, p. 151. Quoted in: W. Piątek, "O różnych sposobach dążenia do specjalizacji sędziów orzekających w sprawach administracyjnych," *Ruch Prawniczy, Ekonomiczny i Socjologiczny*, No. 2, 2020, p. 63.

59 W. Piątek, "O różnych sposobach…," p. 63.

60 P. Butler, "The Assignment of Cases…," p. 85.

61 M. Fabri, P.M. Langbroek, "Is There a Right Judge for Each Case?...," p. 16.

62 M. Fabri, P.M. Langbroek, "Is There a Right Judge for Each Case?...," p. 16.

discussion around electronic case distribution in Poland.[63] M. Fabri and P. M. Langbroek also observed that in European countries, as a rule, judges' specialisation comes before randomisation.[64] This does not mean, however, that specialisation is more significant than impartiality. This comment refers to the fact that randomness in the selection is assured within some limited group of judges, like a competent court, chamber, division or even smaller unit.

For the purposes of the quality and efficiency of judgements, specialised courts are created, individualised in their organisational and functional aspects in order to satisfy modern public demands (e.g., courts for labour disputes in Germany, the Court for Competition and Consumer Protection in Poland).[65] Specialisation may go even further, creating specialised panels or "a narrow specialization" inside a division if it is constituted according to sound criteria that cannot be changed arbitrarily.[66] For example, in Polish ordinary courts cases are primarily distributed to the competent divisions according to the subject matter. Thus, drawing of a panel is done on the level of the division. A similar solution exists in the Swiss Federal Administrative Court, where the president of the division assigns a case to the competent chamber, or to specialised judges with the use of computer software (the previously mentioned Bandlimat).[67] Going a step further, the Georgian lawmaker left the possibility to introduce a narrow specialisation (within division) or even set up specialised judicial benches.[68] The establishment of such a unit does not depend however on the will of the presiding

63 P. Rygiel indicates in similar context that each judge works in a different way and at a unique speed. See: P. Rygiel, "Losowy przydział…," p. 49.

64 M. Fabri, P.M. Langbroek, "Is There a Right Judge for Each Case?...," p. 16. For example, specialisation within the administrative courts is a leading principle for case allocation in Germany. In France, case allocation is a supervisory task of a head of court. See: W. Piątek, "O różnych sposobach…," p. 71 and the literature cited therein.

65 P.P. Serkov, "Specialzed courts and procedure," in: *Justice in the Modern Word. 5th edition*, V. Lebedev, V.M. Khabrieva, Hague: Eleven International Publishing, 2014, p. 494.

66 P. Butler, "The Assignment of Cases…," p. 85.

67 Bandlimat is named after the president of FAC. *Corruption prevention… SWITZERLAND*, p. 32, nb. 121.

68 The Organic Law of Georgia on Common Courts, Article 30.2. Quoted in: *Legal and Technical Analysis…*, p. 15. See also: *FOURTH EVALUATION ROUND. Corruption prevention in respect of Members of Parliament, Judges and Prosecutors. COMPLIANCE REPORT GEORGIA* Adopted by GRECO at its 82nd Plenary Meeting (Strasbourg, 18–22 March 2019), pp. 7 ff, nb. 32–35.

judge, as it can be created only in a situation of excessive caseload by the decision of the High Council of Justice of Georgia.[69]

One exception to this trend of specialisation is Denmark, where all the judges are supposed to be generalists and deal with all kinds of cases.[70] The assignment there is not even made by subject-matter and judges deal with all kinds of cases without any differentiation.[71]

Thus, it follows that the lawmaker considering a case distribution system has to take into consideration what the highest priority in a judicial system is. The answer to that question determines the balance between efficiency (specialisation) in the distribution of cases and the randomness of that process. To optimise the random case assignment, it might be necessary to create smaller units within the division, for which the software selects cases separately. Therefore, the inflexibility of a random distribution of cases in that aspect may be balanced without enhancing the role of the president of a court (division).

5.3 Case complexity in the context of court efficiency

The last problem with electronic case distribution also results from limiting the role of the president of a division and concerns treating cases of varying complexity as similar. Selecting may be done in respect to all of the cases heard in a certain division or according to the subject-matter. In the first situation, there is a little possibility to control the workload of a judge, as it is almost completely random. In comparison, the second one seems to distribute cases equally, however it leads to the problem of the complexity of legal issues and factual circumstances. Sometimes a "thick" case takes a few minutes to adjudicate, while the "thin" one requires spending a few days on it.[72] As cases of the same type may

69 Currently, this solution was introduced to Tbilisi City Court and Tbilisi Court of Appeals in administrative, civil and criminal sections See: *Legal and Technical Analysis…*, supra note 42.

70 This approach is similar to the one presented in the case-law of the Swedish Supreme Court that "All members of the court must be considered to be equally competent to hear any kind of case." See: H. Zahle, *Judicial opinion writing in the Danish Supreme Court (Højesteret)*. "Scandinavian Studies in Law," No. 51, 2007, pp. 561–562.

71 Therefore, the case distribution process in Denmark is fully randomised by a computer. See: M. Fabri, P.M. Langbroek, "Is There a Right Judge for Each Case?...," p. 16.

72 J. Włodarczyk-Madejska, P. Ostaszewski, J. Klimczak, *Efektywność pracy sędziów sądów powszechnych. Wyniki analizy wywiadów* pogłębionych. Analizy wymiaru sprawiedliwości, Warszawa: Instytut Wymiaru Sprawiedliwości, 2019, pp. 69–72.

differ, the second solution, which assumes an equal caseload, may paradoxically distribute cases unequally.

The problem described above is the source of criticism of the Polish System of Random Case Assignment. In secondary acts governing the operation of the Polish ordinary courts, civil cases are marked with a statistical symbol and divided into categories demanding similar amount of work.[73] Likewise, the criterion of the complexity of a criminal case is the number of case files pertaining to it. It might be said that for the purpose of the new system cases were "weighed up."[74] Thus, in the opinion of part of the doctrine, the Minister of Justice is trying to do the impossible – to make objective a thing that is subjective in nature.[75] Furthermore, some judges argue that in the previous system, without statistical assessment of cases, the workload of judges was equal enough, as after some time everyone had a similar number of complex cases.[76]

In trying to reflect on those arguments, a good starting point is to note that weighted caseload systems are not well known and seldom used in Continental Europe.[77] Netherlands and Germany were pioneers (in 1970s), but in the last two decades some studies on this topic were carried out also by Belgium and Switzerland.[78] Currently, the assessment of the resources and working hours that a case in any legal field (or case category) requires are considered in the doctrine as necessary for proper case assignment and allocation of resources.[79]

Nevertheless, the individual nature of each case makes it impossible to precisely predict the length of proceedings. A. Lienhard mentions five ways to measure a case: (a) estimating the workload on the basis of a survey among court clerks and judges, (b) establishing it on the basis of statistics, (c) combining

---

73 Division of cases on categories in listing devices, attachment number 6 to the order of Minister of Justice of 19.06.2019 regarding organisation and scope of activity of court secretariats (Law Journal of Minister of Justice 2019, item 138).

74 The complexity of civil and criminal cases was assessed by a special team created by the Ministry of Justice. See: Order of Minister of Justice of 27.11.2016 regarding establishment of a Team responsible for setting up a system of measuring caseload of judges [weighing up cases] (Law Journal of Minister of Justice 2016, item 204).

75 P. Rygiel, "Losowy przydział…," p. 49.

76 However, there were also positive opinions, as some of the judges appreciated the system for limiting the risk of manipulation of a caseload by the president of the division and considered it necessary.

77 A. Lienhard, D. Kettiger, "Research on the caseload management of courts: methodological questions," *Utrecht Law Review*, No. 1(7), 2011, p. 68.

78 A. Lienhard, D. Kettiger, "Research on the caseload…," p. 68.

79 A. Lienhard, D. Kettiger, "Research on the caseload…," p. 68.

both of the first two methods, (d) interviewing selected judges (e.g. division chairpersons), or (e) asking judges and court clerks to make notes of how long they spent dealing with a case.[80] Later, the author agrees that "Even the most reliable method cannot divert attention from the fact that we are dealing with a mere quantitative record."[81]

It follows that there is no precise method of measuring the complexity of a case type. As a consequence, a judge may be assigned with a complex case that was considered to be simple, which thus causes a higher caseload than was presumed. However, the criticism directed towards this approach is not entirely justified, as usually there are some ways to modify the outcome of allocation. One solution might be leaving some competences to the president of the division to balance the caseload when its necessary. For instance, in some countries there is a right to reassign a case due to excessive workload or the judge's extended absence, or if undue delay is established (e.g. Slovenia[82] or Switzerland[83]). The other idea is to exclude a judge with excessive caseload from the draw (as is the case in Georgia[84]) or to exclude a judge from the assignment of a complex case (with more than 50 volumes of case files) if he/she is currently adjudicating an equally demanding one (the Polish solution).[85] All of these competences are connected with certain objective circumstances, so they comply with art. 6(1) ECHR. Thus, the negative effect of imprecise weighing up of cases may be mitigated by leaving some safeguards which allow the draw to be modified.

Weighing up cases may inevitably cause disproportion in judges' workloads. The creation of a system that entirely realises the requirement of an equal caseload would cause delays in proceedings, thus breaching the right to receive a judgement within reasonable time. Therefore, not only the assessment of a

80 A. Lienhard, "Supervisory Control and Court Management," *International Journal for Court Administration*, No. 1(2), 2009, p. 12. Measuring the workload is necessary, at least to estimate how many judges should be employed in a certain court. Similar research has been conducted in Poland in 2012–2013.

81 A. Lienhard, "Supervisory Control...," p. 12.

82 N. Betetto, "Slovenia," in: *Courts in Evolving societies*, p. 52.

83 *Corruption prevention... SWITZERLAND*, p. 32, nb. 120.

84 According to article 5.5 of the Decision no. 1/56–2017 of the High Council of Justice of Georgia, when the difference among the number of cases assigned to judges with a certain specialisation amounts to 3, the judge assigned the most cases will be removed from the electronic distribution until the above difference decreases.

85 § 48 para. 1 of the Rules of procedure of ordinary courts, Journal of Laws 2019, item 1141.

workload has to be well grounded in the analysis of the court operation, but the lawmaker has to provide the president of a division with some competences to modify the results of a draw.

6. Conclusions

To sum up, the preliminary thesis has been verified positively. The introduction of an electronic case distribution enhances the internal independence of a judge, as it limits the influence of the president of a division. Composing panels with the support of computer software is a pre-established procedure with objective and transparent criteria. The most crucial advantage of that solution is the elimination of arbitrariness, enhancing the neutrality of case assignment. In its basic assumptions, namely randomness and equal caseload, it complies with the requirements of art. 6(1) ECHR.

Nevertheless, there are certain issues that may negatively influence the overall transparency of the procedure, as well as the efficiency of court operations. Firstly, the algorithm that is the core of the IT system which assigns cases should be available for scrutiny by the external subject. The non-transparency of the source code makes it impossible to find out what detailed assumptions are underlying the software and whether they comply with the principles of randomness and equal caseload. Secondly, there has to be a balance between randomness and the efficiency of the court operations. The procedure should be organised in a way that enables specialisation to be included in the draw criteria. Therefore, it might be necessary to create smaller units within the division, for which cases are drawn separately. Finally, the distribution system has to be flexible, which means there ought to be a possibility to modify the results of a draw in certain circumstances. Such an objective situation would be the excessive caseload of a judge, extended absence, undue delay in his cases, or exclusion from the draw of a complex case, if a judge is currently handling a difficult one.

As a final remark, it should be noted that electronic case distribution, like any other system, is susceptible to manipulation and cannot completely eliminate corruption. Traditional ways of distributing cases may still meet the demands of the countries with a legal culture at a high level, as well as a high level of trust in the courts. However, the advantage of benefits when it comes to internal independence, with a rather low cost in court efficiency, makes the electronic system universal. Weighing up its pros and cons, generally it should be assessed positively, as the next valuable automation of the public sector.

References

Publications

Aarli, Ragna, "China," in: *Courts in Evolving societies. Sino-European Dialogue between Judges and Academics*, ed. by Aarli Ragna and Anne Sanders, Leiden: Brill Nijhoff, 2021, pp. 21–32.

Aarli, Ragna, and, Wenche Elizabeth Arntzen, "Norway," in: *Courts in Evolving societies. Sino-European Dialogue between Judges and Academics*, ed. by Aarli Ragna and Anne Sanders, Leiden: Brill Nijhoff, 2021, pp. 71–84.

Aikens, Right Hon Sir Richard, "UK – England and Wales," in: *Courts in Evolving societies. Sino-European Dialogue between Judges and Academics*, ed. by Aarli Ragna and Anne Sanders, Leiden: Brill Nijhoff, 2021, pp. 59–70.

Betetto, Nina, "Slovenia," in: *Courts in Evolving societies. Sino-European Dialogue between Judges and Academics*, ed. by Aarli Ragna and Anne Sanders, Leiden: Brill Nijhoff, 2021, pp. 43–58.

Butler, Petra, "The Assignment of Cases to Judges," *New Zealand Journal of Public and International Law*, No. 1(1), 2003, pp. 83–114.

Fabri, Marco, and, Philip M. Langbroek, "Is There a Right Judge for Each Case? A Comparative Study of Case Assignment in Six European Countries," *European Journal of Legal Studies*, No. 2(1), 2007, available online at: http://hdl.handle.net/1814/7713.

Gaier, Reinhard, and, Anne Sanders, "Germany," in: *Courts in Evolving societies. Sino-European Dialogue between Judges and Academics*, ed. by Aarli Ragna and Anne Sanders, Leiden: Brill Nijhoff, 2021, pp. 33–42.

Haÿduk-Hawrylak, Izabela, Bartłomiej Kołecki, and, Anna Wleklińska, *Prawo o ustroju sądów powszechnych. Komentarz, 3rd edition*, Warszawa: C.H. Beck, 2018.

Hooper, Laural, Dean Miletich, and, Angelia Levy, *Case Management Procedures in the Federal Courts of Appeals,* 2nd edition, Washington: Federal Judicial Center, 2011.

Kluth, Winfried, "Die Rolle des Richters in der Verwaltungsgerichtsbarkeit vor dem Hintergrund ihres Funktionswandels," in: *Entwicklungen im Verwaltungsprozessrecht.* Kluth Winfried, and, Klaus Rennert (Hrsg.), Halle-Leipzig: Universitätsverlag Halle-Wittenberg, 2009, pp. 147–152.

Kociołowicz-Wiśniewska Bogna, and, Bartosz Pilitowski, *Ocena polskiego sądownictwa w świetle badań* Vol. 2.: *Bilans efektów reform wymiaru sprawiedliwości w latach 2017–2019*, Toruń: Fundacja Court Watch Polska, 2019.

Łazarska, Aneta, *Niezawisłość sędziowska i jej gwarancje w procesie cywilnym*, Warszawa: Wolters Kluwer, 2018.

Lessig, Lawrence, *Code and Other Laws of Cyberspace*, New York: Basic Books, 1999.

Lienhard, Andreas, "Supervisory Control and Court Management," *International Journal for Court Administration*, No. 1(2), 2009, available online at: https://doi.org/10.7892/boris.38122.

Lienhard, Andreas, and, Daniel Kettiger, "Research on the caseload management of courts: methodological questions," *Utrecht Law Review*, No. 1(7), 2011, pp. 66–73.

Machnikowska, Anna, *O niezawisłości sędziów i niezależności sądów w trudnych czasach. Wymiar sprawiedliwości w pułapce sprawności*, Warszawa: Wolters Kluwer, 2018.

Nowicki, Marek Antoni, *Wokół Konwencji Europejskiej. Komentarz do Europejskiej Konwencji Praw Człowieka*, Warszawa: Wolters Kluwer, 2017.

Perritt, Henry H. Jr., "Lawrence Lessig, Code and Other Laws of Cyberspace," *Connecticut Law Review*, No. 3(32), 2000, pp. 1061–1064.

Piątek, Wojciech, "O różnych sposobach dążenia do specjalizacji sędziów orzekających w sprawach administracyjnych," *Ruch Prawniczy, Ekonomiczny i Socjologiczny*, No. 2, 2020, pp. 63–76.

Pytlewska, Mirosława, "System Losowego Przydziału Spraw jako gwarancja bezstronnego prawa do sądu w kontekście zaleceń Unii Europejskiej," *Prawo w Działaniu. Sprawy Cywilne*, No. 40, 2019, pp. 265–280. DOI: 10.32041/pwd.4008.

Rygiel, Paweł, "Losowy przydział spraw cywilnych w sądzie drugiej instancji," *Przegląd Sądowy*, No. 2, 2019, pp. 39–56.

Serkov, Peter Pavlovich, "Specialized courts and procedure," in: *Justice in the Modern Word. 5th edition*, Lebedev, Vyacheslav Mikhailovich, and, Taliia Khabrieva, Hague: Eleven International Publishing, 2014, pp. 493–497.

Włodarczyk-Madejska, Justyna, Paweł Ostaszewski, and, Joanna Klimczak, *Efektywność pracy sędziów sądów powszechnych. Wyniki analizy wywiadów pogłębionych. Analizy wymiaru sprawiedliwości*, Warszawa: Instytut Wymiaru Sprawiedliwości, 2019.

Zahle, Henrik, "Judicial opinion writing in the Danish Supreme Court (Højesteret)," *Scandinavian Studies in Law*, No. 51, 2007, pp. 560–57.

Jurisprudence

European Court of Human Rights

Decision of ECtHR, 9.7.2001, *Posokhov v. Russia*, No. 63486/00.

Judgment of ECtHR, 8.7.2008, *Sutyagin v. Russia*, No. 30024/02.

Judgment of ECtHR 5.10.2010, *DMD Group a.s. v. Słowacja*, No. 19334/03.

Polish Supreme Administrative Court

Judgment of Supreme Administrative Court, 27.02.2014, I OSK 2014/13, publ. http://orzeczenia.nsa.gov.pl.

Sources of law

Law amending the Law on the system of ordinary courts and certain other laws of 12.07.2017 (Journal of Laws 2017, item 1452).

Division of cases on categories in listing devices, attachment number 6 to the order of Minister of Justice of 19.06.2019 regarding organisation and scope of activity of court secretariats (Law Journal of Minister of Justice 2019, item 138).

Decision no. 1/56–2017 of the High Council of Justice of Georgia.

Constitution of Spain, English version available at: https://www.boe.es/legislacion/documentos/ConstitucionINGLES.pdf (accesse date: 10.04.2021).

Constitution of Belgium, English version available at: https://www.dekamer.be/kvvcr/pdf_sections/publications/constitution/GrondwetUK.pdf (access date: 10.04.2021).

Constitution of Germany, English version available at: https://www.btg-bestellservice.de/pdf/80201000.pdf (access date: 10.04.2021).

Explanatory statement to Rules of Minister of Justice of 4.12.2017 r. amending Rules of procedure of ordinary courts.

The Constitution of the Republic of Poland of 2.4.1997 (Journal of Laws 1997, No. 78, item 483 with subsequent amendments).

Act of 27.07.2001 on Law on the system of ordinary courts (Consolidated text: Journal of Laws 2020, item 2072).

Regulation of the President of Poland of 5.08.2015 – Rules of procedure of voivodeship administrative courts (Journals of Laws 2015, item 1177).

Order of Minister of Justice of 27.11.2016 regarding establishment of a Team responsible for setting up a system of measuring caseload of judges [weighing up cases] (Law Journal of Minister of Justice 2016, item 204).

Regulation of the Minister of Justice of 18.6.2019 – Rules of procedure of ordinary courts (Journal of Laws 2019, item 1141).

Regulation of the President of Poland of 4.07.2020 – Rules of procedure of Supreme Administrative Court (Journal of Laws 2020, item 1202).

Internet sources

Izdebski, Krzysztof, *Jawność przydzielania sędziów do postępowań. Ważne zwycięstwo, ale droga do jawności jeszcze daleka*, 22.12.2020, https://epf.org.pl/pl/2020/12/22/jawnosc-przydzielania-sedziow-do-postepowan-wazne-zwyciestwo-ale-droga-do-jawnosci-jeszcze-daleka/ (access date: 10.04.2021).

Moody, Glyn, *Code is law: why software openness and algorithmic transparency are vital for privacy*, 10.02.2021 https://www.privateinternetaccess.com/blog/code-is-law-why-software-openness-and-algorithmic-transparency-are-vital-for-privacy/ (access date: 10.04.2021).

Reports, analysis, and recommendations

Automating Society Report 2020, October 2020, Bertelsmann Stiftung. Available online at https://automatingsociety.algorithmwatch.org (access date: 10.04.2020).

Draft Recommendation CM/Rec (2010) of the Committee of Ministers to member states on judges: independence, efficiency and responsibilities – Explanatory Memorandum.

FOURTH EVALUATION ROUND. Corruption prevention in respect of Members of Parliament, Judges and Prosecutors. EVALUATION REPORT SWITZERLAND. Adopted by GRECO at its 74th Plenary Meeting (Strasbourg, 28 November – 2 December 2016).

FOURTH EVALUATION ROUND. Corruption prevention in respect of Members of Parliament, Judges and Prosecutors. COMPLIANCE REPORT GEORGIA Adopted by GRECO at its 82nd Plenary Meeting (Strasbourg, 18–22 March 2019).

Georgian Democracy Initiative, *Legal and Technical Analysis of the New System of Case Distribution in General Courts.*

Nussberger, Angelika, *European Commission for Democracy Through Law (Venice Commission). Comments on European Standards as Regards the Independence of The Judicial System: Judges*, Strasbourg, 2008, available online at: https://www.venice.coe.int/webforms/documents/default.aspx?pdffile=CDL-JD(2008)006-e.

Recommendation CM/Rec (2010)12 adopted by the Committee of Ministers of the Council of Europe on 17 November 2010 and explanatory memorandum.

Report from the audit of the District Court in Toruń held on 11.09.2018, https://torun.so.gov.pl/container//sprawozdanie.pdf (access date: 10.04.2021).

Supreme Audit Office, *Post-audit statement. P/19/038 Realizacja projektów informatycznych mających na celu usprawnienie wymiaru sprawiedliwości*, https://www.nik.gov.pl/kontrole/wyniki-kontroli-nik/pobierz,lwr~p_19_038_202002111434591581428099~id1~01,typ,kj.pdf (access date: 10.04.2021).

The Ministry of Justice of New Zealand website, *Criminal legal aid assignments – information & criminal case reports*, https://www.justice.govt.nz/about/lawyers-and-service-providers/legal-aid-lawyers/criminal-legal-aid-assignments-information-and-criminal-case-reports/ (accesse date: 10.04.2021).

Wojciech Piątek[1]

Administrative supervision as a tool for building trust in the courts and judges

Abstract: The aim of the chapter is to analyse various factors which are responsible for fostering trust in the courts and judges. The starting point for the research is the connection between trust and supervision, including its consequences for the evaluation of courts within societies. These two terms remain in a correlation, in the sense that an adoption of supervision can make a court's adjudication more effective and professional for parties to the proceedings. For the achievement of this goal, supervision measures should be adopted with a high level of restraint, in order not to violate judicial independence, which is the basic element for fostering trust in the courts. The adoption of supervision should remain under the court's verification and be transparent. Public control of the adopted supervision is performed by the media, which assures foreseeability of the undertaken decisions, but may have a negative influence the proper application of the supervision rules. Additionally, in the present situation of the Covid-19 pandemic, when many restrictions are imposed on citizens, the use of supervision measures may strengthen trust in the courts through the efficient review of the restrictions. All the state powers should be interested in fostering the trust placed in the courts. Only independent courts which benefit from a high level of trust can exercise their role of shaping the rule of law.

Keywords: supervision over courts and judges, trust in courts, judicial independence, pandemic, media

1. Introduction

Trust is an essential element of all social relations, including relationships within the legal order, between a client and his or her lawyer, the state and the citizen, the court and the parties to the case. A high level of trust in the courts and judges is an indispensable precondition for the acceptance of and compliance with court decisions.[2] The courts' adjudication is based on the respect and trust

---

1 Wojciech Piątek, PhD, Professor of Law at Adam Mickiewicz University in Poznań, (Poland). ORCID – 0000-0002-3494-1912.

2 A lack of trust in the court system may negatively affect the enforcement of judicial decisions and, in that limited sense, also the proper functioning of the state at large. Trust also plays crucial role in cooperation between states aimed at recovering public claims. See Piątek, W., "Zasada zaufania," in: *Współpraca państw członkowskich*

placed in the state and its institutions.[3] The behaviour of members of the public towards courts and judges can be influenced by their perception of the judicial system. If citizens perceive the decision-making and delivery of service by the courts as fair and just, they respond more positively to the judicial assertion of authority.[4] They are more likely not only to accept the court's decisions but also to litigate in court instead of relying on dispute resolution alternatives that exist in the shadow of the law.

The trust placed in the courts is affected both from within the judiciary and by external actors. The outside view is shaped by the media, which reports on the courts' decision-making and individuals' dealings with courts.[5] From an inside perspective, trust in courts is connected with the court's structural organisation and functioning. Since the primary purpose of administrative supervision is to organise the adjudication as professionally as possible, the adoption of specific supervision measures may affect, positively or negatively, the level of trust enjoyed by courts and judges.[6] Even a non-decision may also affect the trust placed in the courts.[7] In that sense, trust and supervision over the courts are related.

The aim of the analysis in this chapter is to define and critically examine this relationship, to assess the potential that the adopted administrative supervision has for shaping the public's trust in and respect for the courts. The analysis will

---

UE przy odzyskiwaniu wierzytelności podatkowych, ed. by J. Olszanowski, W. Piątek, Warszawa: Wolters Kluwer, 2016, pp. 42 ff.

3 Trust is itself significant for these institutions. A bad reputation may damage the justice system's ability to attract the best staff, which may have an effect on the court's efficiency. See Van de Walle, S., "Trust in the justice system: a comparative view across Europe," *Prison Service Journal*, 2009, No. 183, p. 26.

4 In such situations, citizens are also more likely to engage in dispute resolution with courts. See Ryser, A., "Swiss justice in comparison. An outline of the Swiss judicial system according to the approach by Delvin and Dodek," *Schriftenreihe zur Justizforschung*, 2018, No. 17, p. 77.

5 It is necessary to distinguish between individuals who had personal contacts with courts in their own disputes or as witnesses, and people who gain knowledge about the courts from media and other persons. Unfortunately, the statistics usually do not respect this distinction.

6 E.g. interference with judicial independence stemming from the abuse of supervisory competences can reduce the level of trust in the judiciary and the willingness to follow the court's decisions.

7 E.g. in cases where there was a perceived overreach or breach of duty by a judge but the supervisory bodies took no disciplinary measures.

answer the following questions: What kind of trust ought to exist between the judges and parties to the case, or between the courts and the society as a whole? How can courts and judges strengthen the level of trust the general public affords them? How do administrative supervision measures shape trust that the general public place in the courts and judges? It is also worth analysing what other factors affect trust in courts among citizens, and what kind of relations exist between them and administrative supervision.

The analysis presented in this chapter is divided into six parts. In the first part, trust is explored as a normative category. In the second part, selected administrative supervision measures are critically examined for their impact on the trust in the courts and judges. The third part analyses the competences of legal entities responsible for the performance of courts. In the fourth part, other non-supervisory factors that may help build trust in courts are presented. In the fifth part, the correlation between trust in the courts and the influence of the media is investigated. In the final part, trust in courts will be investigated under the extreme conditions created by the global Covid-19 pandemic. The pandemic led to a demand on courts for a new and innovative approach to adjudication as well as communication with citizens.

2. Trust as a normative and sociological category

Trust can be generally defined as a belief that a person or an institution can be trusted, that the information given by someone is accurate.[8] In other words, trust is a belief that somebody or some institution (e.g. a court) will act according to a predetermined set of rules, which are expected by this person and are favourable for him or her.[9] The building of trust takes time, but the loss of trust can be sudden. From a court, it demands professionalism and sensitivity to concrete human needs. From the parties to the proceedings, it requires openness and cooperation with the judicial institution. Since trust is a bi-directional relationship, the view from the bench should be not omitted. The attitude of the courts towards the public and parties to the case cannot be appropriately defined as trusting. Instead, courts should be receptive to the parties' actions and needs,

8 *Słownik języka polskiego*, Vol. X, ed. by Doroszewski, W., Warszawa: Wydawnictwo Naukowe PWN, 1968, pp. 844–845, *Uniwersalny słownik języka polskiego*, Vol. IV, ed. by Dubisz, S., Warszawa: Wydawnictwo Naukowe PWN, 2006, p. 908.

9 Chmielewski, J., *Zasada budzenia zaufania w ogólnym postępowaniu administracyjnym*, Warszawa: WoltersKluwer, 2018, p. 60, Uusitalo K., *How to maintain and increase public confidence in the judiciary*, Sofia: Themis 2019, p. 5.

while being critical at the same time. These qualities will make it possible to build trust in courts.

Besides many other applications of trust, it has a normative potential for the improvement of values like legal certainty, the foreseeability of law and the uniformity of its application. A need for legal certainty has accompanied human beings for hundreds of years. Trust is an important factor in all human interactions. It concerns both the creation and application of the law. Individuals in democratic states have a right to live under a system which operates within the rule of law. Courts are responsible for applying the law, which concerns substantive and procedural law, and the determination of rights and obligations, combined with an organisation of legal conduct in which the parties of the proceedings feel they are treated professionally.

These values are enshrined in EU law. The Charter of Fundamental Rights of the EU[10] stipulates in Article 47 the right to a fair trial and public hearing within a reasonable time by an independent and impartial tribunal previously established by law.[11] Each of these values is crucial for shaping trust in the courts and can be regarded as a basic element for assessing public intuitions concerning the courts. Courts build trust in a democratic society for the proper discharge of duties and the timely delivery of justice.[12] An institution that is unable to resist external intervention or pressure that threatens independent judgment,[13] and which cannot eliminate external influence on the outcome of the proceedings that encroaches upon a strict interpretation of the law,[14] will be not trustworthy.

---

10 Official Journal of the EU 2012/C 326/02.

11 The right to a fair trial is also protected by the Article 6 para. 1 of the European Convention on Human Rights and the jurisprudence of the ECtHR. According to the jurisprudence of the ECtHR, the judiciary plays a special role in society as the guarantor of justice. The judiciary must enjoy public confidence to be successful in carrying out its duties. See Judgment of ECtHR, 23.06.2016, *Baka v. Hungary*, No. 20261/12, para. 164. See also Judgment of ECtHR, 23.04.2015, *Morice v. France*, No. 29369/10, para. 128–131, where the ECtHR stated that courts may be a subject to personal criticism within the permissible limits, and not only in a theoretical and general manner. When acting in their official capacity they may thus be subject to wider limits of acceptable criticism than ordinary citizens.

12 Judgment of ECtHR, 24.2.1994, *Fey v. Austria*, No. 14396/88, para. 30.

13 Judgment of ECJ, 31.1.2013, *H.I.D., B.A. v. Refugee Applications Commissioner and others*, C 175/11, para. 96–97.

14 Judgment of ECJ, 19.9.2006, *Graham J. Wilson v. Ordre des advocates du barreau de Luxembourg*, C 506/04, para. 52.

Without trust, courts would be unable to settle the disputes that human beings view as significant.

The state's obligation to build trust in its institutions among citizens has its fundaments in national legal orders. The principle of the citizen's trust in the state is an element derived from the democratic normative character of the Polish state, which is declared in Article 2 of the Constitution.[15] According to the jurisprudence of the Constitutional Tribunal (hereinafter: also CT), this principle affects the role of the state and relationships between the state and individuals.[16] The principle of legal certainty means that an individual can plan his or her life, knowing her interests are protected in law.[17] The principle of the foreseeability of the law means that an individual can act with trust, that her conduct will not be judged by a new standard which he or she could not have anticipated before acting.[18] It also contains a general prohibition against creating false and illusory rights.[19] Finally, the uniformity of jurisprudence is a component of the principle, because it ensures that parties to the case can expect consistency in the application of the law.

Analysing trust in the courts from a normative perspective, some procedural institutions play a very important role in shaping this value. It is worth mentioning the possibility of the disqualification of judges. The primary function of judicial disqualification is to ensure impartiality of the process and the final judgment. This value has fundamental importance for the acceptance of court decisions.[20] There are also other procedural institutions that can be analysed from the perspective of strengthening trust in the courts and judges.[21] Each contact

---

15 The Constitution of the Republic of Poland of 2.4.1997 (Journal of Laws 1997, No. 78, item 483 with subsequent amendments).

16 Judgment of the Polish Constitutional Tribunal, 19.11.2008, Kp 2/08, OTK-A 2008, No. 9, item 157.

17 Judgment of the Polish Constitutional Tribunal, 13.11.2013, K 2/12, OTK-A 2012, No. 10, item 12.

18 Judgment of the Polish Constitutional Tribunal, 25.11.1997, K 26/97, OTK 1997, No. 5–6, item 64, judgment of the Polish Constitutional Tribunal, 21.12.1999, K 22/99, OTK 1999, No. 7, item 166.

19 Judgment of the Polish Constitutional Tribunal, 10.01.2012, P 19/10, OTK-A 2012, No. 1, item 2, judgment of the Polish Constitutional Tribunal, from 08.01.2013, K 18/10, OTK-A 2013/1/2.

20 For that reason, the possibility of disqualifying a judge from a concrete dispute is an obligatory element of each statute which regulates judicial procedure.

21 From the perspective of building trust in courts, public hearings play a significant role. The quality of judicial reasoning also has crucial importance. Additionally, each instruction about the legal consequences of individual's initiative which can lead to

between a court and parties to the case during the pre-trial procedure, public trial and the issuance of a judgment can be regarded as a chance for shaping trust in the court's functioning. In other words, the principle of trust protection has extra importance over other rules characteristic for the proper course of the proceedings. At every stage of the proceedings, courts can build and strengthen trust in their impartiality and high-quality decision-making.

Trust in the courts may be analysed from a sociological perspective. There are many sociological surveys concerning the level of trust in courts and reasons for their public support or lack thereof. In Poland, a straightforward question focused on citizens' trust in the courts has been posed for years in surveys prepared by the Public Opinion Research Center.[22] In the last ten years, the level of trust in Polish courts has hovered stably above 40 %.[23] In the broader European context, the CEPEJ reports offer data on the public perception of judicial independence. With regard to the question about judicial independence, which is not the same as trust, but which constitutes an element that undoubtedly affects the level of confidence in the courts, it is clear that West-European legal systems score higher than jurisdictions in Central and Eastern Europe. While in Denmark, Austria and Finland more than 80 % of the general public view the level of judicial independence to be very good or fairly good, in Slovakia and Croatia, it is less than 30 % of the respondents.[24] Among the reasons for the recorded

---

the avoidance of negative consequences may have a positive impact on the perception of the courts and judges.

22 The Center was established in 1982. It conducts research for Polish public administration bodies, as well as various other interested institutions: local government, the press and television, industry and advertising agencies. For more details, see "Public Opinion Research Center. Solid and Professional." https://www.cbos.pl/EN/about_us/about_us.php (access date: 23.10.2020). The research should clearly distinguish between personal and mediated contact with the court system.

23 In 2010, 44 % citizens trusted, 45 % did not trust and 12 % were non-decided. See Boguszewski, R., "Zaufanie społeczne. Komunikat z badań," 2010, No. BS/29/2010. https://www.cbos.pl/SPISKOM.POL/2010/K_029_10.PDF (access date: 23.10.2020). In 2016, 45 % citizens trusted, 42 % did not trust and 13 % were non-decided. See Omyła-Rudzka, M., Zaufanie społeczne. Komunikat z badań," 2016, No. 18. https://www.cbos.pl/SPISKOM.POL/2016/K_018_16.PDF (access date: 23.10.2020). In 2020 42 % citizens trusted, 45 % did not trust and 13 % were non-decided. See Omyła-Rudzka, M., "Zaufanie społeczne. Komunikat z badań," 2020 No. 43; (access date: 23.10.2020).

24 The 2020 EU Justice Scoreboard, Publication Office of the EU 2020, p. 41. The same phenomenon can be observed in Switzerland, where the confidence in the judiciary is high. See Ryser, A., Swiss justice in comparison. An outline of the Swiss judicial system

negative perception, the survey highlights the low prestige of judicial work, and pressure from economic and political interests.[25] These reasons are connected with the administrative supervision measures used with courts, because the purpose of judicial supervision is the quality control of judicial decision-making. Supervisory overreach, however, may be perceived by the public as undue pressure and interference in court cases, which will result in lower levels of trust. In other words, although the level of trust towards the courts is determined by various factors, including historical and cultural grounds,[26] administrative supervision does have an impact. Administrative oversight may lead to external pressure on courts from other areas, mainly the executive and state authorities, and adversely affect its perceived judicial independence.

Trust in the sociological sense will be significant for the analysis presented in this chapter, for assessing the potential of supervision to increase the trust placed in courts. This perspective is crucial for answering the questions formulated in the introduction. It was stated in the analysis that the adoption of supervisory measures might have an impact (positive or negative) on the social trust placed in the courts and judges. In this regard, it is also worth considering if the high confidence enjoyed by the courts in Denmark or Austria is due to special supervision measures and the structural design of their judiciary.

3. Trust in the courts and measures of administrative supervision

Considering the great importance of trust for passing and applying the law, a pertinent question is how the administrative supervision over courts and judges may play a positive role in strengthening the trust placed in courts and judges. The aims of this supervision are to organise the court's adjudication so that it is effective, in the sense of ensuring the professional and meritocratic protection of individual rights.[27] It is essential for the supervision to identify those areas of the

according to the approach by Delvin and Dodek, *Schriftenreihe zur Justizforschung* 2018, No. 17, p. 77. The opposite situation can be observed in Slovakia, where 72 % of Slovak people expressed that they do not trust the courts. See Horvat, M., *Questionnaire "administrative supervision over courts and judges,"* Bratislava, 2020, unpublished, p. 3.

25 The 2020 EU Justice Scoreboard, Publication Office of the EU 2020, p. 41.

26 For such reasons some countries are viewed as "high-trust" societies with high public confidence in the judiciary. See Andersson-Trontti, J., Harakka, K., Pyöriä, M., *How to maintain and increase public confidence in the judiciary*, Sofia: Themis 2019, p. 3.

27 Fischer, C., *Disziplinarrecht und Richteramt*, Frankfurt am Main: Erlanger Schriften zum öffentlichen Recht, 2012, No. 2, pp. 42 ff.

court's functioning which are unprofessional and problematic, and to eliminate these weaknesses so that the courts can adjudicate properly.[28] In that sense, the adoption of supervision measures may lead to strengthening the trust that individuals place in the courts.

Supervision measures have diverse natures and effects. One group is aimed at establishing the facts in the court's functioning or in a concrete case.[29] It is a basis for undertaking measures that can eliminate defects in the court's functioning. Another group is aimed at the adoption of concrete measures which would eliminate identified imperfections in order to organise more efficient and professional adjudication.[30] The adoption of these measures constitutes the core of supervision. They can be undertaken with regard to various entities in the court system, beginning with judges, and then various members of court administration and court presidents, but they cannot encroach on the sphere of their independence. All groups of employees who are responsible for effective adjudication can be subject to administrative supervision. This aim is the only one that justifies this kind of interference.

---

28 Therefore it is beneficial for the strengthening of the public confidence in the judiciary, if judges inform themselves of society's expectations of the judicial system and of complaints about its functioning. See the para. 20 of the recommendation CM/Rec (2010)/12 of the Committee of Ministers to member states on judges: independence, efficiency and responsibilities.

29 For these reasons court's presidents may order an inspection of whole or in separate parts of courts. See Article 37b para. 2 of the Law from 27 June 2001 on the structure of the ordinary courts (Journal of Laws 2020, item 365 with subsequent amendments). The scope of supervision in the Austrian judiciary is determined in article 76 para. 1 Court Organization Act (Gerichtsorganizationsgesetz) of 27.11.1896 (Journal of Laws 2020 I, item 135). The first part of it provides for control of the court's functioning.

30 For that reason the court presidents in Poland can admonish judges for their improper administrative activities which violate the right course of proceedings. See Article 37 para. 3 of the Law from 27.6.2001 on the structure of the ordinary courts, Journal of Laws 2020, item 365 with subsequent amendments. Similar competence is entrusted to the court`s presidents in Denmark, which may issue a warning to a judge guilty of neglect or carelessness in the performance of his or her duties. This covers only less grave cases, as the Danish Penal Code lays down criminal sanctions (a fine or up to 4 months of prison) for judges and other public servants guilty of "gross or repeated neglect or carelessness" while performing in their public capacity. See articles 47–49 of the Danish Administrative of Justice Act (Lov om rettens pleje), Journal of Laws 2014, No. 938 and the article 157 the Danish Penal Code (Straffeloven; Journal of Laws 2015, No. 873).

Supervision measures can be initiated *ex officio* and at the request of interested entities, mainly parties to the proceedings.[31] A second core element of supervision comprises the possibility of reaction without any external impulse.[32] It is important to react to defects in the court's functioning as quickly as possible. A lack of reaction from the authorities responsible for exercising supervision can lead to lowering the trust placed in these entities and the whole judiciary. The same negative result may be reached following poor response to individual claims concerning imperfections in the court's functioning.

A common feature of such supervision is its administrative nature. The supervision is not aimed at affecting the adjudicative competences of courts, since adjudication is the basic function of the third state power. It is evident that a judge must be entirely independent and free from pressure in adjudication.[33] All court activities which involve the basic function are aimed at organising it as professionally as possible. In that sense, even administrative supervision which does not interfere in adjudication still has an impact on its existence. The possibility of making a clear division between adjudication and non-adjudication in court competences is questionable.[34] From this perspective, administrative supervision influences all spheres of court activity. Its adoption should be restrained in order

31 Citizens' complaints and motions in Poland concerning the court's activities should be resolved without undue delay. They cannot concern the sphere in which judges are independent. See article 41a-41e of the Law of 27.06.2001 on the structure the ordinary courts, Journal of Laws 2020, item 365 with subsequent amendments. While in Poland the court president hears the claims, in Denmark they are lodged to the Special Appeal Court (Den Særlige Klageret) within 4 weeks after the complainant has become aware of the circumstances that gaverise to the complaint. See Article 49 of the Danish Administrative of Justice Act. In Austria, according to article 78 para. 1 Court Organization Act, the claims are determined by the court president. If a claim concerned the court president's activity, the President of the Supreme Court is responsible for its determination.

32 It is a characteristic feature of supervision stressed in the doctrine of administrative law. See Szewczyk, M., *Nadzór w materialnym prawie administracyjnym*, Poznań: Wydawnictwo Naukowe UAM, 1995, pp. 44–46.

33 This basic principle is declared by legislators in many countries. E.g. in article 73 para. 2 of the Austrian Court Organization Act it is stated that all authorities involved in the administration of justice are obliged to avoid violating judicial independence.

34 According to statements of some authors, it is not entirely possible. See Wiederin, E., "Gedanken über die richterliche Unabhängigkeit," in: *Unabhängigkeit der Rechtsprechung. Nach außen und innen*, ed. by M. Neumayr, Wien: Manz, 2019, pp. 10–11, Martin AC, W., "Court Administrators and the Judiciary – Partners in the Delivery of Justice," *International Journal for Court Administration*, 2014, No. 2, pp. 14–17.

to not violate judicial independence, and should be precisely aimed at eliminating obstacles or imperfections in the court's functioning. Striking an appropriate balance between these values is crucial for inspiring trust in courts.

The adoption of supervision measures *ex officio* can lead to inefficiencies in the court's adjudication being eliminated. Such activity is usually initiated by representatives of the court's authorities, who identify the imperfections in the court's organisation and functioning.[35] This kind of supervision performed from inside the judiciary system has two main advantages. Firstly, an internal perspective is broader than an external one, and it can give more information about the court's activity and the reasons behind the undertaken activities.[36] Secondly, if the impulses come from inside the court's structure, it raises less controversy over judicial independence than if pressure comes from outside the structure, mainly from the executive power. Considering the division of powers and the necessity of ensuring a high level of judicial independence, every interference from outside can raise doubts and concerns about the level of court independence.

Supervision over the courts and judges may sometimes lead to lower levels of trust in the courts. The first and most serious reason for this is conflict with judicial independence, which is a core element for each court's functioning. From this point of view, it is disputable that court presidents should have the right to supervise public hearings and to demand that judges eliminate administrative delays in a concrete dispute.[37] There is also doubt as to whether presidents should have the right to review the uniformity of judgments.[38] Such competences might

35 In Denmark, one of those competences is a warning that can be issued by the court president to a judge, for his or her improper or indecent behaviour. See Article 48 para. 1 of the Danish Administration of Justice Act. In Poland a warning is one of disciplinary measures which may be issued to a judge. See Article 109 para. 1 of the Polish Law on the structure of the ordinary courts.

36 For the same reasons, it is clear that a disconnection between the external authority (executive power) which allocates resources to the judiciary and is accountable for the outputs from those resources is a recipe for inefficiency and waste. Martin AC, W., "Court Administrators and the Judiciary – Partners in the Delivery of Justice," *International Journal for Court Administration,* 2014, No. 2, p. 8.

37 Article 22 § 1 and 3 of the Law of 25.07.2002 on the system of administrative courts (Journal of Laws 2017, item 2188 with subsequent amendments). This kind of regulation is unknown to the Danish and the Austrian legislators.

38 This kind of competence is characteristic for the Austrian legislator. According to Article 9 § 2 of the statute on the Federal Administrative Court (Journal of Laws I 2020, No. 24 with subsequent amendments), it is the responsibility of the Court's President to ensure that the judiciary is as uniform as possible, while fully preserving the judicial independence of the judges.

be understood only as non-executive measures of shaping the proper course of proceedings and ensuring the uniformity of jurisprudence. Beyond the regulation of law, it is significant how these competences are exercised in practice. If they are not exercised,[39] or are used only in a non-executive manner,[40] then they may not lower trust in public institutions and the courts.

Internal competences		**External competences**
1) Based on direct observation of the court's functioning (internal perspective) 2) Capable of quick reaction to observed imperfections 3) Less controversial for safeguarding the judge's independence	Supervision over courts and judges	1) Based on following the court's activity from the external point of view (external perspective) 2) Capable of reacting after the time necessary to establish what the current state of affairs is 3) Leads to doubts concerning judicial independence
Inspiring more trust in judicial systems – legal regulations in Austria and Denmark		**Inspiring less trust in judicial systems – legal regulations in Poland and Slovakia**

The poor adoption of administrative supervision may change a court's activity in a negative way. A reason for this could be the lack of professionalism of an entity that is responsible for applying a supervisory measure. It is hard to give a straightforward answer regarding how such danger could best be limited. Firstly, supervision measures should be adopted with a high level of restraint to avoid violating judicial independence. This ability is dependent on the level of the legal culture in each country. It is better to refrain from the adoption of supervision measures than exercise such competences and cross the border beyond which judges should be entirely independent. Secondly, supervisory measures should remain under the court's control, by identifying remedies against the adopted

39 The aforementioned competence from Article 22 § 1 and 3 of the Law on the system of administrative courts is not exercised in practice.

40 The competence of the Austrian court presidents is exercised in this manner. See Eckhart, R., "Zur Unabhängigkeit von Richtern der Ordentlichen Gerichtsbarkeit", *Österreichische Juristische Zeitschrift*, 2016, No. 11, p. 493.

restrictions in each concrete case. Especially when supervision becomes part of non-judicial competences, they should remain under court's verification at the final stage of their adoption. Thirdly, the public control of an adoption, which is performed by the media, and which assures the foreseeability of the undertaken decisions, may influence the adoption of the supervision rules. The adoption of supervision measures should not be excluded from media information, since this is the best option for ensuring transparency in court adjudication. This process has a positive influence on shaping trust in the courts and judges. Increased transparency leads to an avoidance of misunderstanding and confusion in the communication between courts and citizens.

4. Which entities are responsible for exercising supervision over courts and judges?

Fostering trust in the courts and judges is also linked with public entities responsible for exercising supervision over the judiciary. Supervisory competences might be granted to the judiciary, to the executive power, or to a separate state agency.

From the analysed point of view, the most controversial option is entrusting supervisory competences to the executive power.[41] This practice raises controversy due to the principle of the separation of powers, because it can give too much power to one branch of the state authorities, at the expense of another branch, the judiciary, which should be separated from legislative and executive powers when fulfilling its obligations.[42] The aims of the executive power are not identical with ensuring effective court adjudication.[43] Courts also adjudicate in disputes where the executive power is one of the parties to the proceedings. If the executive power's competences with regard to the courts are diversified and

---

41 According to Article 9 of the Polish Law on the structure ordinary courts, administrative supervision over courts is exercised by the Minister of Justice.

42 According to Article 173 of the Constitution of the Republic of Poland, courts and tribunals constitute separate powers and shall be independent from other branches of power. This means that the court's competences should not be exercised by other authorities. See the judgment of the Polish Constitutional Tribunal, 19.06.2005, K 28/04, OTK-A 2005, No. 7, item 81.

43 For that reason, the majority of adjudication competences are delegated to the Polish Ministry of Justice judges. See Article 9a § 2 the Polish Law on the structure ordinary courts.

complex, then it is understandable that interferences in the operation of the courts raise questions concerning judicial independence and impartiality.

As stated above, the most appropriate solution from the perspective of shaping trust in the courts is entrusting supervisory competences over the judiciary inside the judicial power. The adoption of supervisory competences by judges or court presidents with regard to other judges is less controversial than entrusting these competences to entities outside the judiciary. There is no necessary connection between more efficient supervision over courts and entrusting this competence to the executive power. Evidence that there is no connection between these components is provided by comparing the supervision exercised over the Polish ordinary judiciary and the administrative judiciary. It is simply not possible to conclude that the ordinary judiciary, which the Ministry of Justice supervises, is more professional than the administrative judiciary, supervised by the President of the Supreme Administrative Court (SAC).[44] If the disputes resolved by ordinary and administrative courts are compared, it is not possible to say that one kind of court is more effective than the other. Undoubtedly, the supervisory measures undertaken by the President of the SAC can efficiently eliminate every inefficiency in the court's activity.[45] Even if there are no clear advantages to entrusting supervision to the judicial realm, the reason that these competences are located inside the judiciary should be regarded as a sufficient rule for this solution.

It is worth considering the creation of a public service that would be separate from the executive and judicial powers and responsible for properly organising court activity. This solution has been adopted in Scandinavian countries, which decided to create agencies that are separate from the executive power and which are responsible for supporting the courts and judges in adjudication.[46] The main

44 From the statistical point of view it is not possible to conclude that the ordinary courts in Poland adjudicate more swiftly. In contrast to this thesis, in the literature it is argued that the administrative courts, specially at first instance level, are swifter and more efficient than the ordinary courts. See Skoczylas, A., "Kwestia zasadności odrębnej regulacji ustroju sądów administracyjnych w Polsce," *Iustitia* 2011, No. 4, https://www.kwartalnikiustitia.pl/kwestia-zasadnosci-odrebnej-regulacji-ustroju-sadow-administracyjnych-w-polsce,923 (access date: 23.10.2020).

45 An example of this thesis was the reaction of the President of the SAC to the pandemic crisis in Fall 2020. The practical regulations as to how the courts should determine cases (mainly not in camera) were published on the website of the SAC earlier than the recommendations from the Ministry of Justice to the ordinary courts.

46 In Sweden, the National Courts Administration is responsible inter alia for supporting the courts through changes, by providing development methods and expertise, to

aim of these agencies is to strengthen judicial independence by entrusting the task of exercising supervision over – and providing assistance to – the courts to a newly created institution that has no personal and or leadership connections with other state authorities.[47] Undoubtedly, an institution that is separated from other state powers has greater legitimacy and weight than the Ministry of Justice, or even a court president, to intervene against inefficient administrative practices at a specific court.[48] This kind of intervention is less likely to lower trust in the courts and in the entity that exercises supervisory functions.

From the above-mentioned methods of supervision over judiciaries, the latter solution has the best potential for fostering trust in the courts and judges. Within this kind of regulation, the judicial power is separated from the other state authorities in the best way. At the same time, the Scandinavian scholarly literature stresses the need for openness and transparency of the judiciary.[49] These values create a combination that results in a high level of trust being placed in the courts and judges.

5. Non-supervisory measures feasible for shaping trust in the courts and judges

The use of supervisory measures is only one tool for increasing the trust placed in the courts and judges, and for strengthening their authority. The first and most basic way is for the courts to communicate their decisions clearly, with

refine professional roles and to bring about greater specialisation, delegation and an efficient case preparation organisation. For more details, see the Swedish National Courts Administration, pp. 644–645 https://www.scandinavianlaw.se/pdf/51-31.pdf (access date: 23.10.2020).

47 See the "Presentation of the National Courts Administration and the Norwegian Courts Reforms," *Stockholm Institute for Scandinavian Law 1957–2010*, ed. by Rosseland A., p. 610.

48 This measure is approved in the Norwegian and Danish literature. See the "Presentation of the National Courts Administration and the Norwegian Courts Reforms," in: *Stockholm Institute for Scandinavian Law*, ed. by A. Rosseland, 1957–2010, p. 610. The same explanation is presented by the Danish judiciary. See "A closer look at the courts of Denmark," 2015, p. 7, https://domstol.dk/media/1634/a-closer-look-at-the-courts-of-denmark.pdf (access date: 7.11.2020).

49 "A closer look at the courts of Denmark," 2015, pp. 29–31, https://domstol.dk/media/1634/a-closer-look-at-the-courts-of-denmark.pdf (access date: 7.11.2020).

justifications.[50] There are plenty of initiatives to deepen trust in the courts and judges that do not involve one-way administrative interference in the courts' structure.

The first group of these initiatives is connected with a new philosophy of court management, named the "New Approach."[51] Here, the basic aim is to foster the feeling among the parties to the proceeding that they are being treated respectfully. The unilateral model of court decision is replaced by a model in which the parties are involved in the way in which the proceedings develop.[52] In this model, the parties are more engaged in resolving a dispute and have more influence on the course of the proceedings. There is a chance that such argumentative relations between them and the court will lead to a higher level of acceptance of final judgments and increase the trust placed in the courts.

This model of the relations between the court and the parties to the proceedings is typical for some countries and branches of courts in Western Europe, such as the administrative judiciary in Germany.[53] It is not employed in the Polish administrative courts, where the traditional model of unilateral, nonargumentative contact between courts and citizens is still in place. Introducing changes would be difficult, due to the citizens' expectations, who are sensitive to every symptom of non-impartiality displayed by the judges. A discussion between judges and parties to the proceedings, with many questions and statements, may lead to the belief that the court is not impartial. However, these cultural limitations should not lead to a reluctance to introduce new forms of argumentation and discussion between all the entities engaged in a court dispute. The introduction of the "New Approach" to the Polish judiciary should be prepared with caution, since this new approach to relations is new for Polish citizens.

---

50 This tool is still regarded as significant, but it is not sufficient to maintain confidence in the judiciary. See Andersson-Trontti, J., Harakka, K., Pyöriä, M., "How to maintain and increase public confidence in the judiciary," Sofia: Themis, 2019, p. 17.

51 Veburg, A., Schueler, B., "Procedural justice in Dutch Administrative court proceedings," *Utrecht Law Review*, 2014, No. 4, pp. 61–71.

52 Veburg, A., Schueler, B., "Procedural justice in Dutch Administrative court proceedings," *Utrecht Law Review*, 2014, No. 4, p. 68.

53 According to article 104 para. 1 VwGO, during public hearing the presiding judge is obliged to discuss the factual and legal aspects of a dispute with parties. In the literature, a public hearing is defined as an analytic (discursive) form of process. See Kothe, P., in: *Verwaltungsgerichtsordnung*, ed. by M., Redeker, Von Oerzten, H.J., Stuttgart: Kohlhammer, 2014, p. 705.

The second group of initiatives includes single activities which are aimed at bringing the courts closer to citizens. These initiatives are diverse, and concern not only judicial court obligations but also cultural and educational issues. Non-judicial measures open up the possibility of looking at courts from other perspectives, and present the courts as institutions where ordinary people are employed – and this includes judges and court staff. In the Polish SAC, various exhibitions about the history of the Polish administrative judiciary are prepared.[54] In the German Federal Administrative Court, the project "Culture&Judiciary" (Kunst&Justiz) is being realised, with the aim of organising cultural events inside the judicial building.[55] Some courts, including the Conceil d`État in Paris, prepare descriptions of their activity in electronic form.[56] Such activities should be welcomed by all judiciaries, since they bring the work of the courts closer to citizens.

In the second group of initiatives, new ways of communicating between the courts and citizens should be distinguished in the court's official documents. It is well-known that the language used by lawyers contains complex jargon and is hard for citizens to follow. Nevertheless, official documents prepared by the courts should be accessible for everybody. The complexity of these files makes following the court's decisions complicated and has a negative effect on the level of trust in the courts and judges. For that reason, it is necessary to adopt measures that make communication between courts and citizens more understandable. An example of such a practice are the efforts made by the French *Conseil Constitutionnel* and the *Conceil d`État*. More complex papers were restructured with headlines and paragraphs, and long sentences were divided into shorter sections.[57] These changes seem simple and obvious; thus, they

---

54 Additionally, in the SAC lessons on Polish law are conducted and the competitions for the best magistry and PhD dissertations on the supervision of public administration are prepared. For more details, see "Lesson in the court," http://www.nsa.gov.pl/lekcja-w-sadzie.php (access date: 24.10.2020).

55 In the court, such events as concerts or panel discussions are organised. For more details, see "Art&Justice in the Federal Administrative Court," http://www.kunstundjustiz.bund.de/ (access date: 24.10.2020).

56 See "Advise the public authorities," https://www.conseil-etat.fr/le-conseil-d-etat/missions/conseiller-les-pouvoirs-publics (access date: 24.10.2020).

57 Ostrowski, P., "Postulat czytelności orzeczeń sądowych w świetle zmian reguł redakcji orzeczeń francuskiego Sądu Kasacyjnego," *Nauka, Badania i Doniesienia Naukowe. Nauki Humanistyczne i Społeczne*. Część II. Świebodzice 2020, pp. 255–256. The same idea of plain language is realised by the Norwegian National Court Administration. See "Action plan for development of services at the courts and the Norwegian Courts

should be considered by other judiciaries. Resigning from the use of specific formulations in the written justifications of judgments, or even the linguistic correction of official courts documents, would not threaten judicial independence. Such solutions would not interfere in the adjudication process and would help people follow the court's reasoning.

6. Media and trust in the courts

The conventional understanding of the judicial function is that courts do not have a lot in common with the media. Nevertheless, the belief that the only acceptable form of communication with citizens is judicial decision-making has gradually been abandoned.[58] Courts needs the media to provide information, in a professional form, about the activities of the judiciary, to foster trust-building. The media also need the courts to generate information that is important for their audience. The relationship between courts and the media can be mutually beneficial.[59] It should be developed not only to serve the interests of the courts and the media but also to provide citizens with accurate information about the functioning of the judiciary.

From judges' perspective, it is clear that there has been increased attention to the professional presentation and representation of the judiciary. The organisation of the judiciary should be conducted in a way that facilitates the creation of appropriate contact with the media. Although it would not be acceptable to influence the media with regard to the adopted measures of court supervision, it is possible to use these measures to determine how the court interacts with the media, which will, in turn, strengthen public confidence in the judiciary. However, communication with the media needs to be conducted with some

---

Administration. The Moment of Truth," https://www.domstol.no/globalassets/upload/da/domstol.no/domstoladministrasjonen/publikasjoner/veiledere/the-moment-of-truth---e-fil-01042016.pdf (access date: 11.2.2020).

58 Which does not mean that judicial reasoning is not the basic form of communication between courts and parties to the case. See. Aarli, R., "Independent judges and their relationship with the media," in: *The independence of judges*, ed. by Asbjørn Engstad, N., A., Tønder, B., Hague: Eleven International Publishing, 2014, p. 327.

59 It is recommended for all countries to develop a proactive media approach which should be focused on individual court cases as well as the judicial system and principles of law. See the report of the European Network of Councils for the Judiciary entitled "Justice, Society and the Media," 2011–2012, https://www.encj.eu/images/stories/pdf/GA/Dublin/encj_report_justice_society_media_def.pdf, pp. 19 ff (access date: 6.2.2020).

restraint.[60] The adoption of supervision provides an opportunity to develop rules on appropriate contact with the media, to create an internal court organisation dedicated to managing this communication channel, and to convey rules for reporting from inside the courtroom (and during the proceedings). Thanks to such oversight, the rules and customs for contact between judges and the media can be monitored, improved and, if necessary, corrected.

Many courts have their spokespersons or even special sections which are responsible for communicating with the media. It is vital that people engaged in this activity – whether judges, court administration staff, or journalists – should have basic legal knowledge and basic public relations training. Their job is not only to communicate some information to media representatives but to do this in a comprehensible manner.[61] The most dangerous threat to the courts is a lack of understanding of their role and misinformation. To avoid such pitfalls, spokespersons should be accessible to media representatives on request. The initiative to contact media can come from the court as an institution, or even from an individual judge. The purpose of such contact should be the development of solutions which make judicial decision-making clearer for citizens.[62] This practice can lead to the preparation of more professional reports about the work of courts.

There should be clear rules for using communication devices inside courts buildings and during case hearings. These rules vary between legal orders and

60 See para. 19 of the recommendation CM/Rec (2010)/12 of the Committee of Ministers to member states on judges: independence, efficiency and responsibilities. In the explanatory memorandum to the recommendation it is explained that the restraint cannot be precisely quantified. As an example, it is stated that personal appearances by judges in the media to justify their decisions are strongly discouraged.

61 It is worth mentioning that communication with media requires additional skills to those traditionally required by a judge. For that reason, trainings for judges engaged as spokespersons are desired. Additionally, it is important to select a serving judge who has the correct profile and ability. See the report of the European Network of Councils for the Judiciary entitled "Justice, Society and the Media," 2011–2012, https://www.encj.eu/images/stories/pdf/GA/Dublin/encj_report_justice_society_media_def.pdf, pp. 4 ff (access date: 6.2.2021).

62 In the Scandinavian countries, judges who want to make themselves available to journalists are associated in the Judge`s Media Group. They are eager to help the media when statements or explanations are needed from judges. See the Norwegian members of this group, "Media judges," https://www.domstol.no/en/Press-services1/media-judges/ (access date: 6.2.2021).

are determined by many factors, including cultural and historical ones.[63] The rules should make media reporting possible. If this is not permissible during the trial, there are other methods for information to be communicated, like announcements on the court's websites about all hearings, not only final results but also information on the submission of the parties to the case and the court's reasoning, as well as comments prepared by the court's PR staff at the request of media representatives, or even press-conferences.

Under specific conditions, courts and judges can use social media to contact the media and inform the public about their decision-making.[64] It would help not only in improving contact with people who are fluent with these platforms, mainly the young, but also in reacting when a court statement is urgently expected. Social media present the judiciary with a new avenue for communication regarding its activity. This initiative will have the biggest impact in high-profile cases that attract the attention of a large audience that would not otherwise read the court judgment.[65] It is a form of a direct contact between courts and citizens, which makes the reasoning more direct. Nevertheless, the use of social media requires special caution in order not to weaken trust in the courts. It should not violate the ethical code of conduct of the judiciary.[66] Direct contact which provides an opportunity for more personalised and detailed information, or

---

63 In some countries, video recording in courtrooms is prohibited. In other countries, like Netherlands, Romania and Poland audio and video recording is allowed within certain limits. See the report of the European Network of Councils for the Judiciary entitled "Justice, Society and the Media," 2011–2012, https://www.encj.eu/images/stories/pdf/GA/Dublin/encj_report_justice_society_media_def.pdf, pp. 6–11 (access date: 6.2.2021).

64 The German Bundesverwaltungsgericht und the French Conseil d`Etat use Twitter accounts. See https://twitter.com/bverwg_de, https://twitter.com/conseil_etat (access date: 24.10.2021). This form of communication is not used by the Polish Supreme Administrative Court.

65 Perl, H., "Die Akzeptanz der Verwaltungsgerichte," in: *Grundfragen der Verwaltungs- und Finanz- gerichtsbarkeit*, ed. by Holoubek, M., Lang, M., Wien: Linde Verlag, 2017, p. 350.

66 In § 23 of the Polish Ethical Code for Judges it is stated that a judge should use social media with restraint. In another section of the Code it is stipulated that a judge should avoid activities violating trust in his professional career (§ 5 No 2) or in his impartiality and independence (§ 10). A judge should not comment on other cases or future court cases (§ 13). See "Set of Rules for the Professional Ethic of Judges," 2017, No. 25, https://krs.pl/pl/o-radzie/zbior-zasad-etyki-zawodowej-sedziow/591-uchwala-nr-25-2017-krajowej-rady-sadownictwa-z-dnia-13-stycznia-2017-r.html (access date: 7.2.2021).

even an exchange of opinions, can become controversial both from the judge's and the citizen's perspective. Judges may be engaged in the kinds of discussions which will not help to foster trust in them. It is possible that citizens will misunderstand their statements. In extreme situations, the citizen's messages can be offensive or even toxic. In some conditions, it can threaten judicial independence and even be a basis for criminal proceedings. Restraint in using social media does not automatically mean that the avoidance of difficult situations will be more feasible. Nevertheless it increases the chances that such situations will not be frequent and will not lower the trust in courts.

The accessibility of judicial decision-making to the media and society as a whole is conditioned by restrictions on access to published court decisions. In the ideal scenario, the media and society would have free access to the whole database of judgments.[67] For transparency and educational purposes, judgments with their reasons should be published without delay.[68] It would also be beneficial if crucial judgments were presented in plain language to allow citizens without a professional background in law to understand them. The French Council of State does this,[69] but the Polish judiciary is not familiar with such practices. A summary of the main reasons for a judgment in a plain language will be beneficial for the media and citizens interested in access to court reasoning.

It is necessary to stress once again that the presented methods of cooperation between the courts and the media do not mean that the courts can abandon all restraint in their media relations. Such restraint ought not to limit access to information concerning the court's decision-making. Instead, it should focus on establishing clear rules for the release of information. This is a matter of internal court organisation and control of its activity that is exercised by court presidents and other actors responsible for supervision over the courts and judges.

---

67 A good example of this practice is the database of the judgments of the Polish administrative courts, which contains almost all the court judgments, with the exception of those which should be secret for special reasons, like security or state secrets. The database is accessible at the address orzeczenia.nsa.gov.pl

68 Von Bernstorff, A., "Die Gerichtsverwaltung in Deutschland und England," *Studien zum vergleichenden Öffentlichen Recht*, 2018, No. 2, p. 210, 320.

69 An example of that is provided by the judgment of the Council of State, 18.5.2020, No. 440366, https://www.conseil-etat.fr/ressources/decisions-contentieuses/dernieres-decisions-importantes/conseil-d-etat-18-mai-2020-rassemblements-dans-les-lieux-de-culte (access date: 26.2.2021), concerning religious freedom during the first wave of pandemic.

7. Covid-19 and trust in the courts

The outbreak of the Covid-19 global pandemic generated renewed interested in the study of trust in the courts and judges. The extreme conditions of the pandemic presented the courts with the unique opportunity to work on their reputation, as court currently adjudicate numerous disputes concerning the influence of the pandemic on human lives. Simultaneously, the present situation may result in increased distrust in the courts if changes in the organisation of the judiciary will be improper, introduced in bad faith, or generally unsuitable to meet the challenge of the times.

One of the most noticeable changes in the delivery of justice during the pandemic has been the increase in the number of proceedings conducted *in camera*.[70] The limitation on contact with parties to the case and circulation of court users for the protection of public health is understandable, but it should not be the go-to measure in all cases. Personal contact between parties to the case and the court is especially significant in criminal cases.[71] For other types of disputes, the dispensation from the requirement of a public hearing may decrease processing times. The aim to accelerate the processing of cases should not be treated as the only goal, however. The use of innovative processes can accelerate the courts' decision-making. For example, courts could save time if discovery proceedings were limited only to documents or other material without the need for personal contact.[72]

In other disputes, the advantage of *in camera* hearings might have been only virtual and could lead to adverse outcomes. Consider the example of a party that wants to participate in the hearing, but the court does not create the possibility for such active participation.[73] Courts should not give up on innovating their

70 Based on the order of the SAC President of Poland, issued on the 16.10.2020, No. 39, all public hearings at the SAC, beginning from the 17.10.2020 were to be dismissed. Disputes which had already been scheduled were heared in camera.

71 The personal presence of the accused during a public trial is regarded by the ECtHR as an indispensable element of a right to a fair trial regulated in Article 6 para. 1 Convention for the Protection of Human Rights and Fundamental Freedoms. See Judgment of ECtHR, 18.10.2006, *Hermi v. Italy*, No. 18114/02, para. 59, judgment of ECtHR, 2.11.2010, *Sakhynovski v. Russia*, No. 21272/03, para. 98.

72 According to Article 106 § 3 of the Polish Law on proceedings before administrative courts, a court may request only documentary proof if it is necessary to resolve substantial doubts and will not extend excessively the proceedings on the case. The administrative courts verify administrative acts on the basis of case files. It is not possible to hear witnesses during public hearings.

73 Public hearing is perceived in the literature as a core element of each proceedings. See Pabel, K., "Die mündliche Verhandlung vor dem Verwaltungsgericht", *Zeitschrift der Verwaltungsgerichtsbarkeit*, 2018, No. 8, pp. 8–9.

decision-making processes. One innovation that could considerably improve the court experience during a pandemic is new, electronic ways of communication that make the procedure as transparent as possible.[74] The pure limitation of public hearings without creating attendance possibilities may lead to a violation of the right to defence and increasing distrust in the courts. In other words, abandoning oral hearings without approval from the parties to the case is controversial, even the circumstances of a pandemic. If there is no way to provide a chance for active participation in a hearing, suspension of the case should be considered. At the very least, this solution would not decrease the trust in courts, unlike deciding cases *in camera*, even if they are heard in a reasonable time.

The pandemic resulted in severe restrictions on fundamental human rights and liberties in many jurisdictions. It is a court obligation to review such restrictions from various perspectives, like the preservation of fundamental rights and freedoms or the principle of proportionality. There are many examples of the courts questioning the imposed restrictions. One group of cases concerned the exclusion of the possibility of participating in religious ceremonies. The complete closure of places of worship was assessed by German and French administrative courts and ultimately judged disproportionate to threats caused by the pandemic.[75] In these cases, courts protected the fundamental rights to religious freedom. In extraordinary circumstances, the courts are faced with the challenge of arriving at a just decision. They need to evaluate the various restrictions imposed on citizens and take into account the protection of their basic rights, so that the restrictions imposed are proportionate to the circumstances.

---

74 It is also possible to organise public hearings in more spacious halls. This possibility was used by the German Bundesverwaltungsgericht in the case concerning building a tunel under the Baltic Sea between Germany and Denmark (Fehmarnbelt tunel). The public trial was organised in the congress centre in Leipzig. See Klohn, A., Zimmermann, B., 23.9.2020, "Fehmarnbelt tunnel put to the test in front of the Leipzig Federal Administrative Court," https://www.lvz.de/Leipzig/Lokales/Fehmarnbelt-Tunnel-vor-Leipziger-BVG-auf-dem-Pruefstand (access date: 7.2.2021).

75 Order of the Federal Constitutional Court in Karlsruhe, 29.4.2020, No. 1 BvQ 44/20, https://www.bundesverfassungsgericht.de/SharedDocs/Entscheidungen/DE/2020/04/qk20200429_1bvq004420.html (access date: 26.2.2021), a judgment of the Council of State, 18.05.2020, No. 440366, https://www.conseil-etat.fr/ressources/decisions-contentieuses/dernieres-decisions-importantes/conseil-d-etat-18-mai-2020-rassemblements-dans-les-lieux-de-culte (access date: 26.2.2021).

Courts also play an essential role in reviewing the penalties imposed on citizens by the state authorities during the pandemic. In Poland, the fines issued by the government in accordance with pandemic restrictions were regarded by the Ombudsman as unconstitutional because the monetary amount was not proportionate to the delict and was too restrictive.[76] For the same reasons, one administrative court quashed a fine received by an entrepreneur who continued his professional activity during the pandemic, contrary to the restrictions.[77] Judicial review of the imposed restrictions may lead to an increase in the trust placed in the courts. Citizens need to know that every order or decision issued by the executive may be subject to an independent court review, which will examine its legality.

The pandemic has also changed the activity of the court administration.[78] Many members of the court staff, including judges, secretaries and assistants, work from home. This situation raises several questions concerning the proper organisation of their professional activity, including mutual contact, personal data protection, or supervision of work done at home. More flexible work conditions create a chance for a better organisation of court obligations. On the other hand, the present situation brings new risks, due to the lack of control and supervision over remote working. It is not possible to organise the whole decision-making process of a court outside of the courthouse.[79] Some activities have to be undertaken inside courts buildings, even during a pandemic. Court authorities must organise the work of the judicial staff efficiently, but with attention to the proper procedure and handling of case files. The use of supervision measures may be essential if the organisation is inadequate.

---

76 Coronavirus. Principles for punishing citizens arise doubts of the Ombudsman, 5.5.2020, https://www.rpo.gov.pl/pl/content/koronawirus-zasady-karania-obywateli-budza-watpliwosci-rpo (access date: 23.10.2020).

77 The court stated that there was no statutory basis for such a ban, which was introduced through an order (under statutory source of law) issued by the government. The judgment of the Voivodship Administrative Court in Opole, 27.10.2020, No. II SA/Op 219/20, published at the website of the judgments of the Polish administrative courts orzeczenia.nsa.gov.pl (access date: 6.2.2021).

78 It is true that court personnel support judges in adjudication, which is crucial to any reform program aimed at strengthening the integrity and capacity of the justice system. See "United Nations Office of Drugs and Crime, Resource Guide on Strenghtening Judicial Integrity and Capacity," 2011, p. 21 in: Martin AC, W., "Court Administrators and the Judiciary – Partners in the Delivery of Justice," *International Journal for Court Administration*, 2014, No. 2, pp. 3 ff.

79 For instance, it is not permissible to take case files away from a courthouse.

8. Conclusions

Trust in the courts is an indispensable requirement for the proper functioning of the judicial system and the rule of law. Trust in courts may buttress the judicial function at every step of the decision-making process. A high level of trust will help the courts fulfil their obligations. A low level of confidence in courts raises questions and increases the potential for non-compliance with their decisions.

Trust in courts is determined by their decision-making and other activities. A basic requirement for the trustworthy decision-making of a court is its independence. If courts are perceived to be dependent, people will not follow their decisions. Not only trust but also the prestige of courts and respect for their adjudication will be undermined. At the same time, courts should be open to citizens and the media. Transparency in courts plays a crucial role in building trust in the judiciary. A combination of these two components, independence and transparency, is indispensable for building trust in the courts. If the decision-making of courts cannot be observed, every measure, even if adopted in good faith, can lower the level of trust in the judiciary. In other words, the adoption of supervision measures can be decisive for shaping trust in the courts in different ways, depending on the intentions and conditions under which it will be used.

In the present situation of a pandemic, the use of supervision measures may strengthen the trust placed in courts through the efficient adoption of such measures that make relations within the judiciary and with citizens possible and meritocratic. There is a need to develop electronic measures of communication between courts and citizens and inside the judiciary. It will be beneficial for courts and citizens to interact via new communication methods like Twitter or Facebook. The pandemic should increase the speed of innovation in the otherwise conservative judicial system. From this perspective, Covid-19 presented the judiciary with a chance for improving its functioning and organisation. Trust in the courts will also be more robust if courts protect the citizens against executive overreach during the pandemic.

The level of trust placed in the courts also depends on the legal culture of each state.[80] The regulation of judicial supervision and protection against unlawful interference in adjudication will not operate as intended if those responsible do not desire to build trust and cooperation between state authorities. To achieve

80 In high-trust societies, the tolerance of mistakes made by the judiciary may be higher than in societies with low trust in the court system. See Aarli, A., "Independent judges and their relationship with the media," in: *The independence of judges*, ed. by Asbjørn Engstad, N., A., B., Hague: Eleven International Publishing, 2014, p. 343.

that desire, judges and members of other state powers are responsible. It is necessary to repeat that building trust in courts is a long process, while squandering it takes very little time.

References

Publications

Aarli, Ragna, "Independent judges and their relationship with the media," in: *The independence of judges*, ed. by Asbjørn Engstad, Nils, Lærdal Frøseth, Astrid, Tønder, Bard, Hague: Eleven International Publishing, 2014, pp. 327–344.

Andersson-Trontti, Jenny, Harakka, Katja, Pyöriä, Matti, *How to maintain and increase public confidence in the judiciary*, Sofia: Themis 2019.

Chmielewski, Jan, *Zasada budzenia zaufania w ogólnym postępowaniu administracyjnym*, Warszawa: WoltersKluwer, 2018.

Doroszewski, Witold, Warszawa: Wydawnictwo Naukowe PWN, 1968.

Dubisz, Stanisław, Warszawa: Wydawnictwo Naukowe PWN, 2006.

Eckhart, Ratz, "Zur Unabhängigkeit von Richtern der Ordentlichen Gerichtsbarkeit", *Österreichische Juristische Zeitschrift*, 2016, No. 11, pp. 492.

Fischer, Claus, *Disziplinarrecht und Richteramt*, Frankfurt am Main: Erlanger Schriften zum öffentlichen Recht, 2012, No. 2.

Horvat, Matej, *Questionnaire "administrative supervision over courts and judges,"* Bratislava, 2020, unpublished.

Kothe, Peter, in: Verwaltungsgerichtsordnung, ed. by Martin, Redeker, Hans-Joachim von Oerzten, Stuttgart: Kohlhammer, 2014.

Martin Martin AC, "Court Administrators and the Judiciary – Partners in the Delivery of Justice," *International Journal for Court Administration*, 2014, No. 2, pp. 3–18.

Ostrowski, Piotr, "Postulat czytelności orzeczeń sądowych w świetle zmian reguł redakcji orzeczeń francuskiego Sądu Kasacyjnego," *Nauka, Badania i Doniesienia Naukowe. Nauki Humanistyczne i Społeczne*. Część II. Świebodzice 2020, pp. 252–259.

Pabel, Katharina, "Die mündliche Verhandlung vor dem Verwaltungsgericht," *Zeitschrift der Verwaltungsgerichtsbarkeit*, 2018, No. 8, pp. 8–14.

Perl, Harald, "Die Akzeptanz der Verwaltungsgerichte," in: *Grundfragen der Verwaltungs- und Finanz- gerichtsbarkeit*, ed. by Holoubek, Michael, Lang, Michael, Wien: Linde Verlag, 2017, pp. 345–353.

Piątek, Wojciech, "Zasada zaufania," in: *Współpraca państw członkowskich UE przy odzyskiwaniu wierzytelności podatkowych*, ed. by Jan Olszanowski, Wojciech Piątek, Warszawa: Wolters Kluwer, 2016, pp. 42–44.

Rosseland, Arvid, "Presentation of the National Courts Administration and the Norwegian Courts Reforms," *Stockholm Institute for Scandinavian Law, 1957–2010*, pp. 608–628.

Ryser, Arabella, "Swiss justice in comparison. An outline of the Swiss judicial system according to the approach by Delvin and Dodek," *Schriftenreihe zur Justizforschung*, 2018, No. 17.

Szewczyk, M., *Nadzór w materialnym prawie administracyjnym*, Poznań: Wydawnictwo Naukowe UAM, 1995.

Uusitalo Kirsti, *How to maintain and increase public confidence in the judiciary*, Sofia: Themis 2019.

Von Bernstorff, Alexander, "Die Gerichtsverwaltung in Deutschland und England," *Studien zum vergleichenden Öffentlichen Recht*, 2018, No. 2.

Wiederin, Ewald, "Gedanken über die richterliche Unabhängigkeit," in: *Unabhängigkeit der Rechtsprechung. Nach außen und innen*, ed. by Matthias Neumayr, Wien: Manz, 2019, pp. 1–15.

Van de Walle, Steven, "Trust in the justice system: a comparative view across Europe," *Prison Service Journal*, 2009, No. 183, pp. 22–26.

Veburg, André, Schueler, Bern, "Procedural justice in Dutch Administrative court proceedings," *Utrecht Law Review*, 2014, No. 4, pp. 56–72.

Jurisprudence

European Court of Justice

Judgment of ECJ, 19.9.2006, *Graham J. Wilson v. Ordre des advocates du barreau de Luxembourg*, C 506/04.

Judgment of ECJ, 31.1.2013, *H.I.D., B.A. v. Refugee Applications Commissioner and others*, C 175/11.

European Court of Human Rights

Judgment of ECtHR, 24.2.1994, *Fey v. Austria*, No. 14396/88.

Judgment of ECtHR, 18.10.2006, *Hermi v. Italy*, No. 18114/02.

judgment of ECtHR, 2.11.2010, *Sakhynovski v. Russia*, No. 21272/03.

Judgment of ECtHR, 23.4.2015, *Morice v. France*, No. 29369/10.

Judgment of ECtHR, 23.6.2016, *Baka v. Hungary*, No. 20261/12.

Polish Constitutional Tribunal

Judgment of the Polish Constitutional Tribunal, 25.11.1997, K 26/97, OTK 1997, No. 5–6, item 64.

Judgment of the Polish Constitutional Tribunal, 21.12.1999, K 22/99, OTK 1999, No. 7, item 166.

Judgment of the Polish Constitutional Tribunal, 19.6.2005, K 28/04, OTK-A 2005, No. 7, item 81.

Judgment of the Polish Constitutional Tribunal, 19.11.2008, Kp 2/08, OTK-A 2008, No. 9, item 157.

Judgment of the Polish Constitutional Tribunal, 10.1.2012, P 19/10, OTK-A 2012, No. 1, item 2.

Judgment of the Polish Constitutional Tribunal, 8.1.2013, K 18/10, OTK-A 2013, No. 1, item 2.

Judgment of the Polish Constitutional Tribunal, 13.11.2013, K 2/12, OTK-A 2012, No. 10, item 12.

Polish Supreme Administrative Court

Judgment of the Voivodship Administrative Court in Opole, 27.10.2020, No. II SA/Op 219/20, orzeczenia.nsa.gov.pl.

Sources of law

The Constitution of the Republic of Poland from 2nd April 1997, Journal of Laws 1997, Nb 78, item 483.

The Austrian Law from 27 June 2001 on the structure of the ordinary courts, Journal of Laws 2020, item 365 with subsequent amendments.

The Austrian Court Organization Act of 27.11.1896, Journal of Laws 2020 I, item 135.

The Austrian statute on the Federal Administrative Court, Journal of Laws I 2020, No. 24.

The Danish Administrative of Justice Act, Journal of Laws 2014, No. 938.

The Danish Penal Code, Journal of Laws 2015, No. 873.

The Polish Law from 27.6.2001 on the structure of the ordinary courts, Journal of Laws 2020, item 365.

The Polish Law of 25.7.2002 on the system of administrative courts, Journal of Laws 2017, item 2188 as am.

The recommendation CM/Rec (2010)/12 of the Committee of Ministers to member states on judges: independence, efficiency and responsibilities.

Internet sources

"A closer look at the courts of Denmark," 2015, pp. 29–31, https://domstol.dk/media/1634/a-closer-look-at-the-courts-of-denmark.pdf (access date: 7.11.2020).

"Action plan for development of services at the courts and the Norwegian Courts Administration. The Moment of Truth," https://www.domstol.no/globalassets/upload/da/domstol.no/domstoladministrasjonen/publikasjoner/veiledere/the-moment-of-truth---e-fil-01042016.pdf (access date: 11.2.2021).

"Advise the public authorities," https://www.conseil-etat.fr/le-conseil-d-etat/missions/conseiller-les-pouvoirs-publics; (access date: 24.10.2020).

"Art&Justice in the Federal Administrative Court," http://www.kunstundjustiz.bund.de/; (access date: 24.10.2020).

Boguszewski, R., "Zaufanie społeczne. Komunikat z badań," 2010, No. BS/29/2010. https://www.cbos.pl/SPISKOM.POL/2010/K_029_10.PDF (access date: 23.10.2020).

"Coronavirus. Principles for punishing citizens arise doubts of the Ombudsman," 5.5.2020, https://www.rpo.gov.pl/pl/content/koronawirus-zasady-karania-obywateli-budza-watpliwosci-rpo (access date: 23.10.2020).

"Lesson in the court," http://www.nsa.gov.pl/lekcja-w-sadzie.php (access date: 24.10.2020).

The judgment of the Council of State, 18.5.2020, No. 440366, https://www.conseil-etat.fr/ressources/decisions-contentieuses/dernieres-decisions-importantes/conseil-d-etat-18-mai-2020-rassemblements-dans-les-lieux-de-culte (access date: 26.2.2021).

The judgment of the Council of State, 18.5.2020, No. 440366, https://www.conseil-etat.fr/ressources/decisions-contentieuses/dernieres-decisions-importantes/conseil-d-etat-18-mai-2020-rassemblements-dans-les-lieux-de-culte (access date: 26.2.2021).

Klohn, A., Zimmermann, B., 23.09.2020, "Fehmarnbelt tunnel put to the test in front of the Leipzig Federal Administrative Court," https://www.lvz.de/Leipzig/Lokales/Fehmarnbelt-Tunnel-vor-Leipziger-BVG-auf-dem-Pruefstand (access date: 7.2.2021).

The Norwegian members of this group, "Media judges," https://www.domstol.no/en/Press-services1/media-judges/ (access date: 06.02.2021).

Omyła-Rudzka, M., "Zaufanie społeczne. Komunikat z badań," 2016, No. 18. https://www.cbos.pl/SPISKOM.POL/2016/K_018_16.PDF; (access date: 23.10.2020).

Omyła-Rudzka, M., "Zaufanie społeczne. Komunikat z badań," 2020 No. 43; https://www.cbos.pl/SPISKOM.POL/2020/K_043_20.PDF (access date: 23.10.2020).

Order of the Federal Constitutional Court in Karlsruhe, 29.04.2020, No. 1 BvQ 44/20, https://www.bundesverfassungsgericht.de/SharedDocs/Entscheidungen/DE/2020/04/qk20200429_1bvq004420.html (access date: 26.2.2021).

"Public Opinion Research Center. Solid and Professional," https://www.cbos.pl/EN/about_us/about_us.php (access date: 23.10.2020).

The report of the European Network of Councils for the Judiciary entitled "Justice, Society and the Media," 2011–2012, https://www.encj.eu/images/stories/pdf/GA/Dublin/encj_report_justice_society_media_def.pdf, pp. 19–20 (access date: 6.2.2021).

The report of the European Network of Councils for the Judiciary entitled "Justice, Society and the Media," 2011–2012, https://www.encj.eu/images/stories/pdf/GA/Dublin/encj_report_justice_society_media_def.pdf, pp. 4–5 (access date: 6.2.2021).

The report of the European Network of Councils for the Judiciary entitled "Justice, Society and the Media," 2011–2012, https://www.encj.eu/images/stories/pdf/GA/Dublin/encj_report_justice_society_media_def.pdf, pp. 6–11 (access date: 6.2.2021).

"Set of Rules for the Professional Ethic of Judges," 2017, No 25, https://krs.pl/pl/o-radzie/zbior-zasad-etyki-zawodowej-sedziow/591-uchwala-nr-25-2017-krajowej-rady-sadownictwa-z-dnia-13-stycznia-2017-r.html (access date: 7.2.2021).

Skoczylas, A., "Kwestia zasadności odrębnej regulacji ustroju sądów administracyjnych w Polsce," Iustitia 2011, No. 4, https://www.kwartalnikiustitia.pl/kwestia-zasadnosci-odrebnej-regulacji-ustroju-sadow-administracyjnych-w-polsce,923 (access date: 23.10.2020).

Final remarks

This research has come to the basic conclusion that administrative supervision may be used as a feasible instrument for making the courts' activity more effective. Supervision, understood as a whole scope of measures focused on the courts' functioning from an administrative perspective (financial, employee-related, technical, connected to the work of judges), can improve the organisation of the courts' adjudication and may lead to an increase in the quality of jurisprudence, the issuance of judgments in a reasonable time, and the creation of effective judicial protection for individuals. It is difficult to imagine the courts functioning properly without any control or corrections of various spheres of their organisation.

At the same time, administrative supervision seems to be a sensible tool for eliminating imperfections in the courts' functioning, because it may be used for the opposite aims, such as the subordination of judicial power to the other two state powers, mainly the executive; or the exertion of pressure on judges to prevent the issuance of expected unfavourable judgments. In such conditions, the judicial power becomes incapable of fulfilling its basic tasks, and individuals no longer view it as trustworthy. Other negative consequences would be a lack of legal certainty and a low level of jurisprudence. To avoid these threats, safeguarding judicial independence has crucial significance. If the courts are dependent on the other state powers or particular individuals, they in fact cease to be courts. In that sense, judicial independence is more important than administrative supervision, because without independence the courts are deprived of their basic feature. This does not mean that supervision over the courts is not necessary and that the courts' activities can be organised without any supervision.[1] Instead, it means that supervision over the courts without the preservation of judicial independence may cause deep damage to the essence of the courts' adjudication. Judicial independence must be treated as a precondition for all forms of supervision over the courts and judges. Those which pose concrete threats, and which will lead to weakened independence, should not be adopted.

1 As S. Haack claims, "a constitutional state without judicial independence is just as inconceivable as a constitutional state without such a minimum of supervision of judges."

Supervision over the courts and judicial independence remain connected in the sense that it is impossible to designate a clear border beyond which supervisory measures should not be applied. The core area of judicial independence does not exist, and each individual dispute concerning the relations between independence and supervision should be solved independently. For countries with lower levels of legal culture – thus in Central and Eastern Europe, including Poland – the level of interference into judicial functions should be more restrictive than for these countries where deep and controversial interference into judicial independence is unimaginable. In other words, there is a need for stronger structural guarantees of judicial independence in countries where this value is violated or may be violated on the basis of populist reasoning. Nevertheless, even countries with more developed and established legal cultures should not avoid reflections concerning mechanisms that safeguard the principles of judicial independence, because their history and legal achievements do not entirely guarantee that deep violations of judicial independence are impossible.[2] In some of these countries, measures are adopted for shaping greater guarantees of judicial independence. The principles of judicial ethics should be based on values such as independence, integrity, dignity, honour, impartiality, restraint, discretion, equal treatment, transparency, humanity, and prudence.[3] Noteworthy examples of this phenomenon are present in the Scandinavian countries, where supervisory functions are excluded from the executive and judicial powers and given to independent administrative bodies, called National Courts Administrations.[4] These bodies, located outside the Ministry of Justice, are responsible for meritocratic court support and services (in various spheres from human resources and communication to information technology and innovations) in order to ensure reasonable and efficient adjudication.

Focusing on subjective matters, the aforementioned independent bodies offer a feasible solution to the organisation of administrative supervision over the courts without posing any major threats to their impartiality. Such bodies are mainly equipped with supervisory competences of executive power. The

---

2 As K. Pabel claims, "is not enough to have the 'perfect' legal framework for the organisation of the judiciary and the independent position of judges with all the requirements emanating from the case law fulfilled. The implementation of the law in every single proceeding with the mind-set of effective independence is at least as important as the legislation itself."

3 M. Horvat, M. Radosa, "Considerations on the supervision exercised over courts and judges."

4 For more about this mechanism, see the paper by M. Sunnqvist in this volume.

supervision is organised by experts from various branches of science, from the representatives of legal science to specialists in electronic communication and media services. Another feasible solution is based on the organisation of supervisory competences inside judiciary, as the presidents of courts have wide knowledge concerning weaknesses in the courts' organisation, and they can counteract them quickly and precisely.[5] The most controversial regulation involves the executive power supervising the courts. External supervision over courts' activities may lead to charges of excessive interference with judicial independence and to a violation of the principle of the division of powers. For these reasons, supervision performed by members of the executive power may be less effective and focus on issues which are not responsible for the courts' imperfections.

Supervision may be treated as an effective tool for eliminating delays in delivering justice. The right to a court hearing within a reasonable time is one of the fundamental components of the right to a fair trial. The duration of the proceedings may be subject to supervision with regard to the correctness of the actions taken by a court or a judge. Any shortcomings in a specific case may result in an order for the matter to be settled immediately. They may also lead to specific disciplinary consequences against the judge hearing the case.[6]

There are different measures of supervision in each of the analysed legal orders. They vary in nature, can be advisory or authoritative, and are aimed at various spheres of the courts' functioning. A common feature is that all legal interference in judicial positions (fines, reduction of salaries, termination of employment) has to remain under the supervision exercised by courts, particularly in disciplinary proceedings.[7] This is regarded as a guarantee of judicial independence and the courts' autonomy.

Currently, technological development is significant for supervisory aims. Such instruments as electronic case distribution may strengthen the courts' independence without simultaneously weakening supervision over them. Creating panels with the support of computer software shapes a pre-established procedure with objective and transparent criteria. The most crucial advantage of this solution is the elimination of arbitrariness, thus enhancing the neutrality of case assignment.[8] It can be also perceived more generally as only one of various

5 As A. Skoczylas observes, the decision-making process concerning the court's internal organisation should be partially assigned to each judge.

6 For more about such mechanisms, see the paper written by A. Paduch in this volume.

7 For more about the various systems of supervision measures, see the paper by J. Olszanowski in this volume.

8 For more on the advantages of this solution, see the paper of I. Gontarz in this volume.

mechanisms which can improve judicial systems and give more detailed information about their functioning and imperfections. Nevertheless, it cannot entirely replace adjudication processes and supervision over them, because they involve and depend on human abilities. The adoption of supervision measures can be supported by electronic measures, but the final decision as to which measure should be adopted in specific circumstances should remain in the human sphere.

If supervision is exercised properly, it can strengthen the trust placed in the courts.[9] The adoption of supervision measures *ex officio* can lead to eliminating the ineffective exercise of the court's adjudication, like delays or other imperfections in the court's functioning. It has a direct impact on the courts' evaluation by citizens. If imperfections are eliminated and citizens receive information about the adopted measures, their perception of justice changes in a positive way.

Contact between the courts and media by means of various forms of communication can be analysed from the perspective of supervision in a broader sense, understood as pertaining to all the measures involved in professional adjudication. In the information era, the courts face the need to communicate the results of their work, including access to jurisprudence for professionals and ordinary people. Supervision in the strict sense, understood as measures aimed at eliminating defined imperfections in the court's organisation, may be adopted in those situations where a court's contact with the media would lead to lowering the trust placed in them. Such threats may arise if judges use social media. Though direct contact provides an opportunity for more personalised and detailed information, or even an exchange of opinions, it can become controversial, both from the judge's and the citizen's perspective. Judges may become engaged in some discussions which will not help to foster trust in them. It is also possible that citizens will misunderstand judges' statements.

In the present situation of the Covid-19 pandemic, the use of supervision may strengthen trust in the courts through the efficient adoption of measures that make relations within the judiciary and with citizens possible and meritocratic. For citizens, the courts' adjudication concerning the scope of restrictions is in many disputes is tied up with basic rights, such as freedom of assembly or religious freedom. Apart from the external sphere, the courts' internal activity had to be reorganised due to the threat posed to health and safety. This also

---

9 For more on the various ways of strengthening trust in the courts, see the paper by W. Piątek in this volume.

involves the adoption of supervision in order to make the courts' adjudication more effective.

In the final conclusion, it is necessary to repeat that although it is not possible to entirely separate supervisory measures from the courts' adjudication and judicial independence, both factors – supervision and judicial independence – are in need of improvement if the courts are to function more professionally. It is a challenge for each state where the rule of law plays a significant role to create such mechanisms which will eliminate imperfections in the courts' functioning without any interference in judicial independence. There is no simple answer as to how to best organise this process. The experiences from various European countries presented in this monograph may be treated as suggestions on how to organise these processes in a professional manner.

About the Authors

Igor Gontarz

Igor Gontarz is a PhD student at the Doctoral School of Social Sciences at the Adam Mickiewicz University in Poznań. His scientific research focuses on the right to information and automation of public administration. He is also an author of a few publications in the field of new technologies and law and a member of research projects devoted to digitalisation of judiciary, algorithms and criminal procedure. Next to the science, he is a town hall associate Email: igor.gontarz@amu.edu.pl

Stefan Haack

Stefan Haack is Professor of Public Law, in particular Constitutional Law, at the European University Viadrina in Frankfurt (Oder) since 2015. From 2009 to 2014, he was Professor of Public Law at the Rheinische Friedrich-Wilhelms-Universität Bonn. His work focuses on constitutional law, constitutional theory, and various areas of administrative law. His most recent publications include the trilogy "Theorie des öffentlichen Rechts" (Volume I: 2017, Volume II: 2019, Volume III: 2021). Professor Haack has taught as a guest lecturer at the universities of Warsaw, Poznań and Kaliningrad. He is a member of renowned academic associations such as "Vereinigung der Deutschen Staatsrechtslehrer", " Societas Iuris Publici Europaei (SIPE)" and "Schönburger Gespräche zu Recht und Staat".

Matej Horvat

Matej Horvat is Associate professor at the Department of Administrative and Environmental Law of the Comenius University in Bratislava, Faculty of Law. His scientific research focuses on various aspects of administrative punishment, e-government, and administrative proceedings. In those areas, he published several monographs and many papers in European and Slovak journals. He is a member of several international (e.g. EU's WE Project and Visegrad Fund) and national (e.g. APVV) research projects focused on preventing combating discrimination, simplification of administrative proceedings or administrative punishment. He is a member of advisory board for appeals procedures at several ministries (central state bodies) in Slovakia. Email: matej.horvat@flaw.uniba.sk

Jan Olszanowski

Jan Olszanowski is Assistant Professor of administrative law and procedure at the Adam Mickiewicz University in Poznań. He is author of papers focused on administrative-, administrative enforcement- and court-administrative proceedings as well as papers about the system of judiciary. He is a member of Justice Administration Research Association He is also the judge of District Court in Poznań. Email: jan.olszanowski@amu.edu.pl

Katharina Pabel

Karharina Pabel is Professor of Law at the Vienna University of Economics and Business, Institute of European and International Law. She is an author of more than 100 papers focused on Austrian, European and international human rights protection, Austrian constitutional and administrative law. Email: Katharina.Pabel@wu.ac.at

Andrzej Paduch

Andrzej Paduch is Assistant Professor of administrative law and procedure at the Adam Mickiewicz University in Poznań. He is an author of papers focused on administrative-, administrative enforcement- and court-administrative proceedings from the comparative and national (Polish) perspective. He is also an attorney. Email: andrzej.paduch@amu.edu.pl

Wojciech Piątek

Wojciech Piątek is Professor of Law at the Adam Mickiewicz University in Poznań. He is an author of more than 100 papers focused on administrative-, administrative enforcement- and court-administrative proceedings from the European, comparative and national (Polish) perspective. He is principal investigator in research projects devoted to supervision over courts and judges, appealability of administrative courts judgments and simplifications in administrative proceedings Visegrad Countries. Professor Piątek conducted research at various European universities like Humboldt University Berlin (DAAD Sholarship) or Ludwig Maximilian University Munich (BAYHOST sholarship). He is a member of international research associations (Research Network of Administrative Science and Justice Administration Research Association). He is also a specialist in the Jurisprudence Office of the Supreme Administrative Court in Warsaw. Email: wojciech.piatek@amu.edu.pl

Matúš Radosa

Matúš Radosa is an internal Ph.D. student at the Department of Administrative and Environmental Law of the Comenius University in Bratislava, Faculty of Law. He is the author of multiple papers focused on electronic public administration.

He is a member of the research team in project devoted to proposal of new legislation of administrative punishment in Slovak Republic. He is also a member of the Slovak Bar Association. Email: matus.radosa@flaw.uniba.sk

Andrzej Skoczylas

Andrzej Skoczylas is Professor of Law at Adam Mickiewicz University in Poznań. Since 2007, head of Chair of the Administrative and Administrative Judical Procedure. He is an author of more than 160 papers focused on administrative-, administrative enforcement- and court-administrative proceedings. He is also a Judge of the Supreme Administrative Court. Email: andrzej.skoczylas@amu.edu.pl

Martin Sunnqvist

Martin Sunnqvist is Associate Professor of Legal History at the Faculty of Law, Lund University, Sweden. He teaches Swedish legal history, comparative European legal history, and procedural law. His main research intrests concern the role and ethics of judges, the rule of law and Rechtsstaat, and other issues relating to the constitutional function of courts. His dissertation (2014) concerned the development of judicial review of legislation in the Nordic countries. He currently (2020-2022) runs a research project about the rule of law and Rechtsstaat in Europe from a historical, EU law and procedural perspective. Another research interest relates to the symbols of justice and judicial decision making. E-mail: martin.sunnqvist@jur.lu.se.

DIA-LOGS

Schriften zu Philosophie und Sozialwissenschaften

Studies in Philosophy and Social Sciences

Edited by

Piotr W. Juchacz

Dia-Logos. Studies in Philosophy and Social Sciences is a peer-reviewed book series publishing valuable monographs and edited volumes on various aspects of philosophy and social sciences. The series is intended to be an interdisciplinary forum of deliberation according to our firm belief that challenges of the contemporary world require common and multilevel research. The *Dia-Logos* series does not represent a single ideology or school of thought, but it is open to different trends and various styles of reflection, trying to understand better the contemporary world. We invite the submission of manuscripts of monographs and edited volumes from academic philosophers and social scientists.

Vol. 1 Piotr W. Juchacz/Roman Kozłowski (Hrsg.): Freiheit und Verantwortung. Moral, Recht und Politik. 2002.

Vol. 2 Norbert Leśniewski/Ewa Nowak-Juchacz (Hrsg.): Die Zeit Heideggers. 2002.

Vol. 3 Marek Kwiek (ed.): The University, Globalization, Central Europe. 2003.

Vol. 4 Ewa Czerwińska-Schupp (Hrsg.): Philosophie an der Schwelle des 21. Jahrhunderts. Geschichte der Philosophie, Philosophische Anthropologie, Ethik, Wissenschaftstheorie, Politische Philosophie. 2003.

Vol. 5 Danuta Sobczyńska/Pawel Zeidler/Ewa Zielonacka-Lis (eds.): Chemistry in the Philosophical Melting Pot. 2004.

Vol. 6 Marek Kwiek: Intellectuals, Power, and Knowledge. Studies in the Philosophy of Culture and Education. 2004.

Vol. 7 Marek Kwiek: The University and the State. A Study into Global Transformations. 2006.

Vol. 8 Andrzej Przylebski (Hrsg.): Das Erbe Gadamers. 2006.

Vol. 9 Ewa Czerwińska-Schupp (ed.): Values and Norms in the Age of Globalization. 2007.

Vol. 10 Tadeusz Buksiński (ed.): Democracy in Western and Post-Communist Countries. Twenty Years after the Fall of Communism. 2009.

Vol. 11 Marek Zirk-Sadowski / Mariusz Golecki / Bartosz Wojciechowski (eds.): Multicentrism as an Emerging Paradigm in Legal Theory. 2009.

Vol. 12 Bartosz Wojciechowski: Philosophical Approach to the Interculturality of Criminal Law. 2010.

Vol. 13 Marek Nowak / Michał Nowosielski (eds.): (Post)transformational Migration. Inequalities, Welfare State, and Horizontal Mobility. 2011.

Vol. 14 Tadeusz Buksiński (ed.): Religions in the Public Spheres. 2011.

Vol. 15 Bartosz Wojciechowski / Piotr W. Juchacz / Karolina M. Cern (eds.): Legal Rules, Moral Norms and Democratic Principles. 2013.

Vol. 16 Ewa Nowak / Dawn E. Schrader / Boris Zizek (eds.): Educating Competencies for Democracy. 2013.

Vol. 17 Tadeusz Buksiński (ed.): Identities and Modernizations. 2013.

Vol. 18 Karolina M. Cern: The Counterfactual Yardstick. Normativity, Self-Constitutionalisation and the Public Sphere. 2014.

Vol. 19 Vito Breda / Lidia Rodak (eds.). Diverse Narratives of Legal Objectivity. An Interdisciplinary Perspective. 2016.

Vol. 20 Marek Woszczek: Platonic Wholes and Quantum Ontology. Translated by Katarzyna Kretkowska. 2015.

Vol. 21 Roman Hauser / Marek Zirk-Sadowski / Bartosz Wojciechowski (eds.): The Common European Constitutional Culture. Its Sources, Limits and Identity. 2016.

Vol. 22 Aigerim Raimzhanova: Hard, Soft, and Smart Power – Education as a Power Resource. 2017.

Vol. 23 Roberto Franzini Tibaldeo / Graziano Lingua (eds.): Philosophy and Community Practices. 2018.

Vol. 24 Marta Soniewicka: After God – The Normative Power of the Will from the Nietzschean Perspective. 2017.

Vol. 25 Tomasz Jarmużek: On the Sea Battle Tomorrow That May Not Happen. A Logical and Philosophical Analysis of the Master Argument. 2018.

Vol. 26 Krzysztof Brzechczyn (ed.): New Perspectives in Transnational History of Communism in East Central Europe. 2019.

Vol. 27 Ewa Nowak: Advancing the Human Self. Do Technologies Make Us "Posthuman"?. 2020.

Vol. 28 Lidia Rodak: Judicial Objectivity. Limits, Merits and Beyond. 2020.

Vol. 29 Tomasz Pietrzykowski: Naturalism and the Frontiers of Legal Science. 2021.

Vol. 30 Wojciech Piątek (ed.): Supervision over Courts and Judges. Insights into Selected Legal Systems. 2021.

www.peterlang.com

www.ingramcontent.com/pod-product-compliance
Ingram Content Group UK Ltd.
Pitfield, Milton Keynes, MK11 3LW, UK
UKHW021832100926
8556IPUK00004B/289

9 783631 836170